IMAGES
of America

FISHKILL REVISITED

I0806163

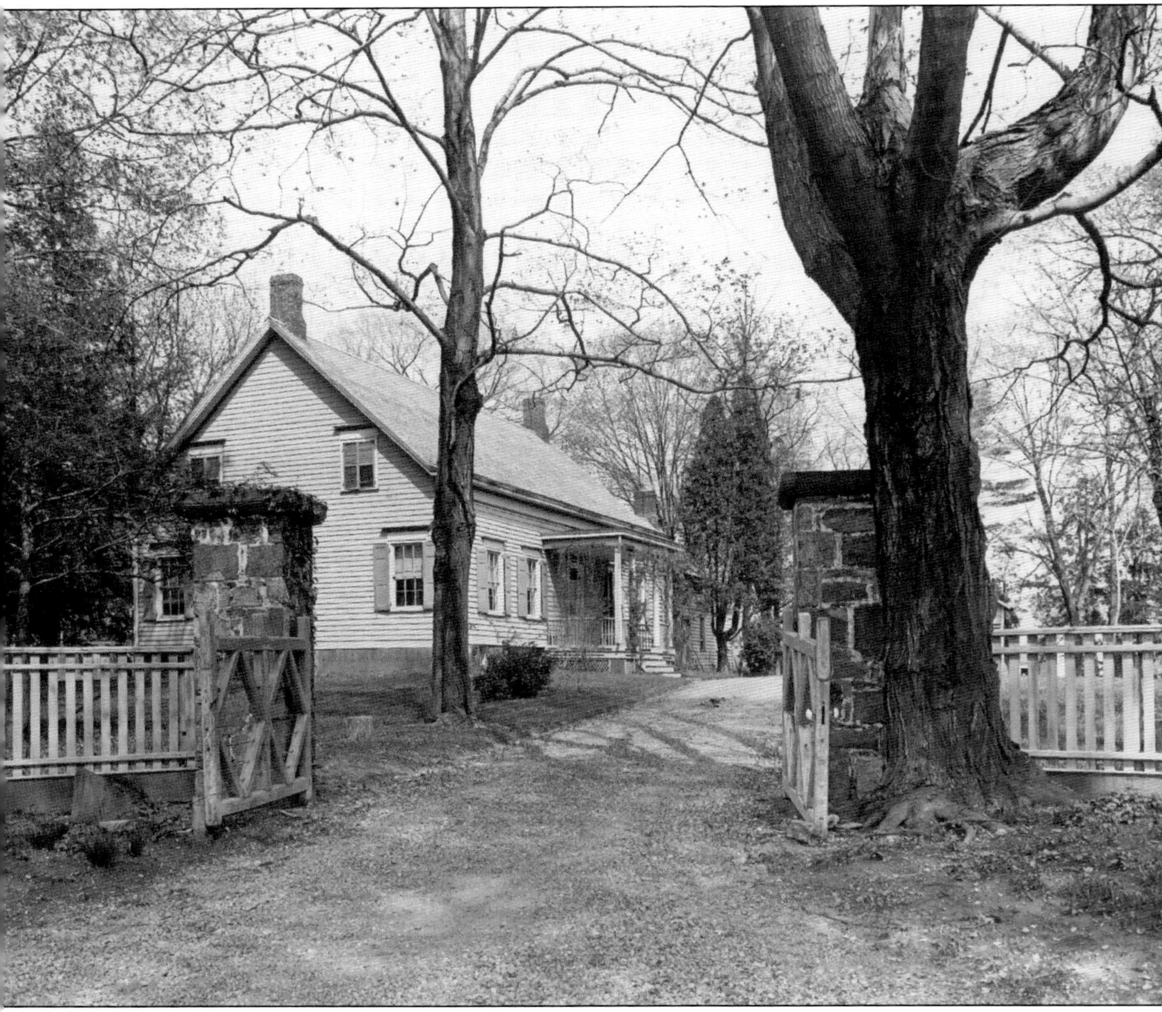

ON THE COVER: Taken around 1913, this photograph offers a welcoming view of the Wharton or Van Wyck House. The home served as headquarters to the Fishkill Supply Depot during the American Revolutionary War. During that time, it was home to Isaac Van Wyck and then later, it passed down to the Hustis and Snook families. Today, it is the site of the Fishkill Historical Society. (Courtesy of the New York State Archives, Education Department, Division of Visual Instruction.)

IMAGES
of America

FISHKILL REVISITED

Tracy Nicole Dunstan
Foreword by Roy Jorgensen

ARCADIA
PUBLISHING

ISBN 978-0-7385-7675-6

Published by Arcadia Publishing
Charleston, South Carolina

Printed in the United States of America

Library of Congress Control Number: 2011934176

For all general information, please contact Arcadia Publishing:
Telephone 843-853-2070
Fax 843-853-0044
E-mail sales@arcadiapublishing.com
For customer service and orders:
Toll-Free 1-888-313-2665

Visit us on the Internet at www.arcadiapublishing.com

To mom and Tisha for everything

Contents

FOREWORD

When the first Arcadia book about Fishkill was published in 1996, it was immediately evident that there was much more that could have been collected for a second book. It has taken 15 years for someone to take on that task.

Fishkill's national significance came about during the American Revolutionary War, when the supply depot and barracks were established for the northern branch of the Continental Army in Fishkill in 1776, enduring until the end of the war in 1783.

The town also flourished during the Civil War, when the woolen mills in Glenham hamlet produced uniforms for the Yankee army. Those mills have long disappeared but were an important part of Fishkill's and America's history.

Fishkill has been the site of a prosperous black community that settled around the time that slavery was abolished in New York State. That community mingled and intermarried with the Native American community, also known as the Wappinger people, long after many from that community had removed to Stockbridge, Massachusetts.

In spite of its manufacturing presence during the War of the Rebellion, the town had been largely an agricultural area that relied on the railroad and the Hudson River to ship supply goods to New York City; it was a breadbasket for the ever growing metropolis. Around 1900, Fishkill was a garden center that started raising flowers for the big-city market. Taking a look at the directories at that time, one can see the great number of garden and greenhouse workers who populated the area.

This second volume of photographs is a welcome addition to the recent books about Fishkill, a town with an odd English and Dutch name.

—Roy Jorgensen
Historical Researcher

ACKNOWLEDGMENTS

This project was completed with the generous help of countless members of the Hudson Valley community. I thank the following: John Ansley, head of Archives and Special Collections, Marist College; Michael Diaz and Emily Bitteker, Mount Gulian Historic Site; Dr. Peter Feinman, Institute of History, Archeology, and Education; Lorraine MacAulay, curator, Madam Brett Homestead; Dr. James Johnson, executive director, Hudson River Valley Institute; Monica Gray and Maria McCashion, New York State Archives; Steve Lynch, president, Fishkill Historical Society; Neil Caplan, Bannerman Castle; Fern Franke; Joan Carol Berube; Thom Johnson; and Wayne Francis.

Special thanks also go to Elaine Hayes, executive director, Mount Gulian Historic Site; Ericka Gerreno, Fishkill United Methodist Church; Heather Henriques; Willa Skinner, historian, Town of Fishkill; Frederick Villforth; Barbara Sparacio; Linda, Trinity Episcopal Church; Erin Vosgien, my kind and efficient editor, who never failed to answer my questions and ease my concerns; Cathy Foley, Fishkill Historical Society; Cheryl Urquhart; Lance A. Ashworth, president, Fishkill Supply Depot; Bob Murphy, president, Beacon Historical Society; Christopher Pryslopski, program director, Hudson River Valley Institute; Andy Villani, Hudson River Valley Institute; Allan R. Way, co-historian, Village of Fishkill; Rachel Buyes; Dr. Rose Mason; Betty Snook; Laurel Snook; and Nicole Famulare and Angela Ricciardi, for attempting to help with last-minute scanning issues.

Also, a very special thank you goes to Roy Jorgensen of the Fishkill Historical Society for graciously allowing me his time and his historical expertise.

Lastly, I would like to thank Lauren Savino, Stephanie Ragonese, Amanda Snook, Kristin Rose-DaCosta, Pam Noga, Amy Hacker, Kathleen Maguire, Kelly O'Connell, the DaCosta family, and of course, my family for their support and encouragement.

INTRODUCTION

Fifteen years ago, in 1996, a group of fourth-graders made the trip down Route 9 from Fishkill Elementary to the Van Wyck Homestead. The students were taking part of the New York State local history requirement, and that year, they learned about the Continental Army, Mount Gulian, Madam Brett, and the many other figures that make up the history of Fishkill. I was one of those students, and I spent that school year learning about Fishkill's history. This experience started what would become a lifelong interest in the subject of history.

Fishkill awaits just 60 miles from New York City and is an area that is rich in US history. Fishkill housed George Washington, captured a Revolutionary War spy, and nursed the War for Independence's wounded. Notably, the town was also home to a large population of blacks along Baxtertown Road; assisted James Brown, a runaway slave; and may have helped in the Underground Railroad. During the Industrial Revolution, mills and factories sprang up in Glenham, and a vibrant population flourished for several decades. In 1873, a fire raged through Main Street in Fishkill, and in 1899, the Village of Fishkill was incorporated. During the 1950s and 1960s, the Fishkill Historical Society was organized and Mount Gulian was reconstructed. Today, Fishkill is a growing and active town that still celebrates its long history.

In 1609, Henry Hudson unearthed the land, which was previously inhabited by the Wappinger Indians. His men sailed on up what would later be know as the Hudson River on the *Half Moon*. The land, located 75 miles from New Amsterdam, fell into Dutch hands and was called Dutchess County. Dutchess County was described as very mountainous, broken by the deep valley of streams, with the land shaped almost like a parallelogram. The Taconic Mountains lie to the east, and the Matteawan or Fishkill Mountains run north and south.

Fishkill was included as part of the Rombout Patent, which was land purchased from the Wappinger Indians in 1685 by Gulian Verplanck and Francis Rombout. The patent contained one third of Dutchess County, roughly 85,000 acres. Fishkill's early growth in the 1680s is attributed to Rombout's daughter, Catharyna Brett. After her husband's death in a boating accident, Catharyna, or Madam Brett, as she is more commonly known, sold tracts of land from the original patent to pay off debts. Afterwards, homesteads sprang up and the area came to life due to available land. By 1776, the village of Fishkill was the largest in Dutchess County.

Fishkill Village had an academy, two churches, one schoolhouse, a hotel, and a printing press. By 1789, the only post road in the state was between New York City and Albany, running through Fishkill, Poughkeepsie, and Rhinebeck. Dutchess had two mail routes that extended though eastern and western borders to New York. Letters were few and carried through private hands. Post riders on horseback carried newspapers from Hartford and Poughkeepsie.

Several important places in Fishkill are the Van Wyck Homestead Museum, First Reformed Protestant Dutch Church of Fishkill, Mount Gulian Historic Site, and Trinity Episcopal Church. Noted historical figures in Fishkill are Enoch Crosby, an American spy who was taken with recruits for the British Army; the Verplanck family, who gave Mount Gulian to the Continental Army so that it could be used as a headquarters of Gen. Fredrich von Steuben during the American Revolution; and James F. Brown.

The Van Wyck Homestead, besides being the current home of the Fishkill Historical Society, is one of the last remaining structures of the Fishkill Supply Depot. Gen. Israel Putnam used it as his headquarters during the Revolutionary War. As a result, several important leaders from that time, such as George Washington, John Jay, and the Marquis de Lafayette visited the house. During the presidency of Franklin Delano Roosevelt, the Van Wyck Homestead was used as a tearoom and was visited frequently by Eleanor Roosevelt as she travelled to her home at nearby Hyde Park.

Enoch Crosby was born in Harwich, Massachusetts, in 1750. He and his family moved to Dutchess County not long after his birth. When Crosby was in his teens, he apprenticed in Putnam County. During the American Revolution, he worked under John Jay for the Committee of Safety, gathering intelligence for the Continental Army. He is noted as the first American "secret agent." The Dutch Reformed Church was the first church built on land that was included in the Rombout Patent. The church was also the site of the mock trial of Enoch Crosby during the American Revolution.

James Brown was born in Maryland and fled to freedom in the north. For reasons unknown to history, James found himself working for the Verplanck family in New York City. Later, he moved with the Verplancks to their home in Fishkill, called Mount Gulian. He worked for many years as their gardener and caretaker, and he eventually learned to read and write. Brown settled comfortably into life in the Hudson Valley. James was an active participant in Beacon as he helped in the church and voted in elections, thus becoming involved in the African American community. James Brown kept a 40-year diary that serves as one of the only sources of information on life in the area. He died on January 14, 1868.

Trinity Episcopal Church was built on land given by Madam Brett during the 1760s. At the time of the American Revolution, Trinity was used as a hospital for Washington's army, and many soldiers are buried in the church burial ground. Fishkill has a long and varied history.

Much has happened in Fishkill during the decade and a half since the first book in the Images of America series was published—for example: the 100th anniversary of Fishkill Elementary, one of the oldest public buildings that is continually in use as a school in New York State; the 250th anniversary of Trinity Church; and the resurgence of Main Street through events like the annual Rock Around the Clock Block Party. Fishkill still has an important role in history and within the state. The town serves as a midway point between New York City and the state capital in Albany. Fishkill also was the setting for the 1990s Paul Newman movie *Nobody's Fool*. Furthermore, Splashdown Water Park and Dutchess Stadium bring hundreds of tourists to the Fishkill area. There is a lot to experience in this small town.

Enjoy this trip back to Fishkill.

—Tracy Dunstan
September 19, 2011

One

A Walk through Fishkill

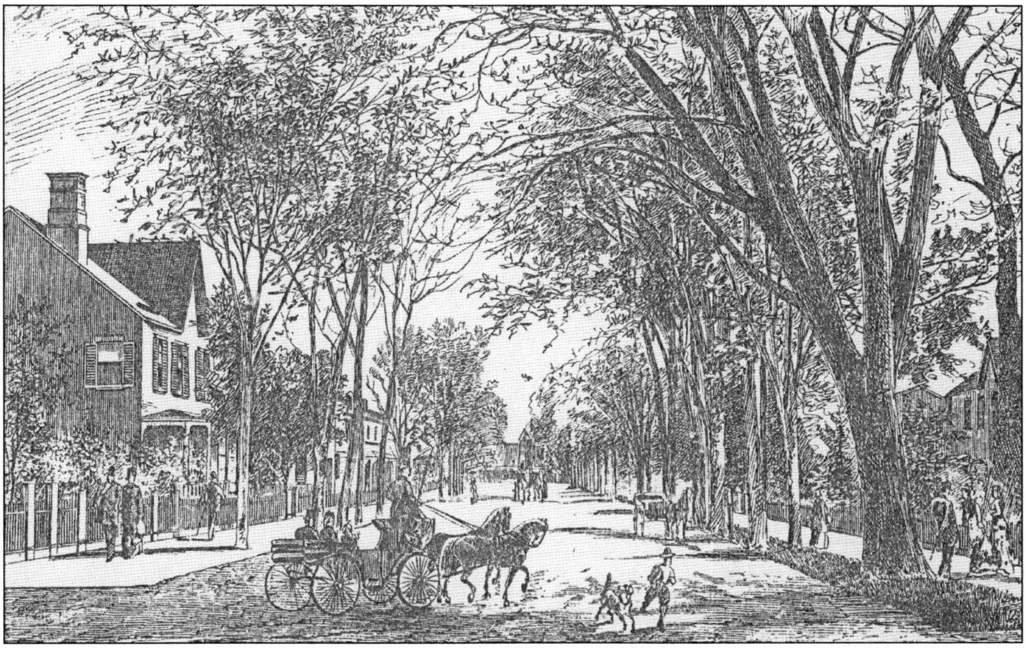

The village of Fishkill is depicted in a 19th century sketch. The image shows the daily activity of village residents during Fishkill's early years. Fishkill was part of the 85,000 acres included in the 1685 Rombout Patent. Fishkill was much larger than it is today, as it included the current town and village of Fishkill; Beacon, which was previously called Matteawan and included Glenham and Dutchess Junction; the town of Wappingers; and parts of Poughkeepsie and LaGrange. (Courtesy of Beacon Historical Society.)

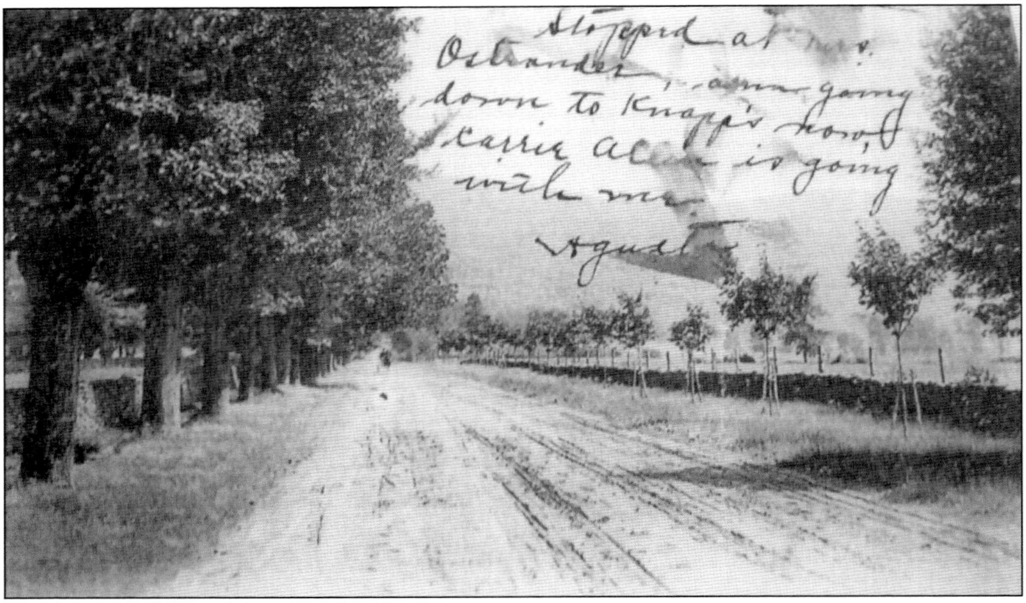

The Old Post Road is shown in this postcard dated July 31, 1905. The front of the postcard reads: "Dear Mama, Stopped at Mrs. Ortanders and I'm going down to Knapp's now, Carrie Allen is going with me. –Augusta." The Old Post Road is approximately the same path that US Route 9 travels today. (Courtesy of Willa Skinner.)

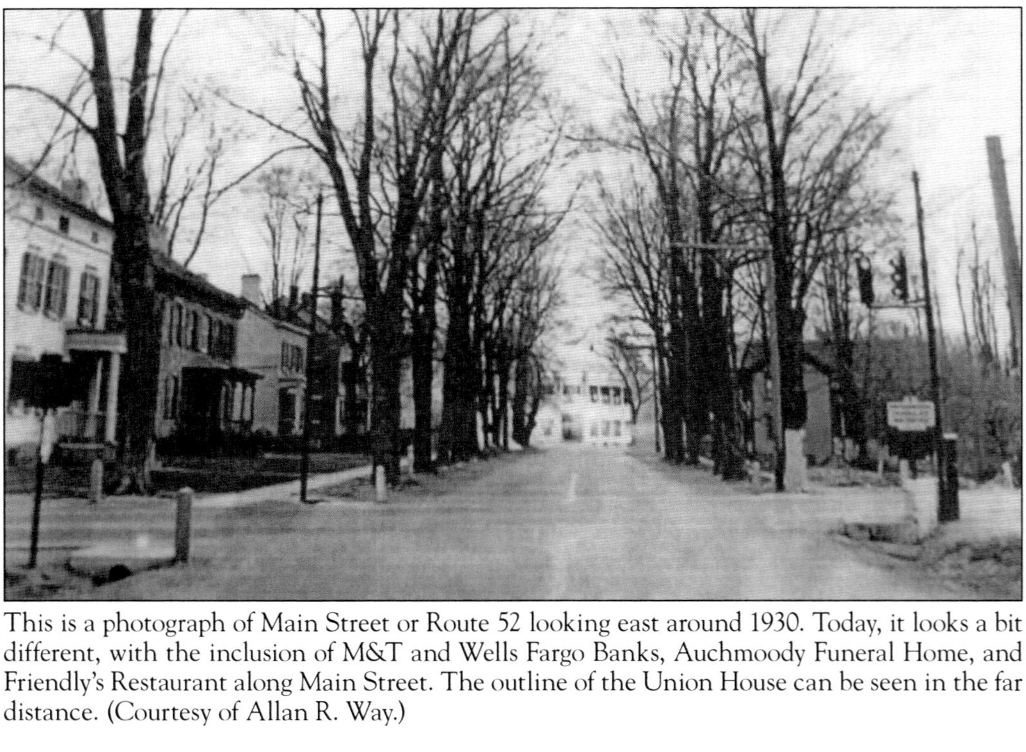

This is a photograph of Main Street or Route 52 looking east around 1930. Today, it looks a bit different, with the inclusion of M&T and Wells Fargo Banks, Auchmoody Funeral Home, and Friendly's Restaurant along Main Street. The outline of the Union House can be seen in the far distance. (Courtesy of Allan R. Way.)

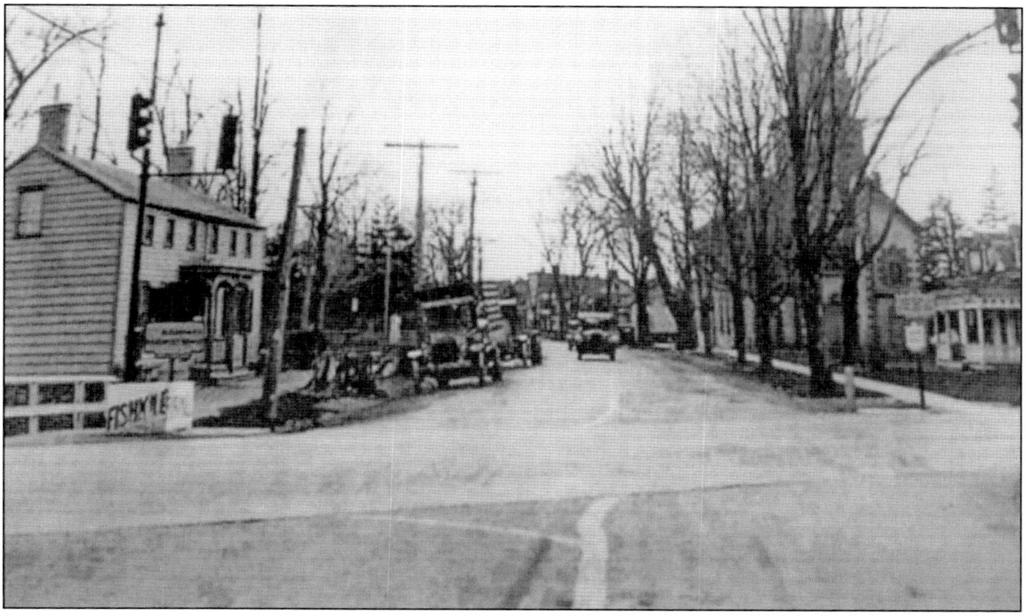

Main Street is depicted facing west in this c. 1930 photograph. This view of Main Street shows just how little Fishkill has changed from this direction. On the right is the Dutch Reformed Church. In the distance are the familiar structures that host several restaurants today. (Courtesy of Allan R. Way.)

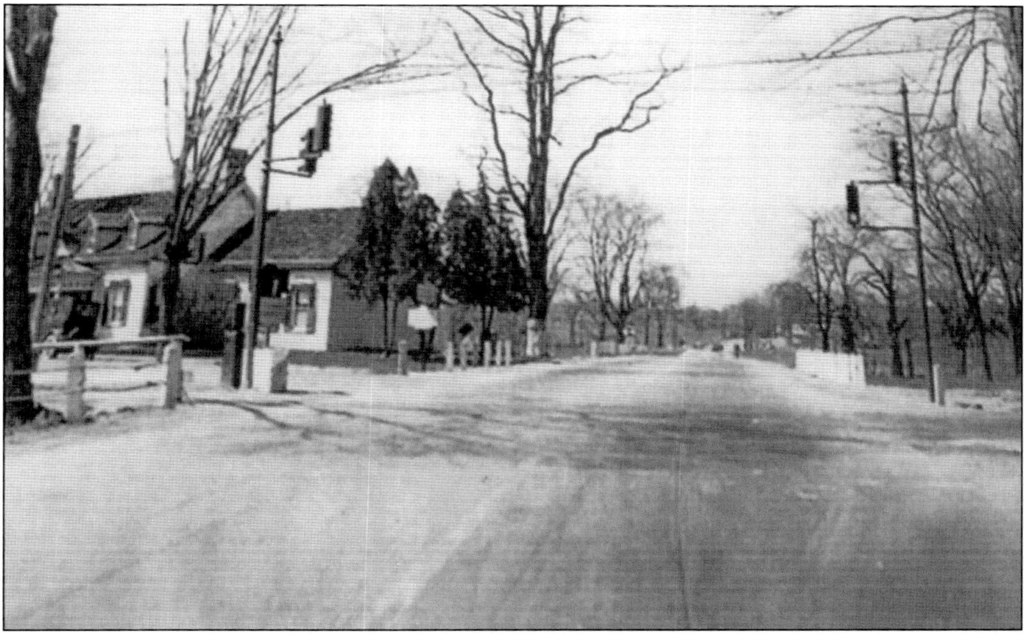

This photograph is a 1930s view of Route 9 and Main Street or Route 52 facing north. The Dutch Reformed Parish House is on the far left and Trinity Episcopal Church would be on the left if the photograph continued. Today, Route 9 is much busier, as it consists of about three lanes on both sides of the yellow line. It is also lined with several shopping plazas, gas stations, and restaurants. (Courtesy of Allan R. Way.)

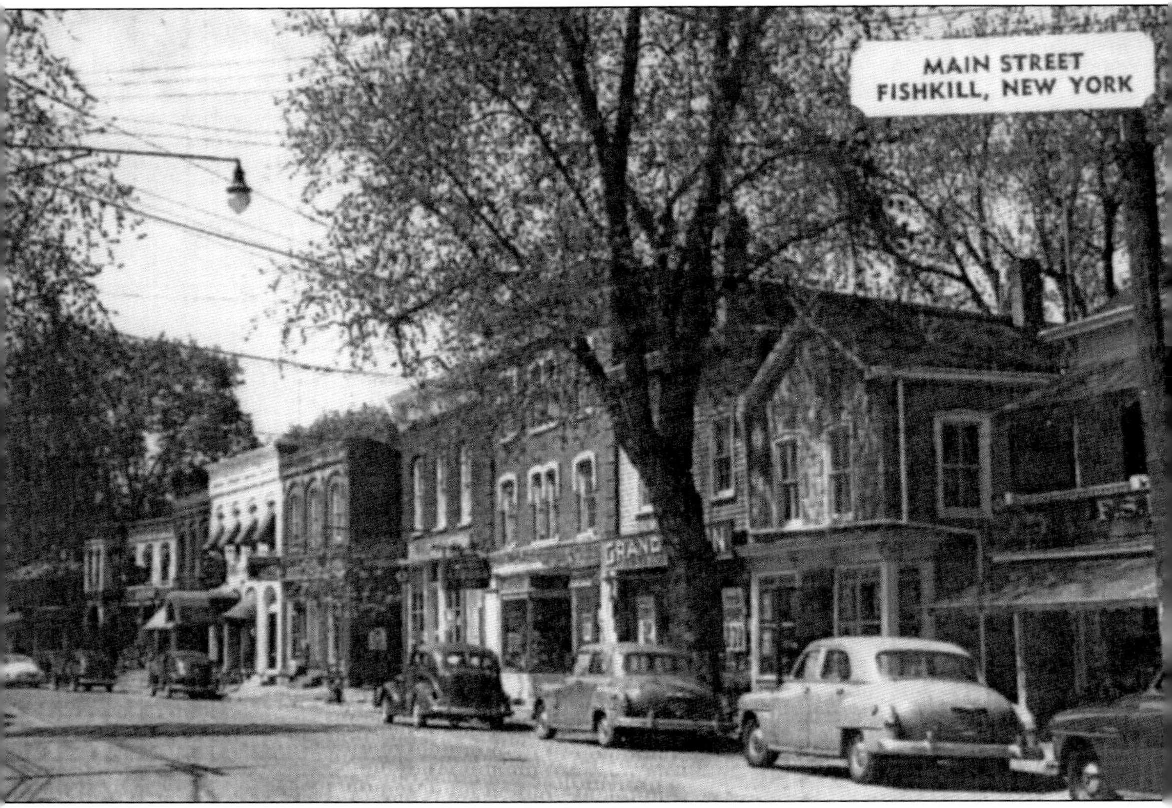

This postcard is of Main Street facing west some time between 1940 and 1950. Today, the store names have changed, yet most of the buildings remain. The western portion of the Fishkill Village District is comprised of three full blocks between Main and Broad Streets. Bedford and Robinson Streets are also included within this area. (Courtesy of Willa Skinner.)

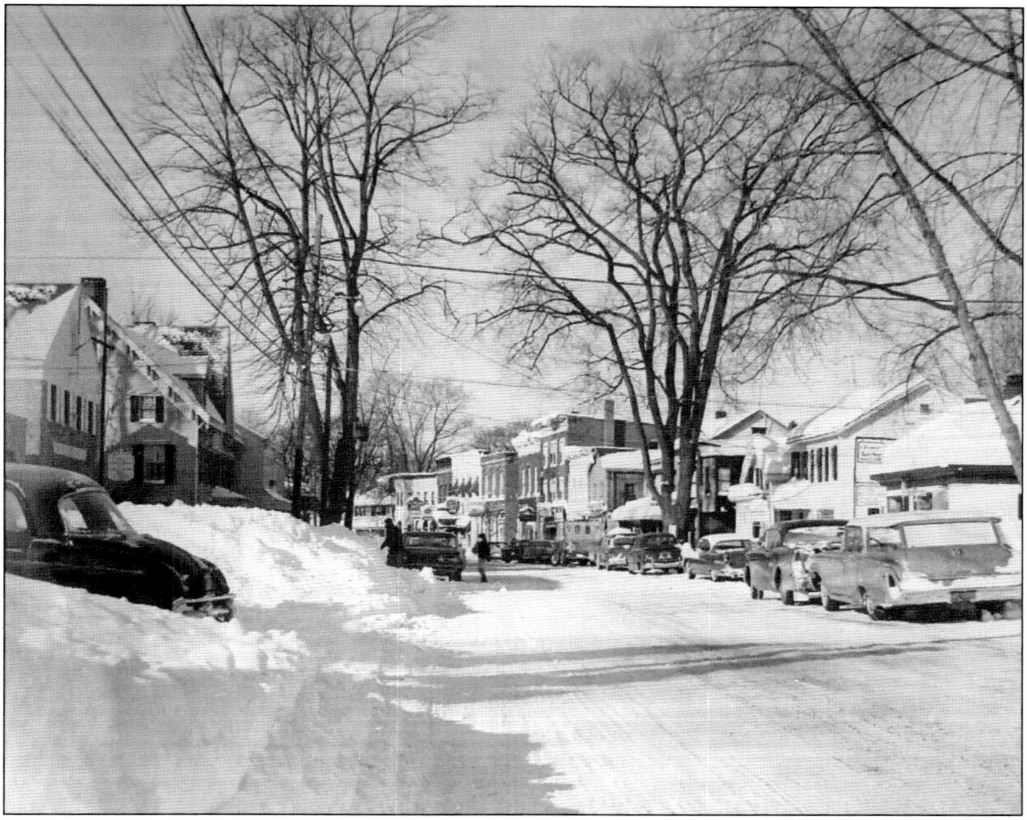

Two people are depicted digging out from a snowstorm on Main Street in 1961. Today, they would be in front of what is known as Cibo Restaurant. A severe snowstorm in March 2010 came through Fishkill and shut the town down for several days. A winter full of heavy snowfall would not be welcomed today; however, in the early part of Fishkill's history, a warm winter meant a decrease in the income for farmers and ice cutters in the area. (Courtesy of the Victor L. Sanko Collection, Allan R. Way.)

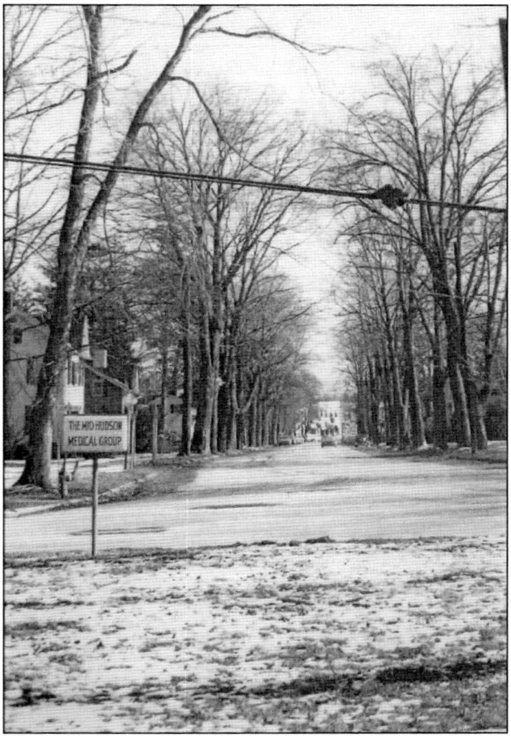

The intersection of Jackson Street and Main Street is shown between 1960 and 1970. The sign for the Mid Hudson Medical Building is on the right corner. The building that is most commonly known as the Mid Hudson Medical Group Building is shown in this photograph. It is located at 24 Jackson Street and 1019 Main Street. (Courtesy of Willa Skinner.)

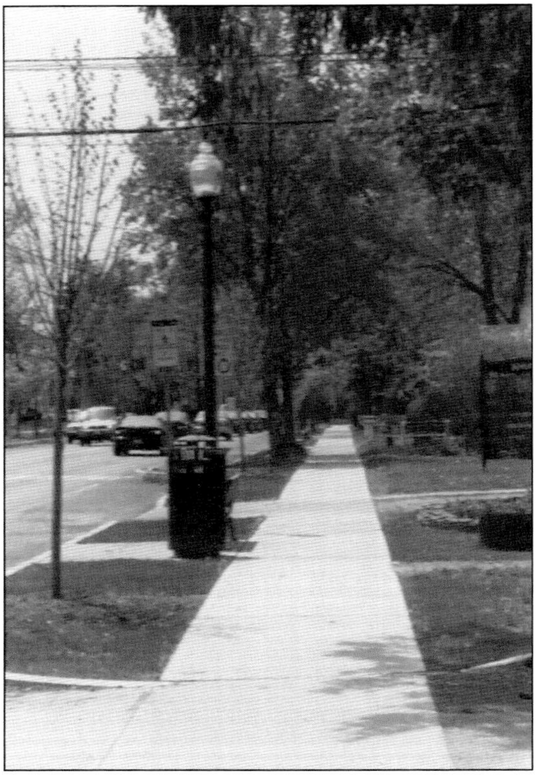

The village is shown in its more modern state around 2006 looking west. The village of Fishkill, which is east of Route 9, contains the properties that front on Main Street where it intersects with Route 9 and Hopewell Avenue and the properties that front on Hopewell Avenue from the junction with Main Street to that with Rappalje Road. (Courtesy of Tisha Dunstan.)

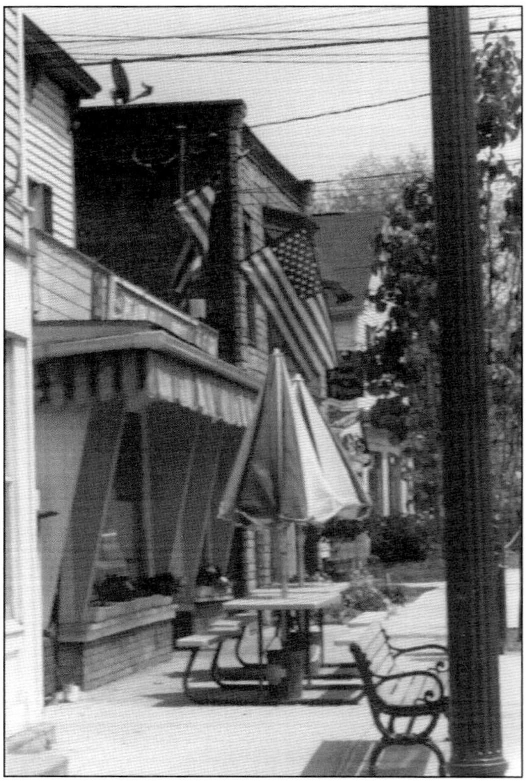

This photograph shows a close-up of the left side of Main Street looking east around 2006. The former Plain and Fancy Delicatessen can clearly be seen on the left. Today, it is the site of the Tomato Café Restaurant. (Courtesy of Tisha Dunstan.)

In this c. 2006 close-up photograph, Main Street is depicted looking west. On December 1, 1875, a fire occurred on Main Street. The fire destroyed the wood-frame commercial district on Main Street between Robinson and Church Streets. (Courtesy of Tisha Dunstan.)

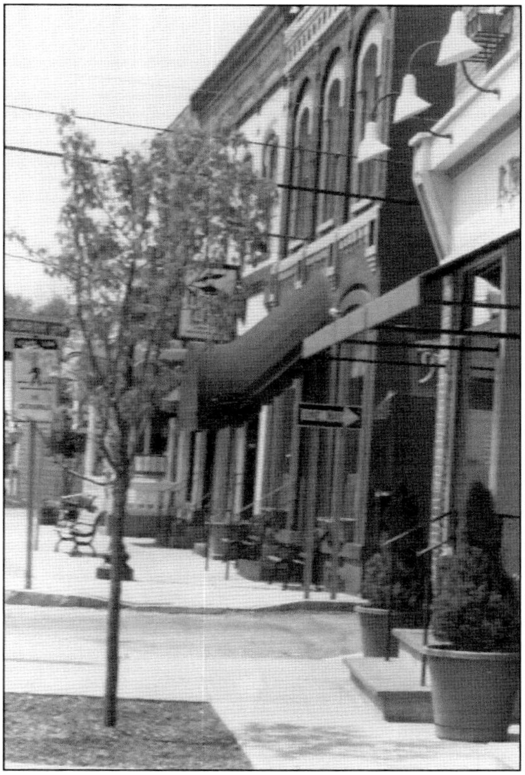

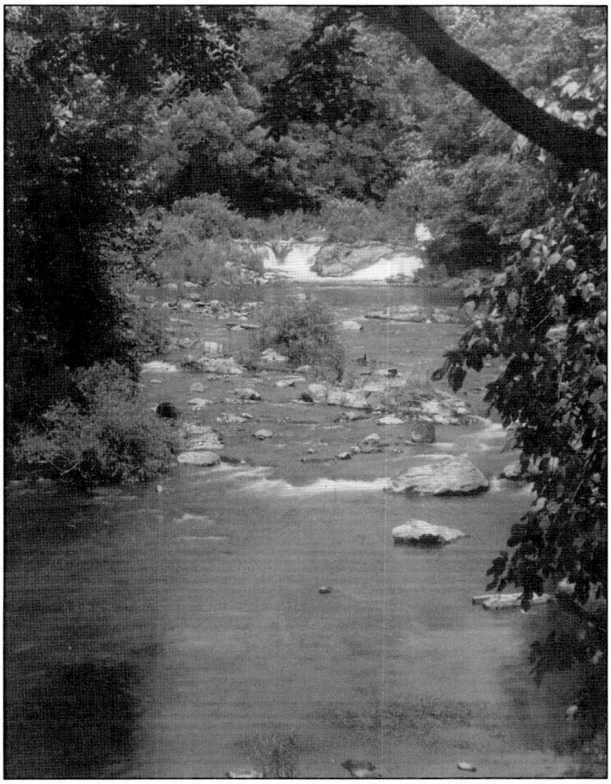

The Brett Hill Falls in Fishkill is pictured in 1930. The Brett family came to what would become Dutchess County in 1709. Catheryna Rombout married Roger Brett when she was 16 years old in 1705. Her mother, Helena Teller Bogardus Van Ball, died four years later and left Brett as the sole heir of the Rombout portion of the 85,000 acres of land known as the Rombout Patent. Catheryna Brett, or Madam Brett as she is known, inherited about 28,000 acres of land that included the Fishkill Creek, land along the river, and the Wappinger Creek. (Courtesy of the Dutchess County Historical Society.)

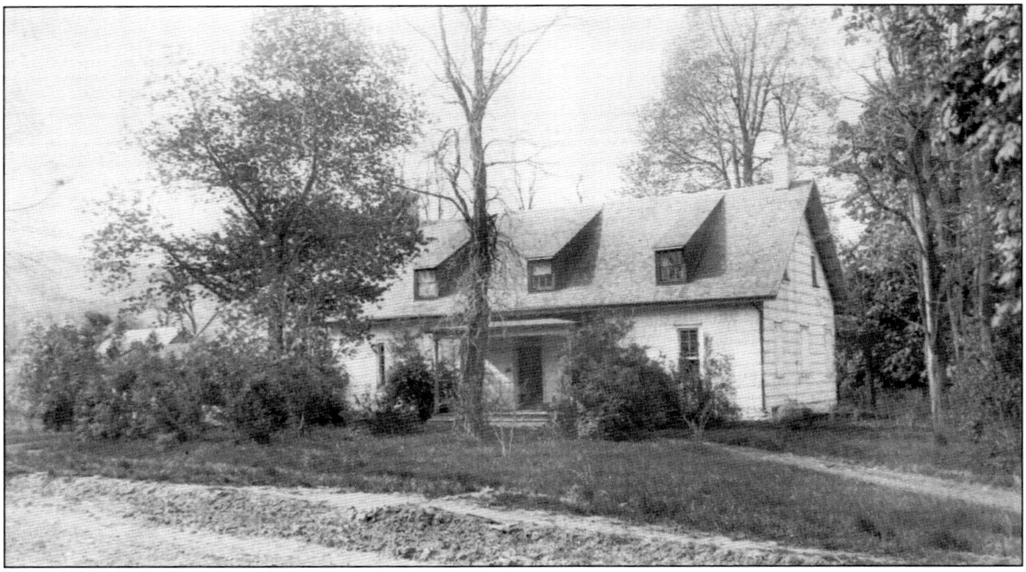

The Teller house, or Madam Brett Homestead, is pictured in a 19th-century photograph. The Teller house is the oldest standing home in the Beacon and Fishkill area and has been listed in the National Register of Historic Places since 1976. It was built in 1709, and the home was slated to be demolished in 1954, but it was saved by the Daughters of the American Revolution and turned into a museum that preserves the history of the Brett and Teller families today. (Courtesy of the Dutchess County Historical Society; photograph by C.A. Palmer.)

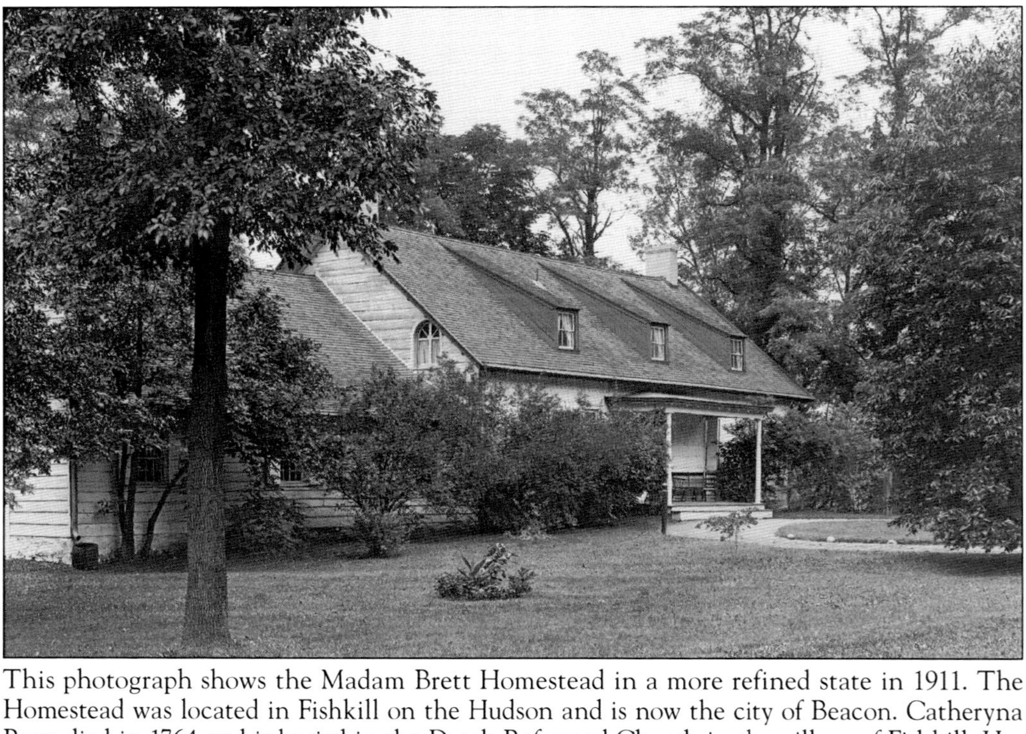

This photograph shows the Madam Brett Homestead in a more refined state in 1911. The Homestead was located in Fishkill on the Hudson and is now the city of Beacon. Catheryna Brett died in 1764 and is buried in the Dutch Reformed Church in the village of Fishkill. Her descendants continued to live in the house until the middle of the 20th century. (Courtesy of the New York State Archives.)

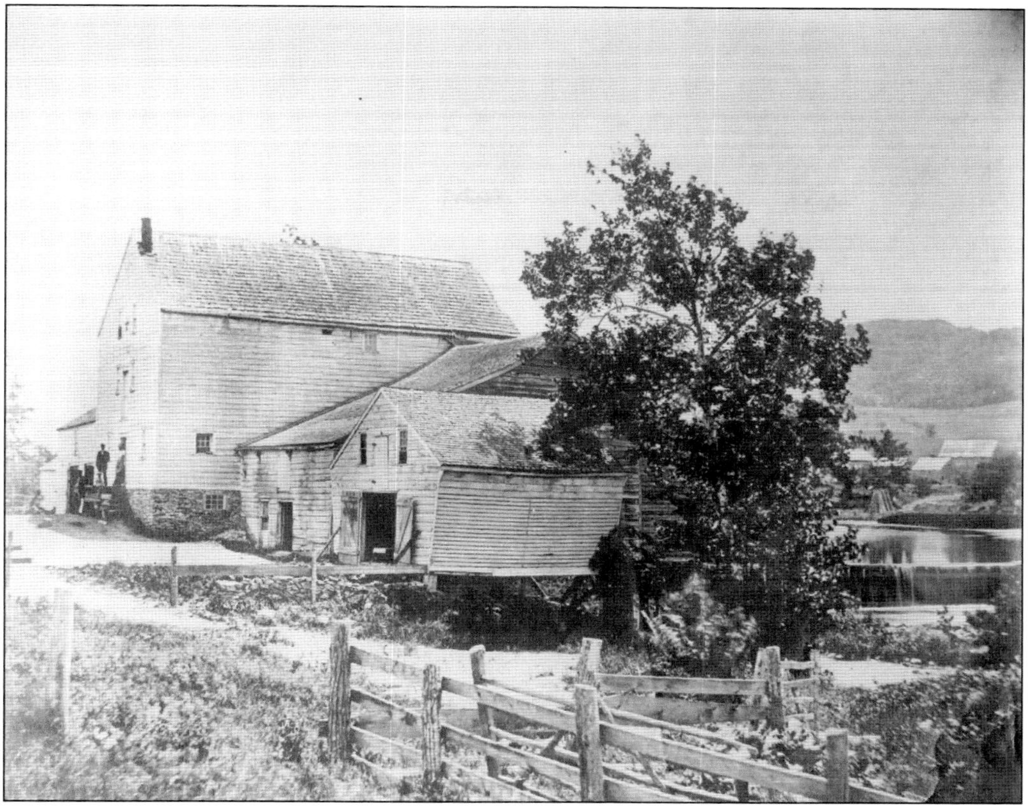

This is the mill at Brinckerhoff. The Brinckerhoff Mill was built by Col. Derick Brinckerhoff on Fishkill Creek in the neighborhood now known as Brinckerhoff. It was built in 1735 and burned in 1777, and George Washington's army rebuilt the mill. George Washington came to Fishkill and set up headquarters in Brinckerhoff's home, which still stands today. (Courtesy of the Dutchess County Historical Society.)

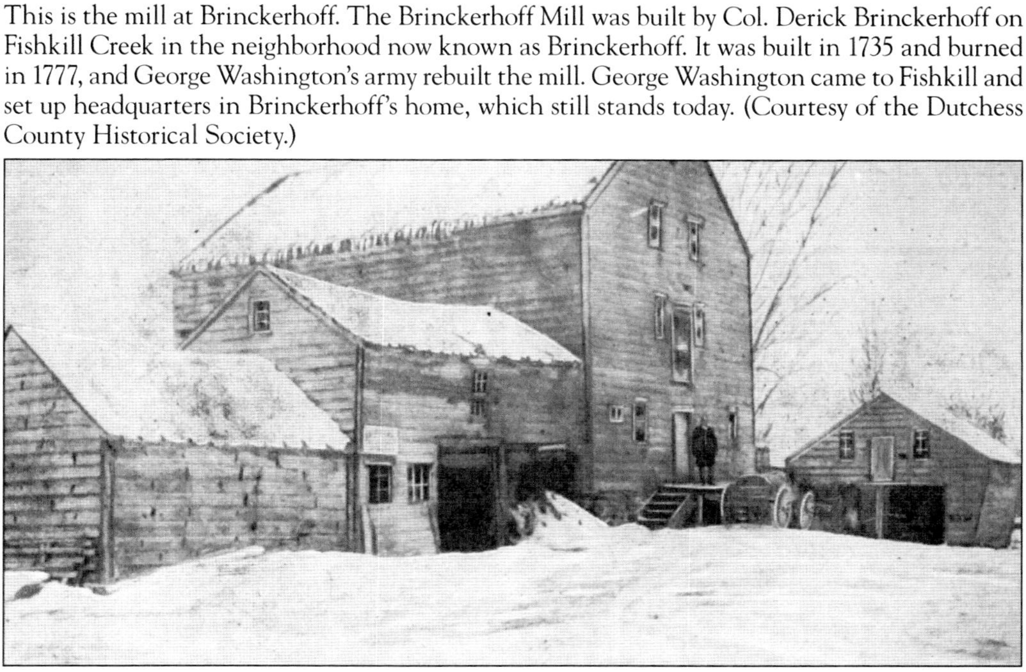

The corner of a mill in Brinckerhoff is shown in this postcard. Derick Brinckerhoff built a mill on Fishkill Creek after Madam Brett loosened her claim to all the mills in the area. Mills were one of the most important forms of business within the Fishkill area. (Courtesy of Betty Snook.)

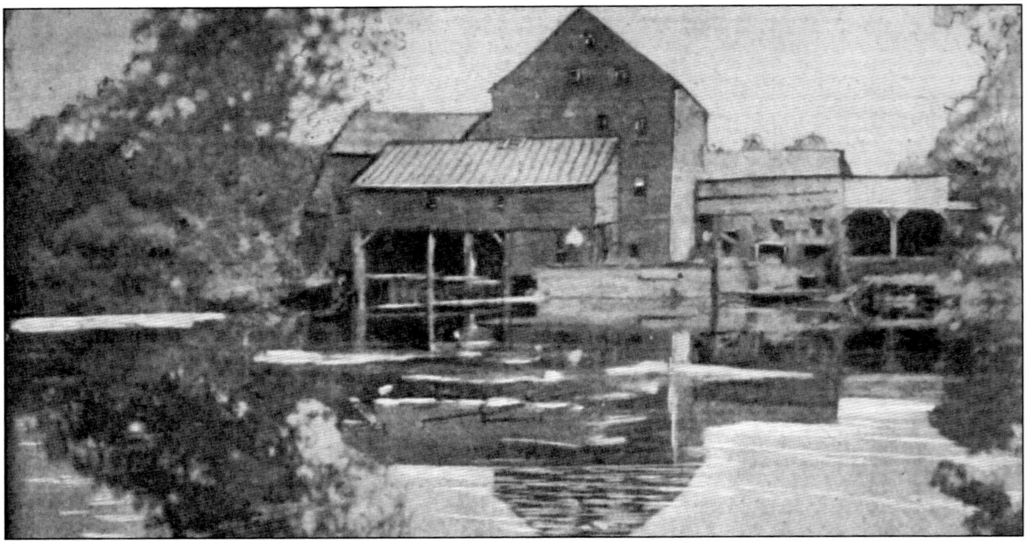

The mill that was built in 1735 is shown in the above postcard. The mill was located at Brinckerhoff and burned down in 1777. George Washington's army rebuilt the mill and used it to grind grain. The second postcard depicts an old gristmill in midsummer. A gristmill is a building in which grain is ground into flour. This mill is an example of a classical mill, as it is water-powered. According to Henry Noble MacCracken's book *Old Dutchess Forever*, "one-third of all the flour shipped to New York came from Dutchess, and her mills ground more than any other." (Both, courtesy of Betty Snook.)

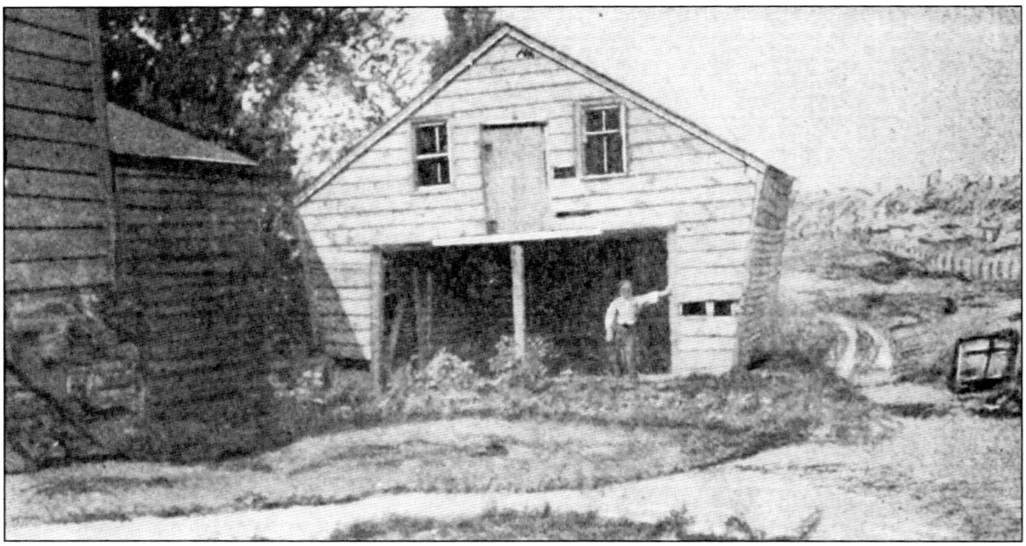

The First Reformed Dutch Church is pictured in the village of Fishkill on Main Street in 1913. The church was erected in 1731. The original building was small and square and only one story in height. The Dutch Reformed Church was the first church built on land that was included in the Rombout Patent. The church was also the site of the mock trial of Enoch Crosby during the American Revolution. (Courtesy of the New York State Archives.)

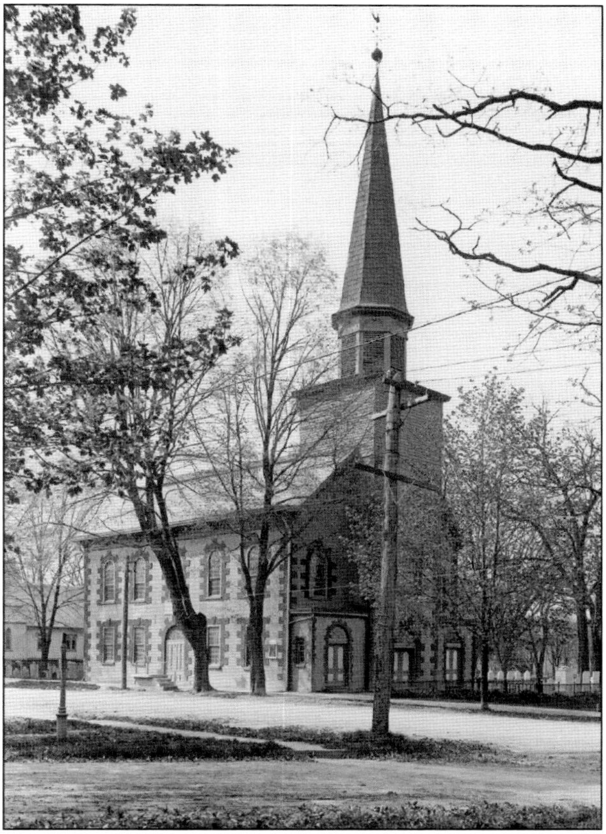

Several people standing in front of the building that once housed the Bank of Fishkill are depicted in this image from the 19th century. The Bank of Fishkill ceased to exist in 1877. It was Fishkill Town Hall between the years of 1944 and 1989. After being on the market for a few years, it is the site of a new wine bar in 2012. The structure has basically remained in the same since the 19th century. (Courtesy of the Beacon Historical Society.)

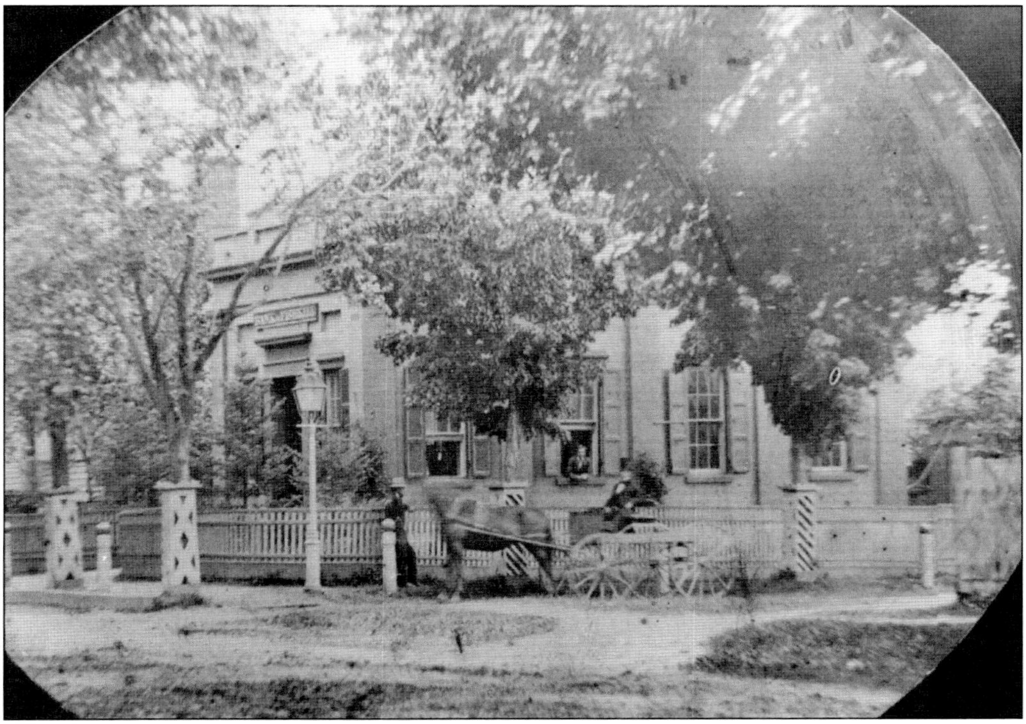

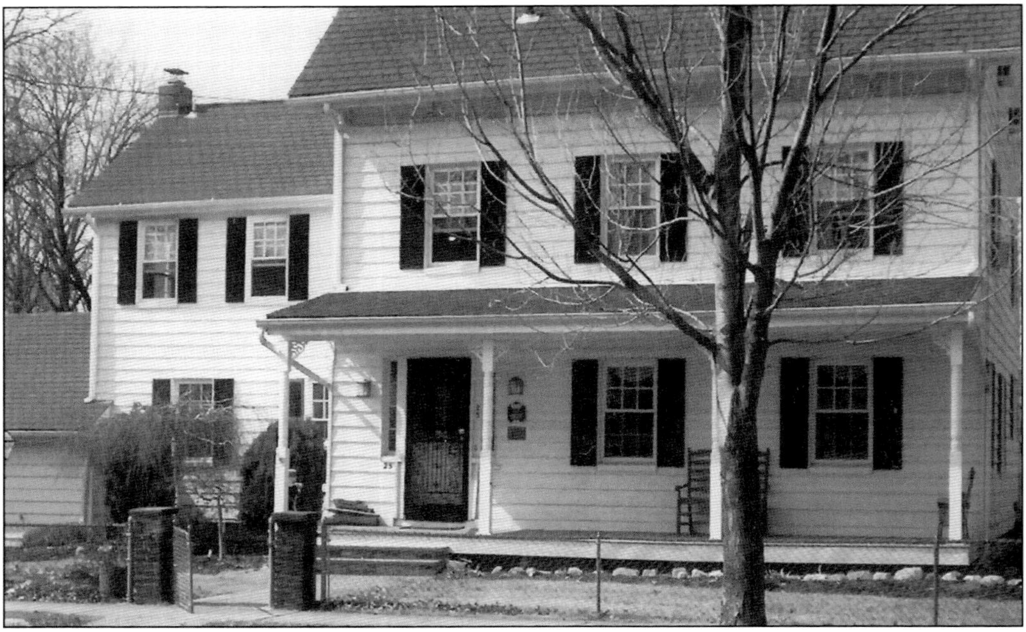

A home at 25 Broad Street is pictured in the 2000s in the village of Fishkill. In the back of the home is an example one of the last standing 19th-century carriage houses. It is hard to say for sure if a branch of the famed Underground Railroad existed in Fishkill. However, the Mason family, former residents of 25 Broad Street, remembers hearing that the home used to be the site of a blacksmith shop and that it had a trapdoor underneath where runaway slaves may have been hidden. (Courtesy of Rachel Buyes.)

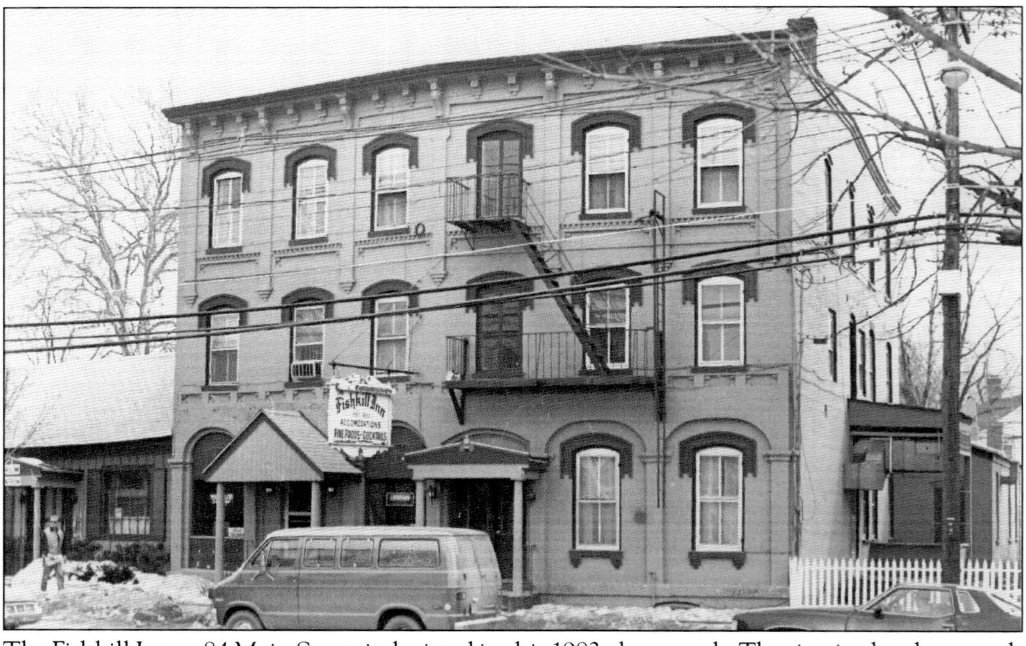

The Fishkill Inn at 84 Main Street is depicted in this 1983 photograph. The sign in the photograph reads, "Fishkill Inn, established 1819. Accommodations, fine foods, and cocktails." The building burned in a fire in 1979. The Fishkill Inn was remodeled in 2001 and became the Union House. Today, it is the site of Sapore Steakhouse. (Courtesy of the Fishkill Historical Society.)

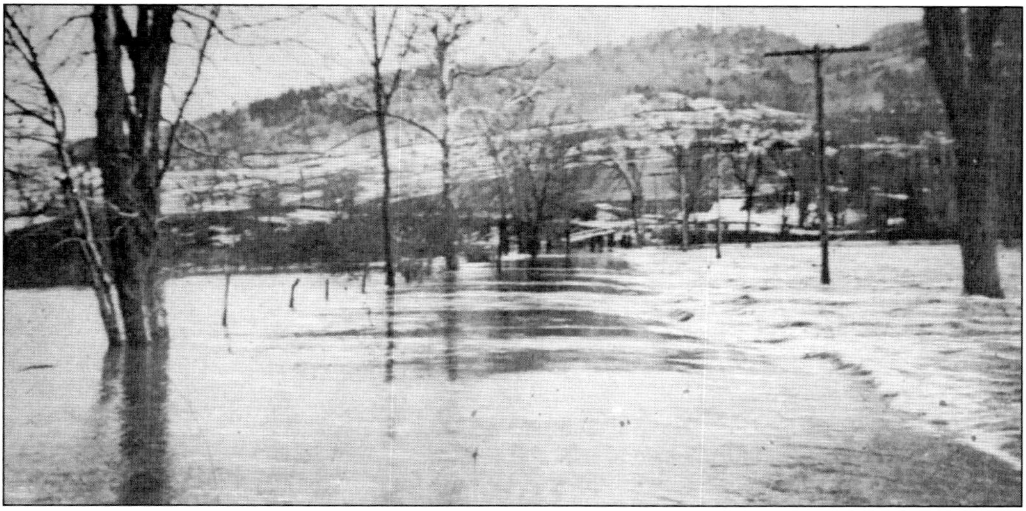

State Road leading to the bridge at Brinckerhoff during a January 1910 flood is depicted in this postcard. State Road connects Route 52 and Cedar Hill Road in Fishkill. Near State Road are the Brinckerhoff home and the Rombout Cemetery. Also near the road is a fork separating Route 52 and Route 82. Brinckerhoff was an important community in Fishkill. At one time, it contained a gristmill, church, academy, and general store. The village took its name from the Brinckerhoff family, the first to settle in this region. Derick Brinckerhoff came from Long Island and purchased 2,000 acres of land from Madam Brett in 1718. (Both, courtesy of Betty Snook.)

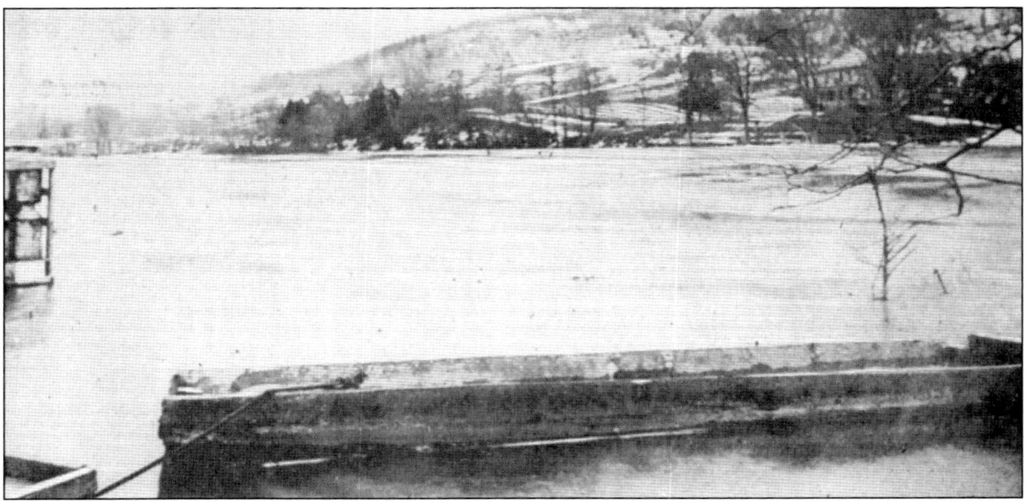

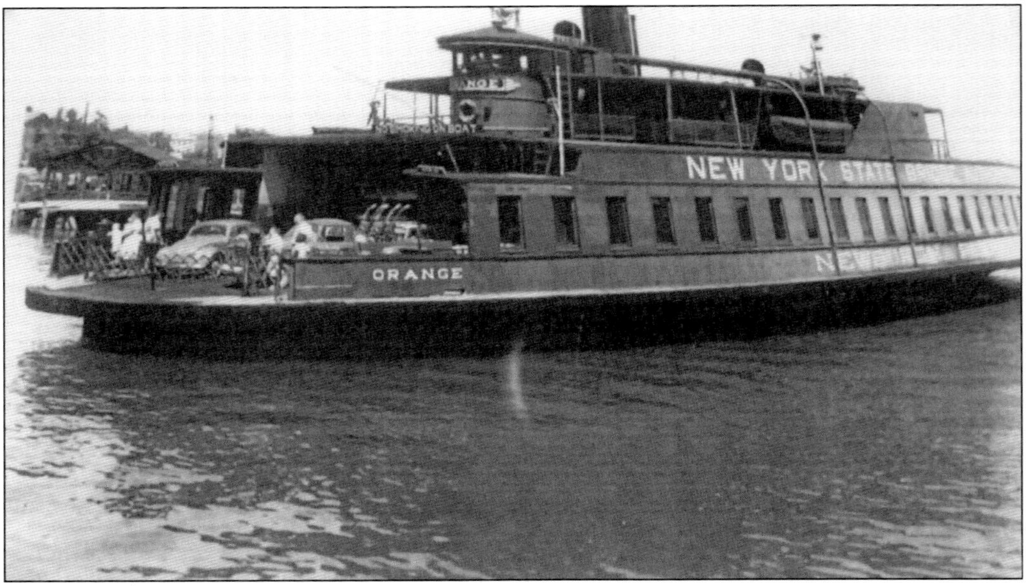

This image made from a slide depicts the last day of the Newburgh-Beacon ferry called the *Orange* in 1963. Ferry service between Newburgh and Beacon, previously called Fishkill Landing, existed in some form since the 1740s. During the 1700s and 1800s, river travel was very common. The ferry service was discontinued during the 1960s. In 2005, the ferries returned to service, and they continue to run as of 2011. (Courtesy of Willa Skinner.)

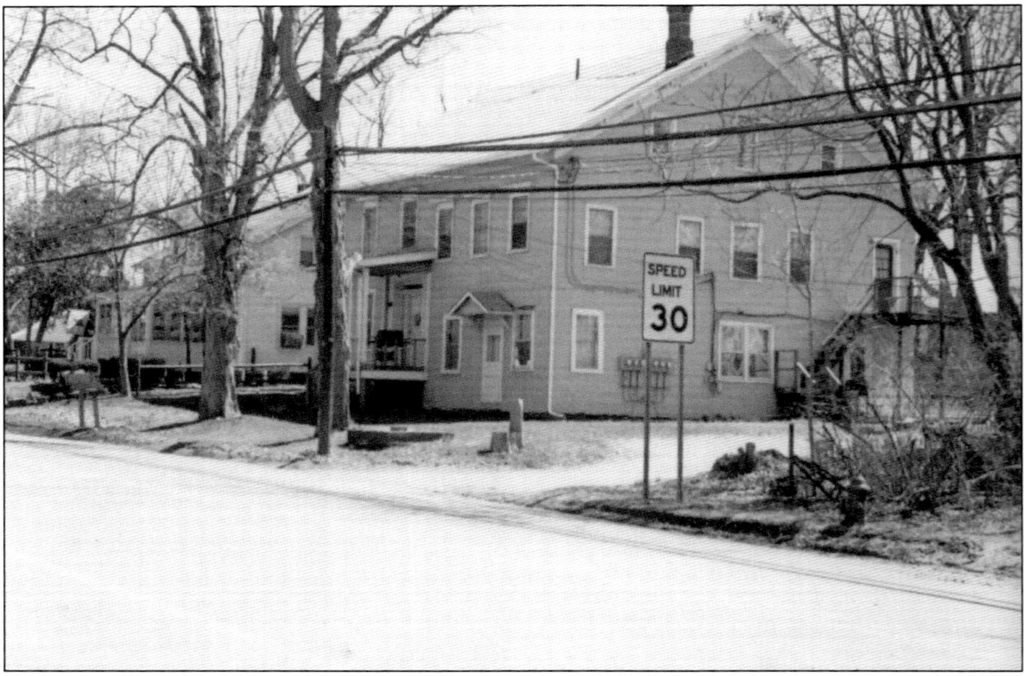

This photograph depicts a home on Route 52 near Shirley Avenue. It was built around 1800, and it was used as a home for indigent people. At that time, it was known as the "Poor House." During the 1900s, the Plumbush family sold it for $1,500 to the Clark family. It was then made into a two-family house during World War II. Trinity Episcopal Church is located near the home. (Courtesy of the Fishkill Historical Society.)

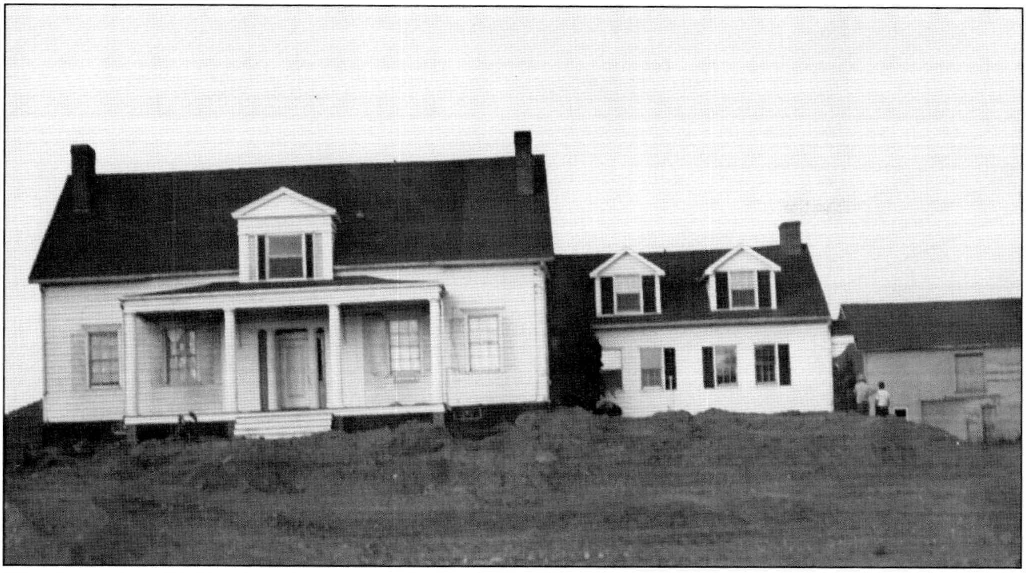

The Cornelius C. Van Wyck house is shown in this photograph at its former location on Route 9. The property was known as the Shaw Farm. Eventually, the Raisch family purchased the house, and they lived there until the mid-20th century. The family sold the house to the Holiday Inn, and it was torn down in 1965. Today, the Ramada Inn stands on the space where this house once stood. (Courtesy of the Fishkill Historical Society.)

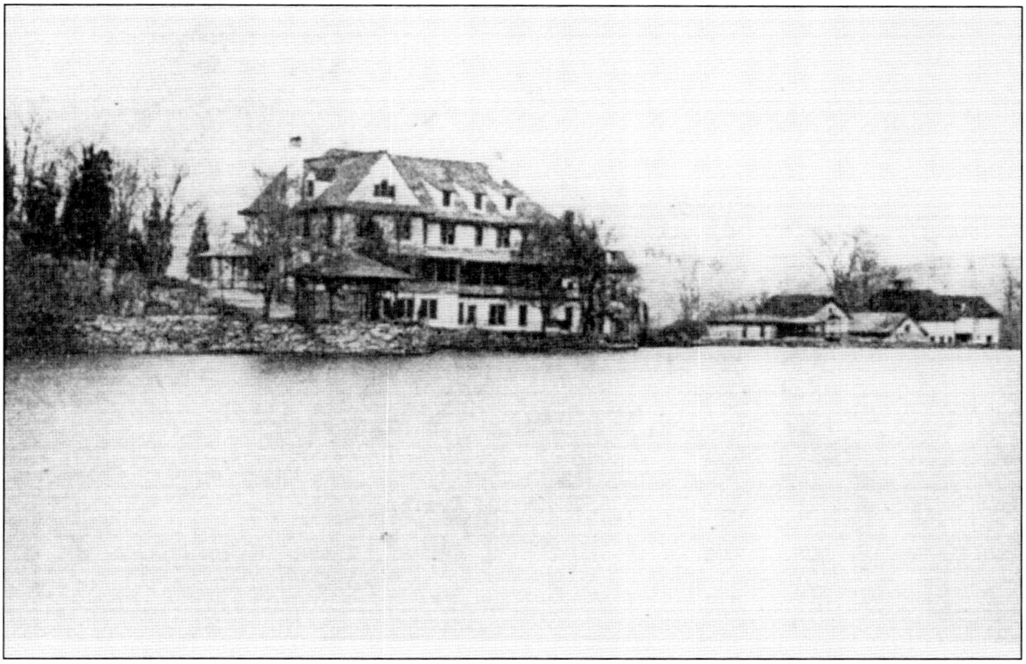

Henry Dubois Van Wyck built the Knickerbocker Lodge, which can be seen in this photograph. The lodge was located on Van Wyck Lane Road. Henry DuBois Van Wyck was born on October 27, 1823, and he built Willow Lake in the late 1800s. The Knickerbocker Lodge was built at Willow Lake, was featured on old postcards, and was considered to be a great location for special occasions. The hotel burned in the 1920s. J.H. Noah Slee acquired the property and built a stone house for his wife, Margaret Sanger. (Courtesy of the Fishkill Historical Society.)

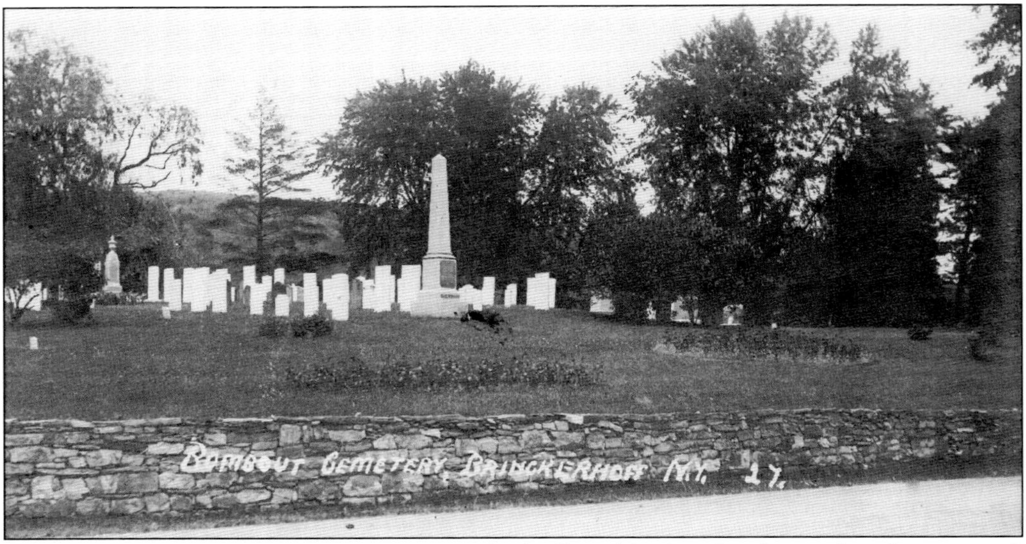

The Rombout Cemetery, located in the Brinckerhoff neighborhood, is depicted in this postcard. The cemetery once housed a Presbyterian church that was erected in the 1740s. The church burned down in 1866 and was not rebuilt. The church also served as a military hospital during the American Revolution. The cemetery has a modern monument to General Lafayette. He stayed at the adjacent Brinckerhoff house during the American Revolution. (Courtesy of Betty Snook.)

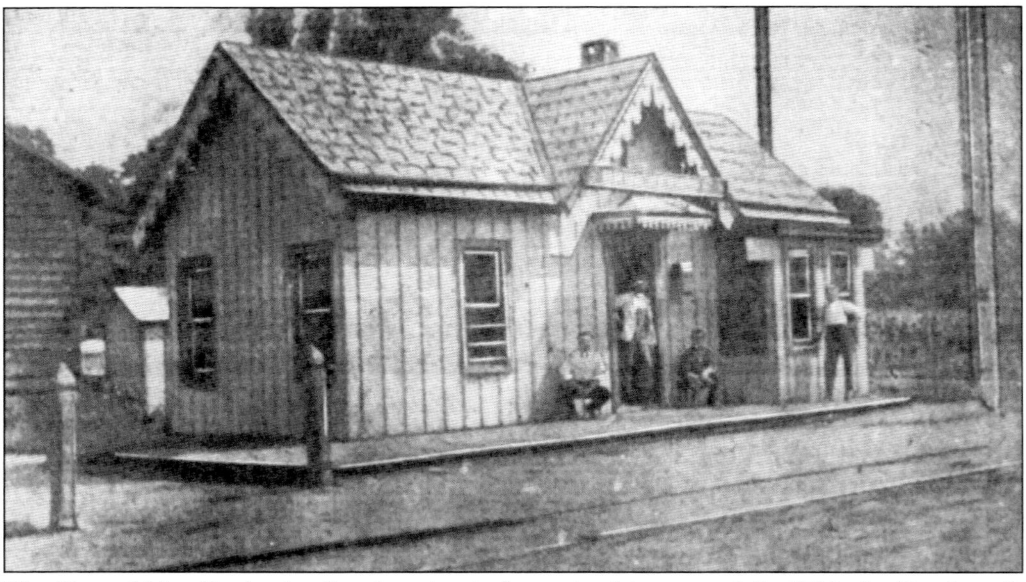
The Central New England railroad station is shown in this postcard. In 1866, the Dutchess & Columbia Railroad was constructed from a station of the Hudson River Railroad (1851) at the mouth of Fishkill Creek, northeast through Dutchess County. Fishkill was a stop along the line. Today, the line is not used. (Courtesy of Betty Snook.)

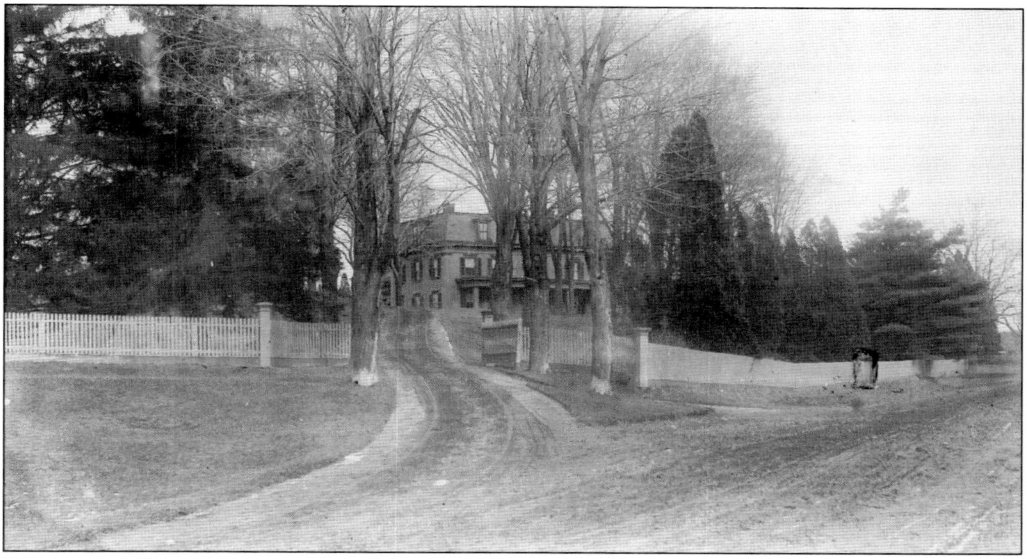

The home of Derick Brinckerhoff is shown in this photograph at Brinckerhoff. The back of the photograph reads "it was given by Reverend Jones at Cold Spring-on-Hudson to Helen W. Reynolds, April 1926." This home is also where the Marquis de Lafayette was ill during the Revolutionary War on the old Burton and Fishkill Road. The home was made of stone. (Courtesy of the Dutchess County Historical Society.)

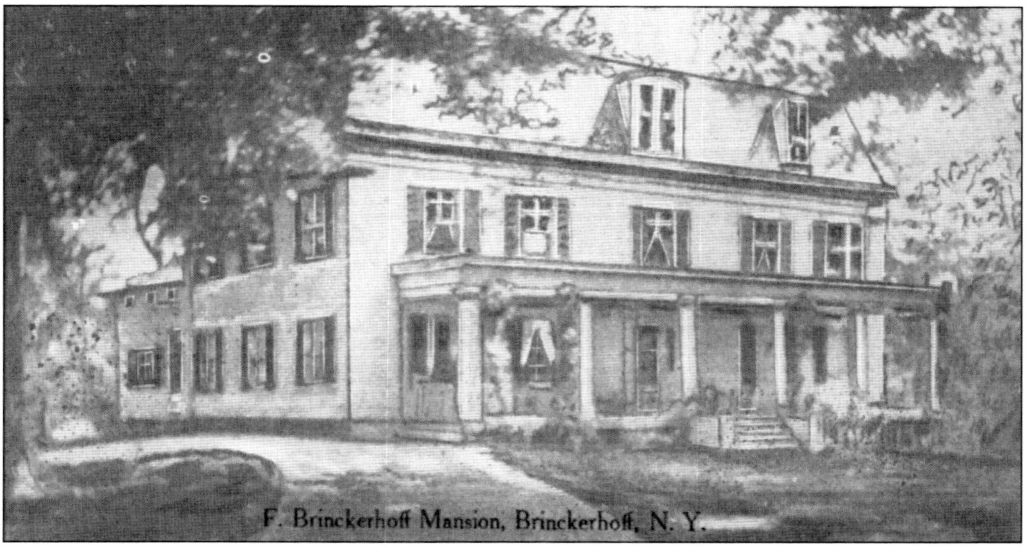

A closer view of the Brinckerhoff home is shown in a postcard. During the Revolution, Abram Brinckerhoff kept a store. A "Fishkill Tea Party" was held in Fishkill during the American Revolution when about 100 housewives of Fishkill and Beekman, commanded by Catharine Schutt and marching in military order, drew up before the Brinckerhoff store and demanded tea at the lawful price of six shillings per pound. Threatened with the destruction of his stock, Brinckerhoff quickly met the demands of the housewives. (Courtesy of Betty Snook.)

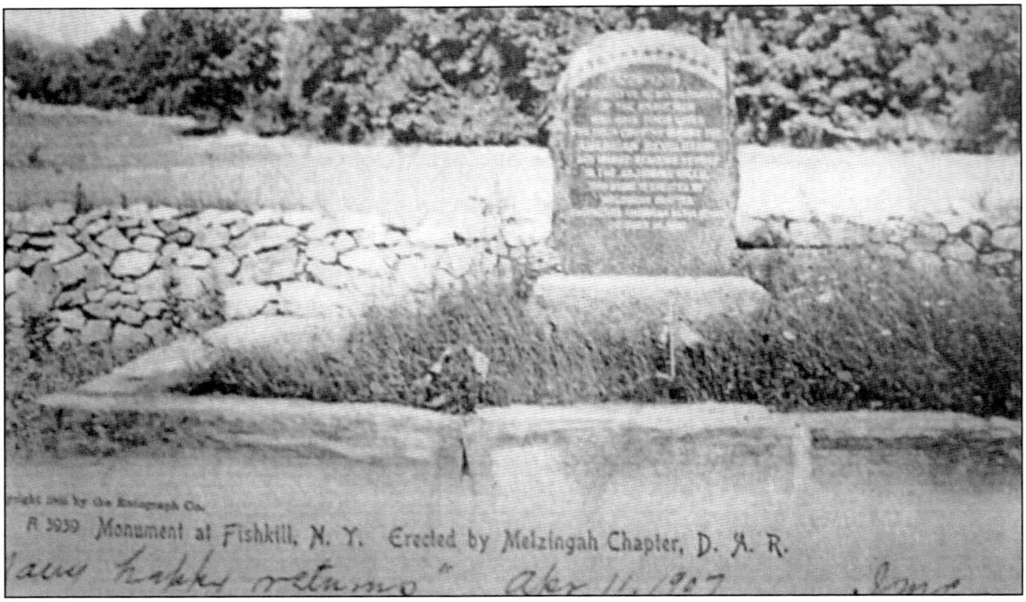

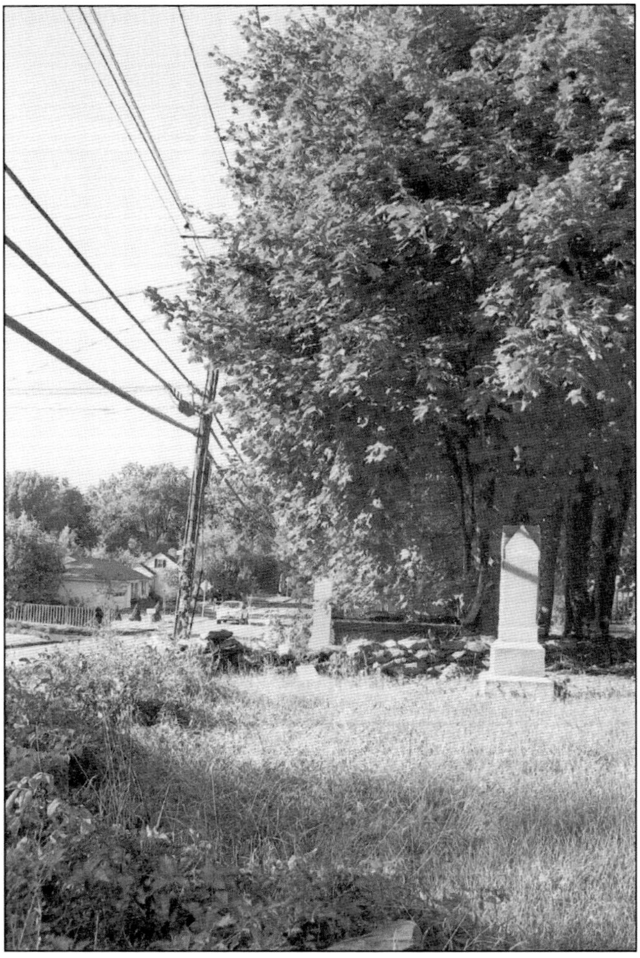

This postcard depicts a monument in tribute to the Continental Soldiers' Burial Ground at the historic Revolutionary War Fishkill Supply Depot that was emplaced in 1897. It is the largest burial ground of Revolutionary War soldiers identified in the United States. (Courtesy of Lance A. Ashworth.)

The black cemetery on Osborne Hill Road is depicted in this photograph. Some of the markers date back to 1832 and mark members of a black church called the Baxtertown AME Zion Church, which was located on Baxtertown Road. The church burned around the 1920s, and it was not rebuilt. The road was settled during the 19th century, making it one of the oldest black neighborhoods in Dutchess County. Wappinger Indians also reportedly lived on Baxtertown Road. (Courtesy of the author.)

Two

FISHKILL'S PEOPLE AND PLACES

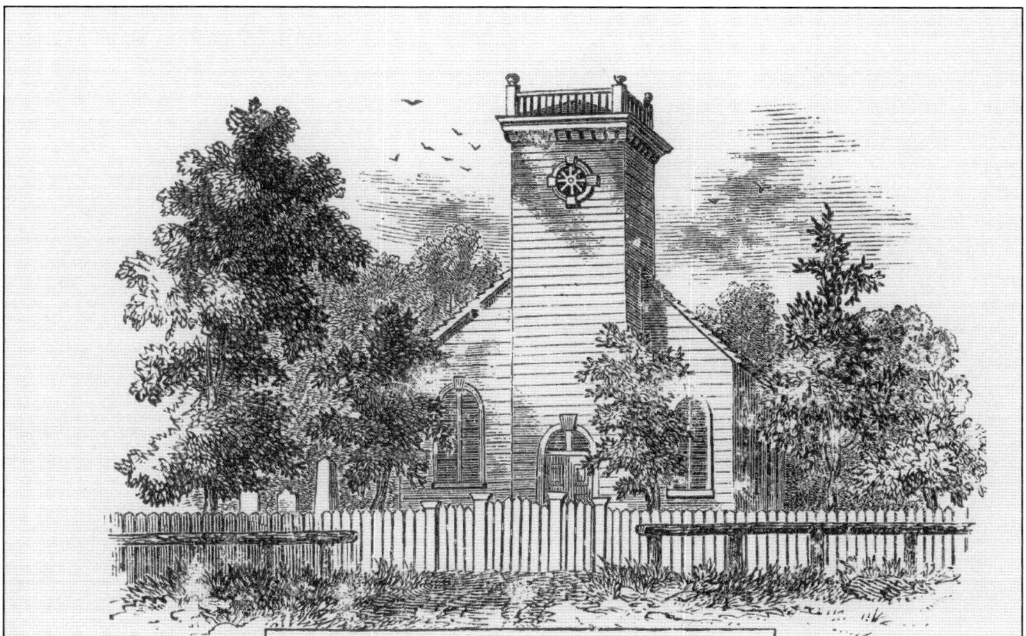

Trinity Episcopal Church in Fishkill is pictured in a drawing before the year 1860. Today, the church looks essentially the same as when it was built, except for the steeple and tower that is depicted in this drawing. The steeple was removed in 1803 because it was deemed unsafe. The remaining lower portion of the steeple tower was removed in 1860. (Courtesy of the Dutchess County Historical Society.)

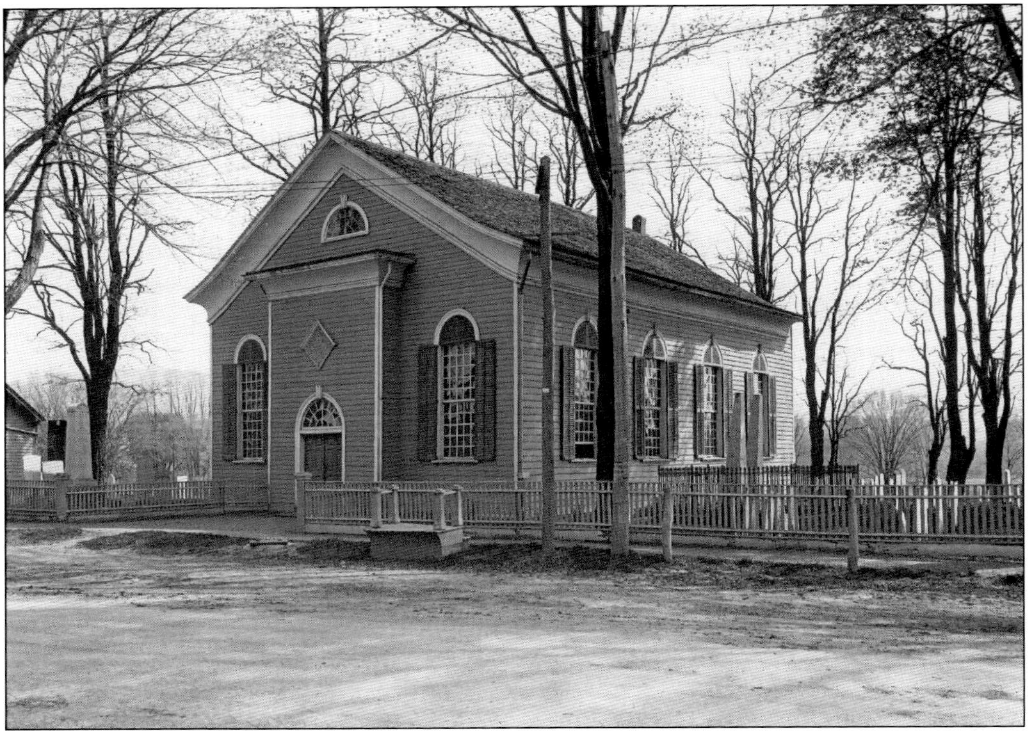

Trinity Episcopal Church is depicted in a 1913 photograph. This photograph shows the church as it currently looks. The church is located on the left side of Route 9 on Route 52 towards Brinckerhoff. (Courtesy of the New York State Archives.)

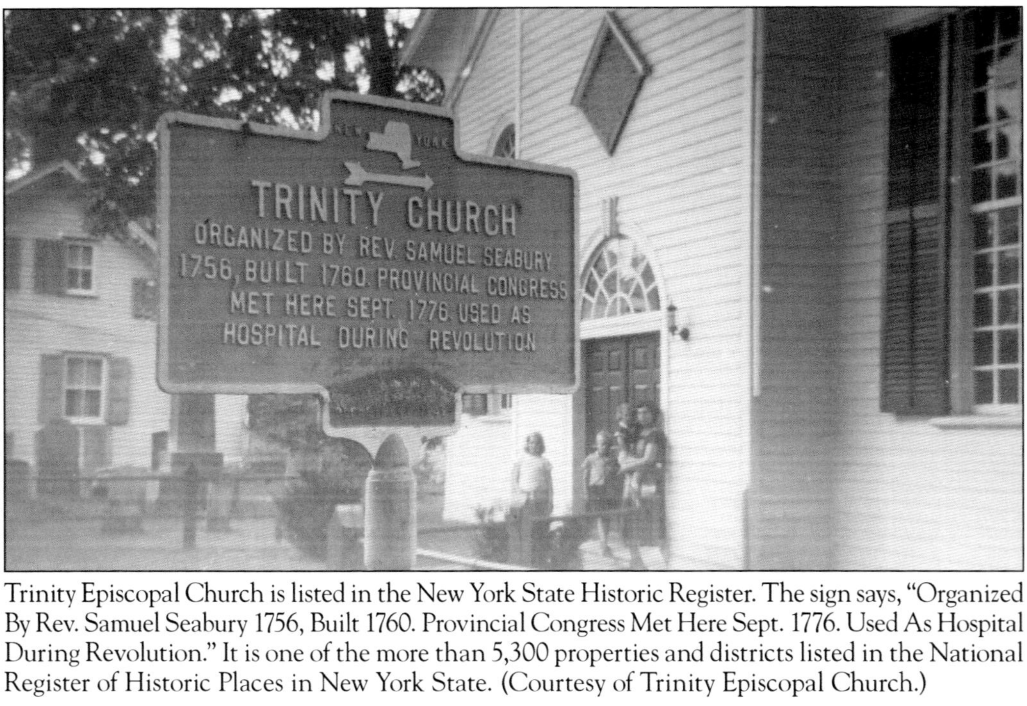

Trinity Episcopal Church is listed in the New York State Historic Register. The sign says, "Organized By Rev. Samuel Seabury 1756, Built 1760. Provincial Congress Met Here Sept. 1776. Used As Hospital During Revolution." It is one of the more than 5,300 properties and districts listed in the National Register of Historic Places in New York State. (Courtesy of Trinity Episcopal Church.)

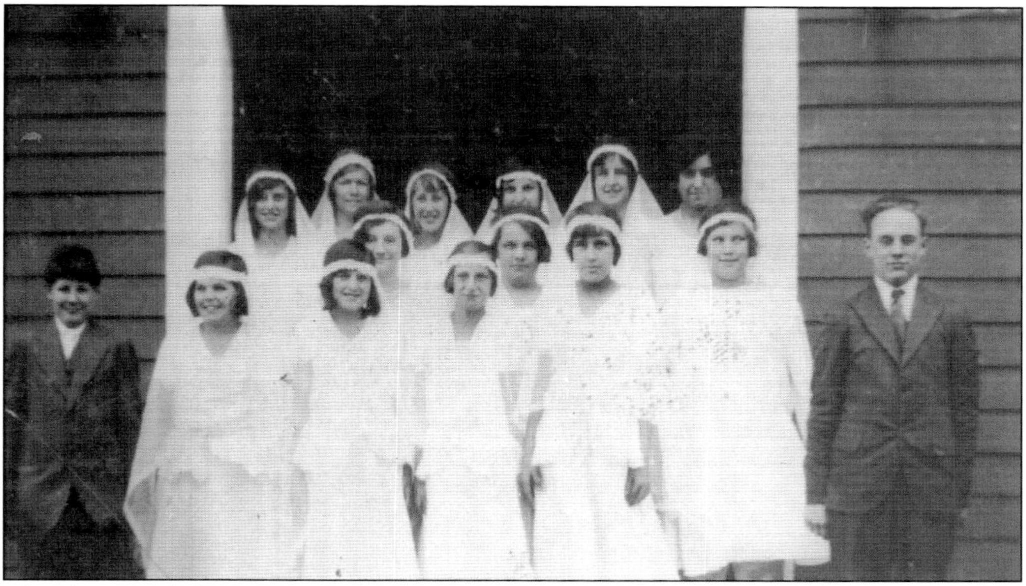

This photograph shows a group of girls as they receive their first communion in 1955. They stand in front of a painted Trinity Episcopal Church. From the photograph, it appears as if the church is painted a darker color than its current tan. Communions are still held at the church. (Courtesy of Trinity Episcopal Church.)

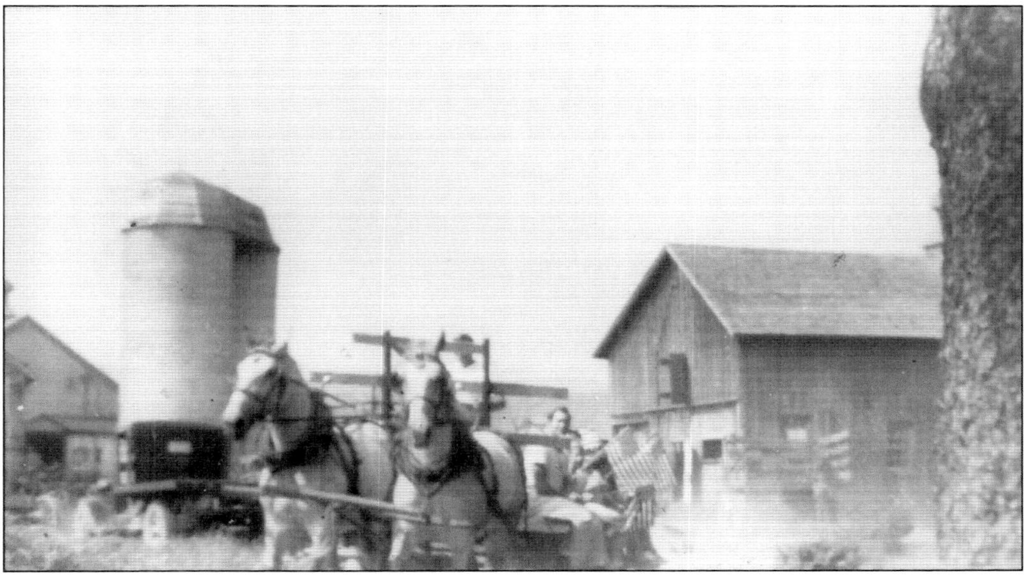

A Sunday school picnic at Fishkill Farms is depicted in this 1942 photograph. The Trinity Episcopal Church records hold a first account of someone who attended the picnic. The person wrote, "On the third Thursday in May 1931, we had our first ham supper and party at the house of Arthur D. Hoose at Fishkill Farms. This became an annual event. In 1942, we discontinued the supper but continued the annual card parties." (Courtesy of Trinity Episcopal Church.)

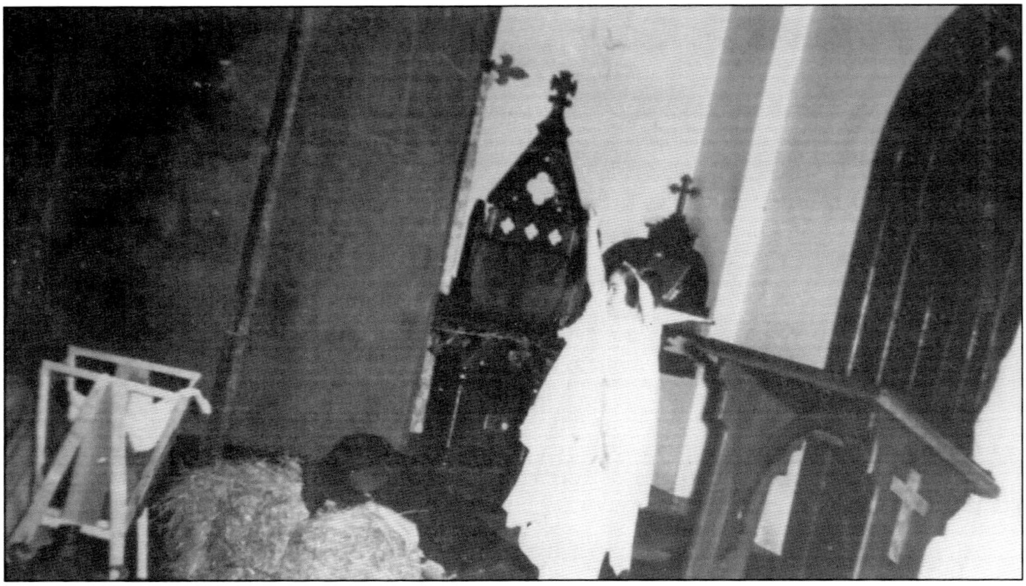

This photograph shows the 1941 depiction of the Nativity scene during the annual Christmas pageant. The priest still plans the Christmas pageant. Trinity Fishkill Episcopal Church has had 29 priests, including the current rector, Rev. Jean Campbell. The church was incorporated under the New York State Religious Law in 1784. (Courtesy of Trinity Episcopal Church.)

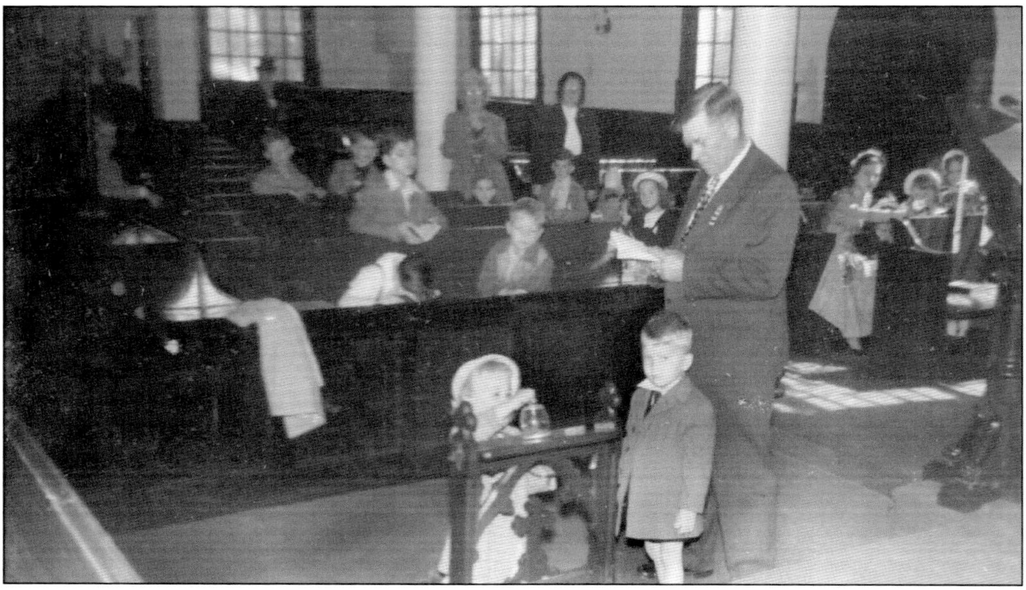

A father and son are shown attending Trinity Episcopal Church in this December 1955 photograph. Madam Brett gave land for Trinity Episcopal Church to James Duncan and Richard Southard as trustees in 1767. The original church building was occupied around 1769 and is still used for worship services today. (Courtesy of Trinity Episcopal Church.)

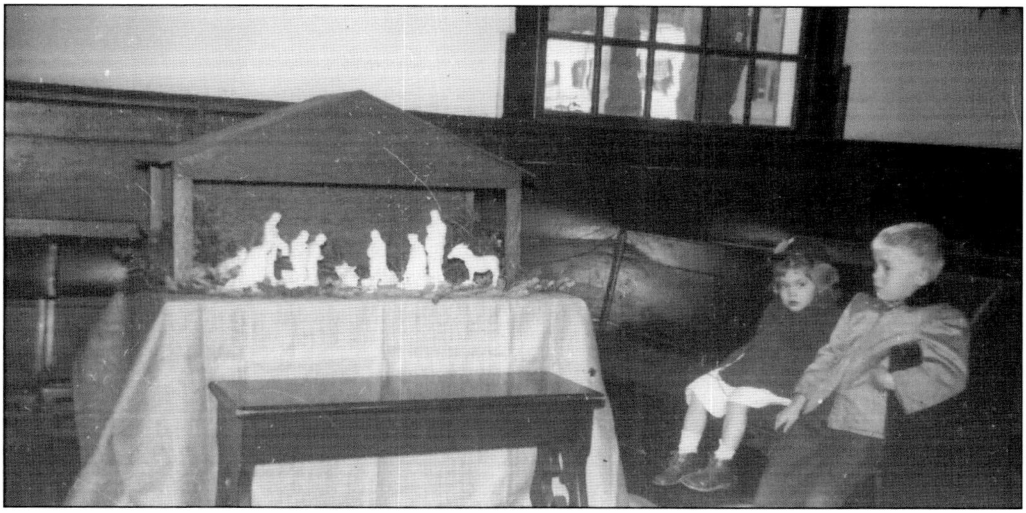

Two children look on in this photograph as Trinity Episcopal Church prepares the Christmas crèche in 1955. The Christmas crèche is one of the oldest Christmas traditions, demonstrating a three-dimensional artistic representation of the birth of Jesus. According to the church records, "At Christmas for several years, Edna Hoose, Arthur Hoose, and Nathan Hoose directed the pageant of the Nativity in the church." (Courtesy of Trinity Episcopal Church.)

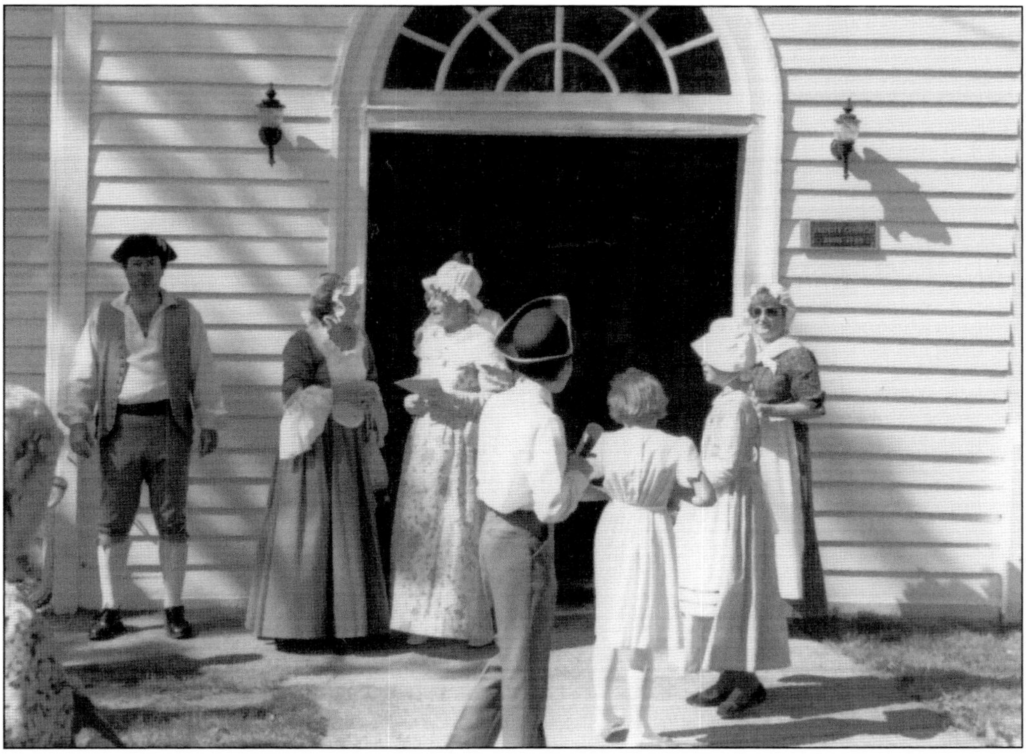

Several people dressed in costume stand in front of Trinity Episcopal Church. Trinity served as a hospital for Washington's army until at least 1781. It is not know if the church was used during the smallpox epidemic that ravaged the army at Fishkill. At the time of the Revolution, Trinity did not have pews, making it easier for it to be used as a hospital during the war. (Courtesy of Trinity Episcopal Church.)

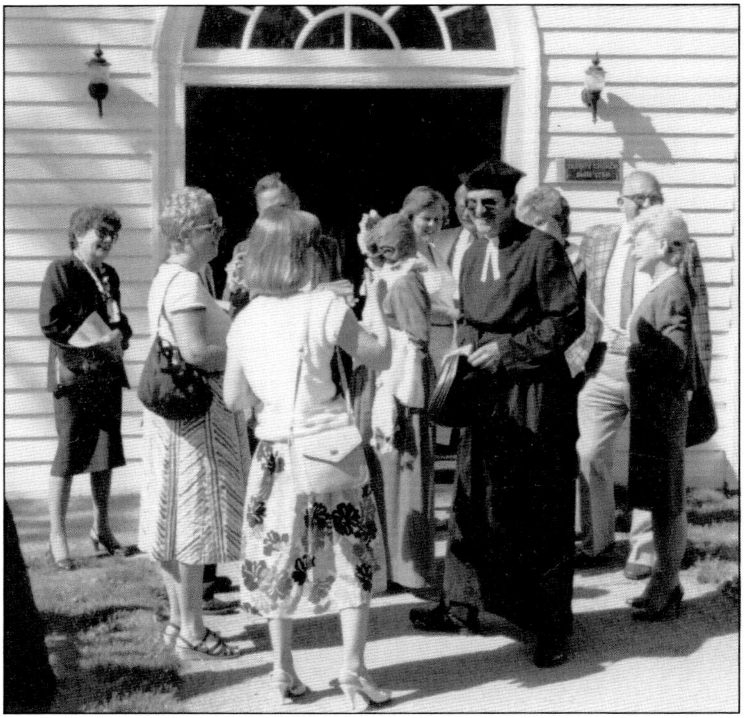

This photograph shows several people standing in front of Trinity Episcopal Church in 1986. In 1755, Rev. Samuel Seabury traveled from Long Island to Dutchess County in search of spreading the Episcopal Church. When he arrived to Fishkill, there were about 13 dwellings, another church, a tavern, and a schoolhouse along the main road. Seabury might have been dressed similar to the main depicted in this photograph. (Courtesy of Trinity Episcopal Church.)

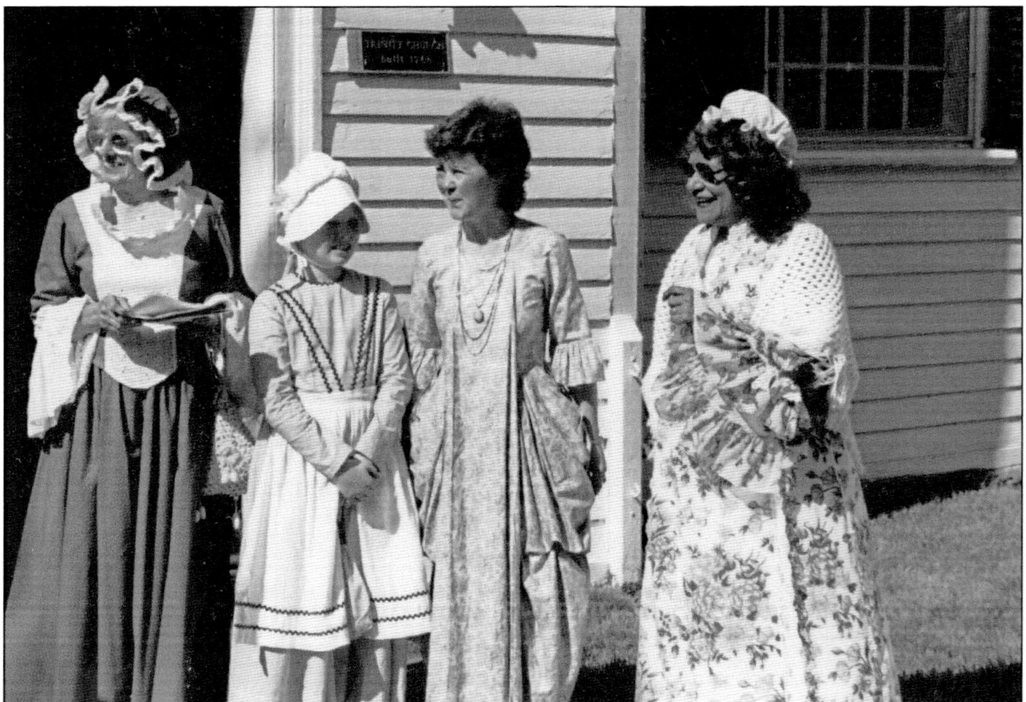

This photograph shows four women as they stand in front of Trinity Episcopal Church. They are celebrating Colonial Day in 1986. In 2006, the church celebrated its 250th anniversary and had similar colonial celebrations. The woman on the far right is Deacon Vivian Seipp, who served the church for many years. (Courtesy of Trinity Episcopal Church.)

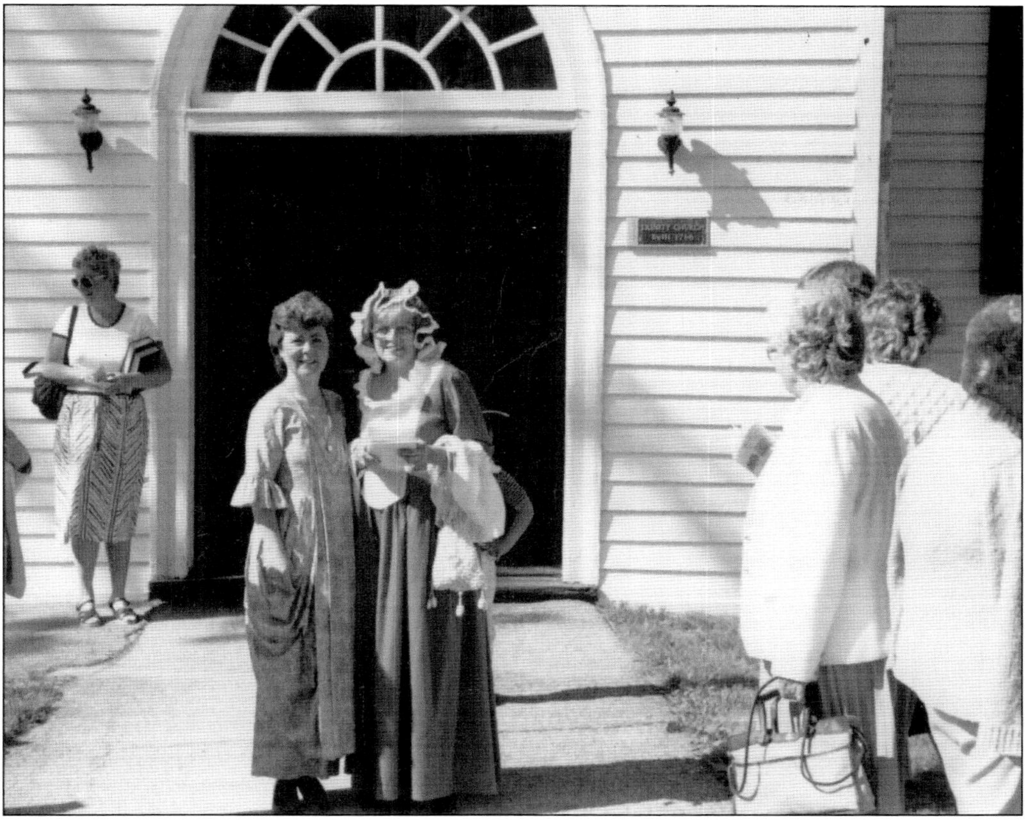

This photograph shows Trinity Episcopal Church parishioners celebrating Colonial Day in May 1986. Trinity Episcopal Church was closed after the Declaration of Independence. However, there is evidence that the congregation continued to hold home services, omitting prayers for the English king because doing so might offend patriots. The reverend at the time was John Beardsley, who was a loyalist. (Courtesy of Trinity Episcopal Church.)

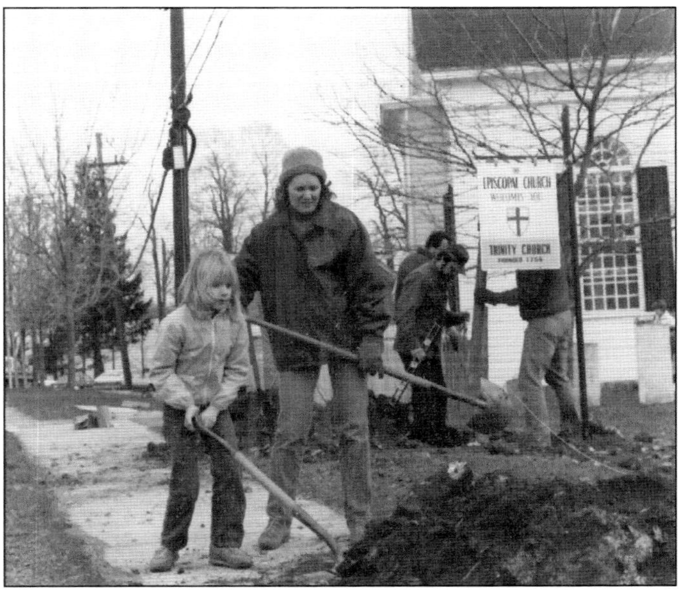

A mother and daughter stand together in this photograph in front of Trinity Episcopal Church. Samuel Verplanck, who had a local housed called Mount Gulian (used as General von Steuben's headquarters during the Revolution), gave Trinity a 140-acre glebe (a farm) at Stormville in 1785. The glebe was sold in 1955, and the proceeds were used to help finance the construction of Trinity's parish house, which was updated as depicted in this 1984 photograph. (Courtesy of Trinity Episcopal Church.)

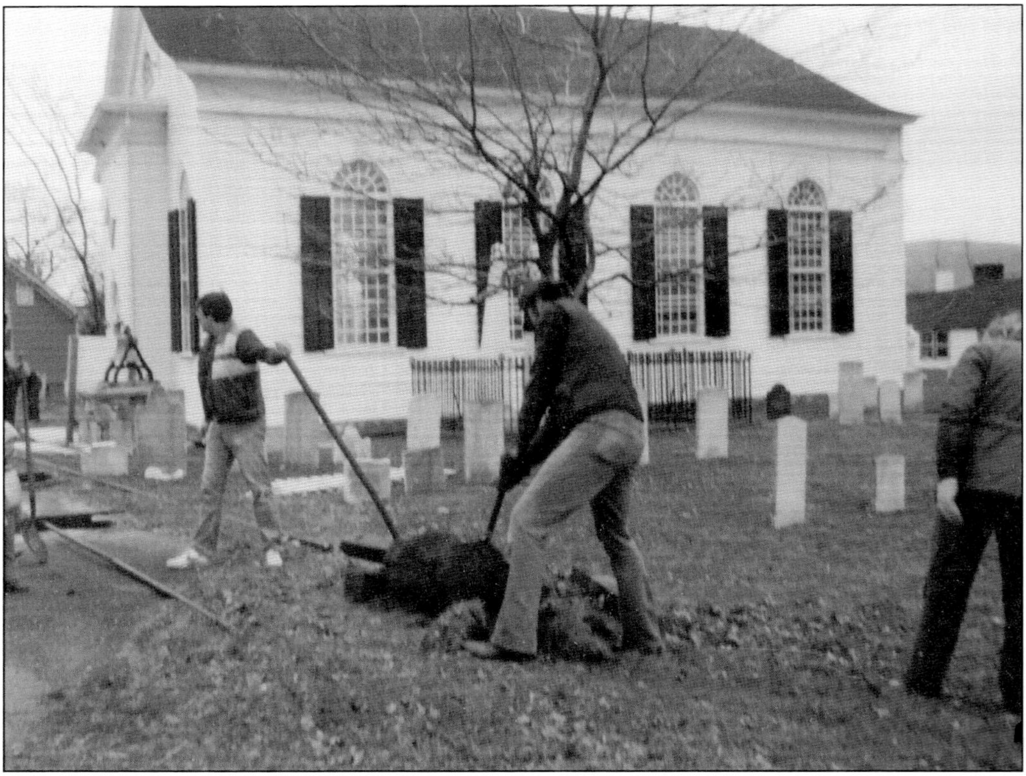

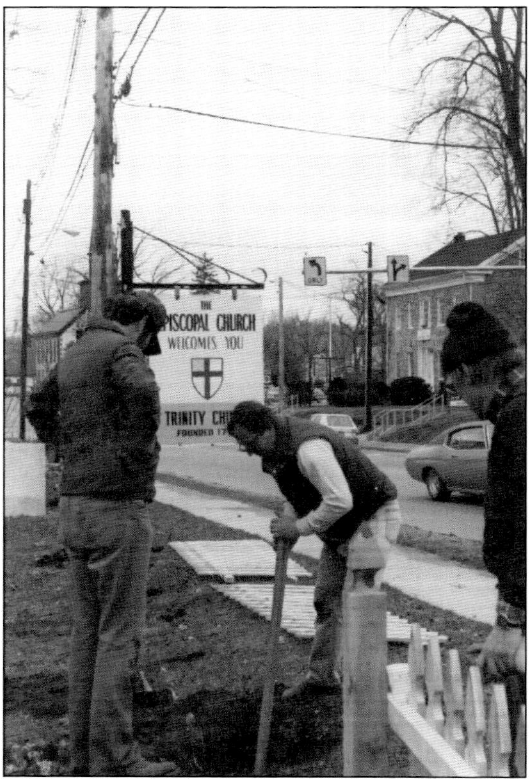

In April 1984, Trinity Episcopal Church underwent construction to its grounds. In the background of the photograph is Trinity Episcopal Church. The techniques used to construct Trinity Episcopal Church are similar to those used to build Dutch barns. The building is a rectangle about 42 feet by 60 feet. Ten smoothed tree trunks are mounted vertically on masonry foundations and joined at the top by timbers. The church likely did not have the glass windows that are shown here when it was first built. (Courtesy of Trinity Episcopal Church.)

This photograph shows a man repairing the fence in front of Trinity Episcopal Church. Constructed in 1768, according to church records, Trinity Episcopal Church is a rectangular, one-and-a-half-story frame edifice covered by a gable roof that flares gently at the eaves. Notable features are a fanlight and semicircular-headed windows. The interior was restored in 1963. (Courtesy of Trinity Episcopal Church.)

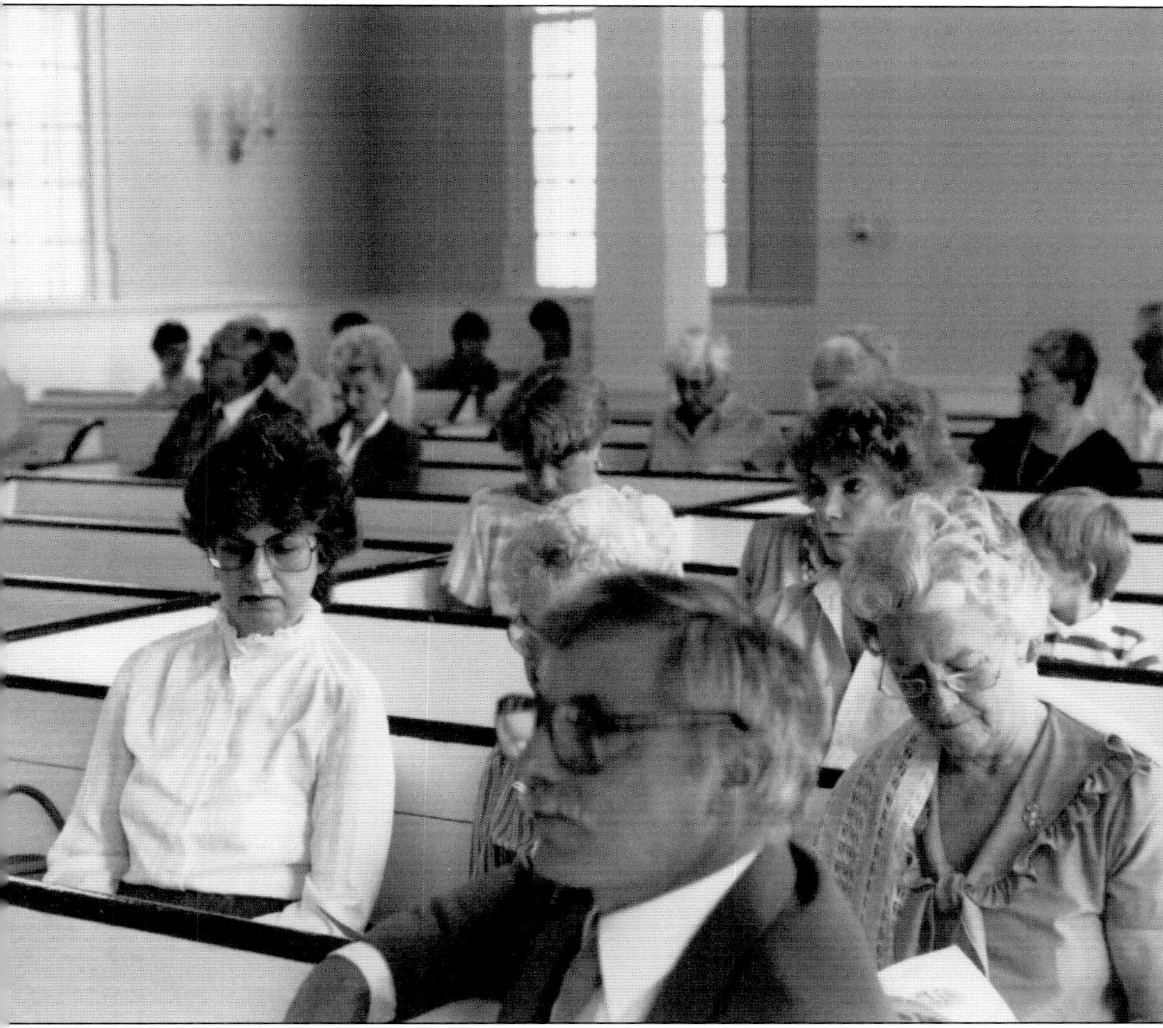

Several parishioners sit in pews during a church service during the 1980s. As mentioned, Trinity did not have pews when it was first constructed, making it easier for it to be used as a hospital during the Revolutionary War. (Courtesy of Trinity Episcopal Church.)

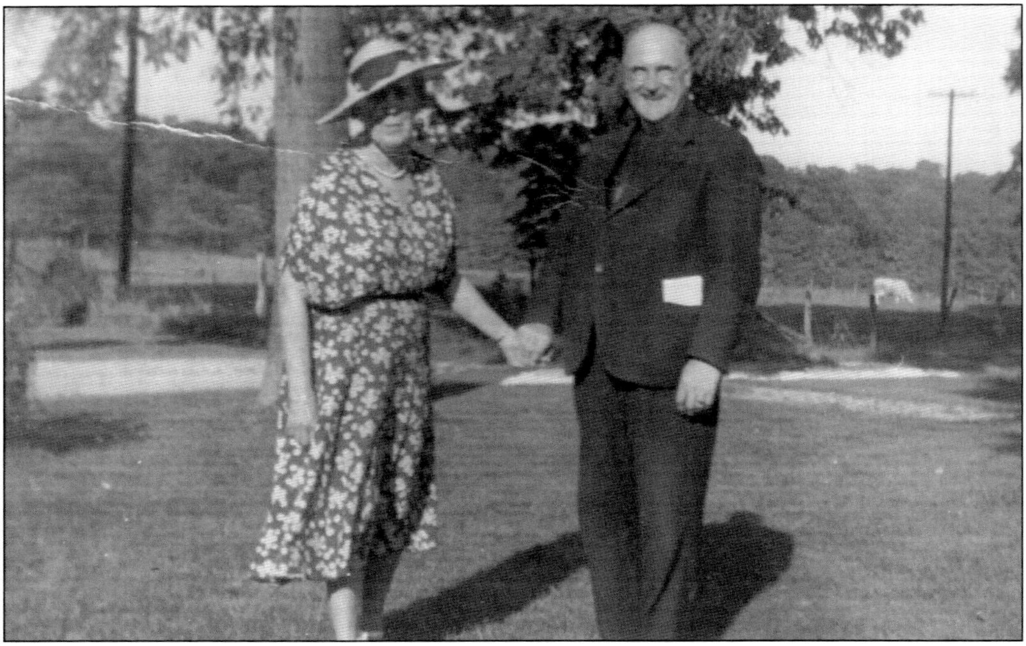

This photograph depicts the Rev. John B. Myers and his wife standing near Trinity Episcopal Church in 1941. He was the rector from 1938 to 1952. While the state convention was meeting in Fishkill at the beginning of the American Revolution, it met at the church in September 1776. However, the church was deemed to not be in fit condition, as there was a dearth of seats and other necessities. The convention then moved to the nearby Dutch Reformed Church. (Courtesy of Trinity Episcopal Church.)

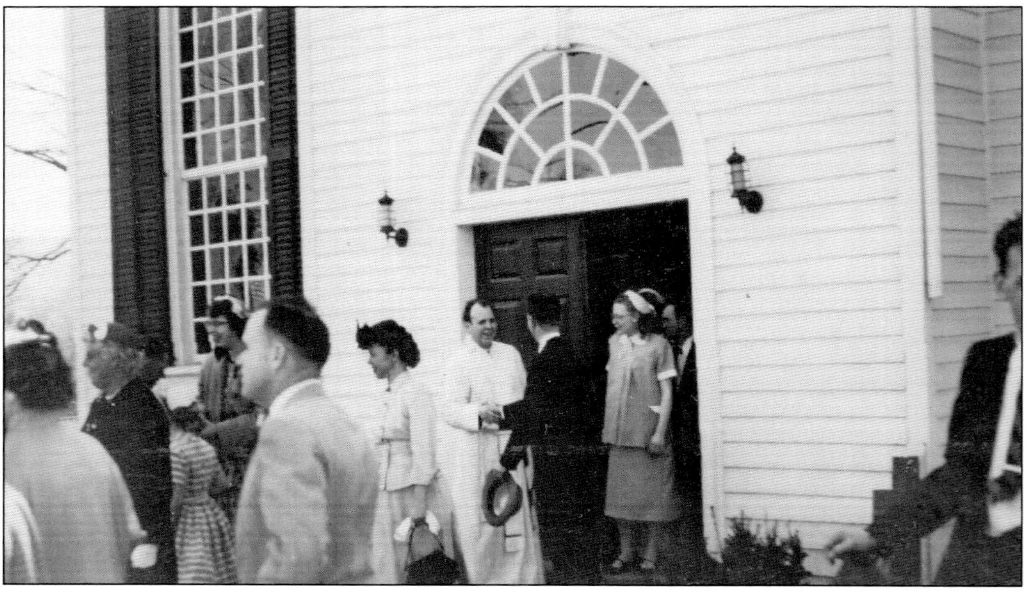

The Trinity Episcopal Church congregation files out of the building in this photograph after Easter services in 1943. Several of the people in the photograph look as if they are heading off to "Coffee Hour," which is held in the parish house. Coffee Hour is an activity held after services that allows members to socialize and partake in the provided food and beverages. (Courtesy of Trinity Episcopal Church.)

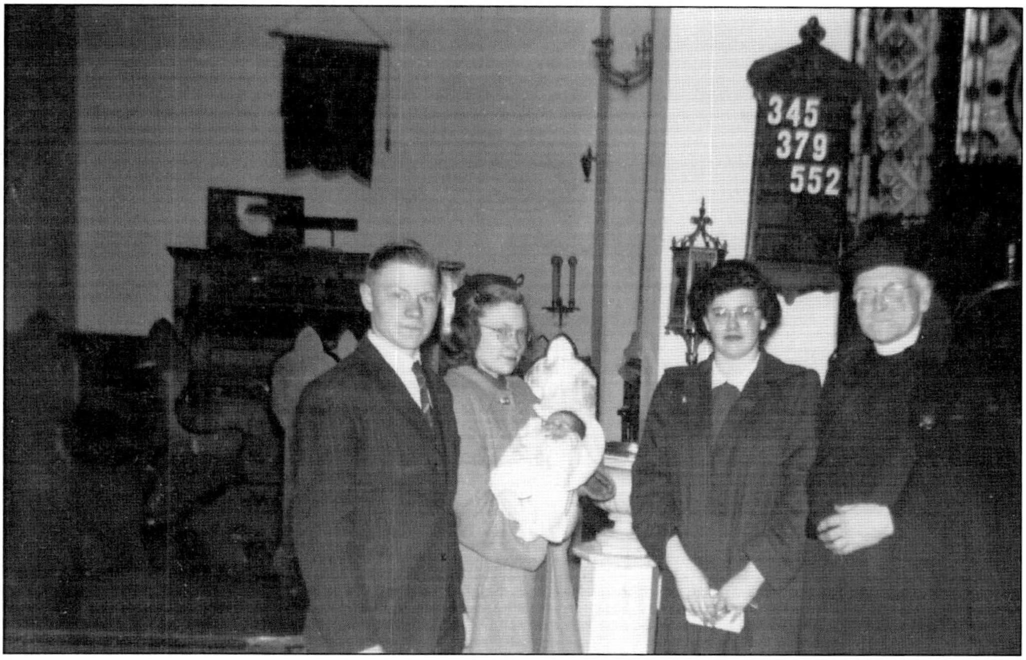

A couple, the rector, and presumably the baby's godmother stand for a photograph in 1952. Baptisms in the church are held during the service. The congregations sing hymns from the hymnal books. The hymns used for the baptism depicted in the photograph can be seen in the right corner: 345, 379 and 552. (Courtesy of Trinity Episcopal Church.)

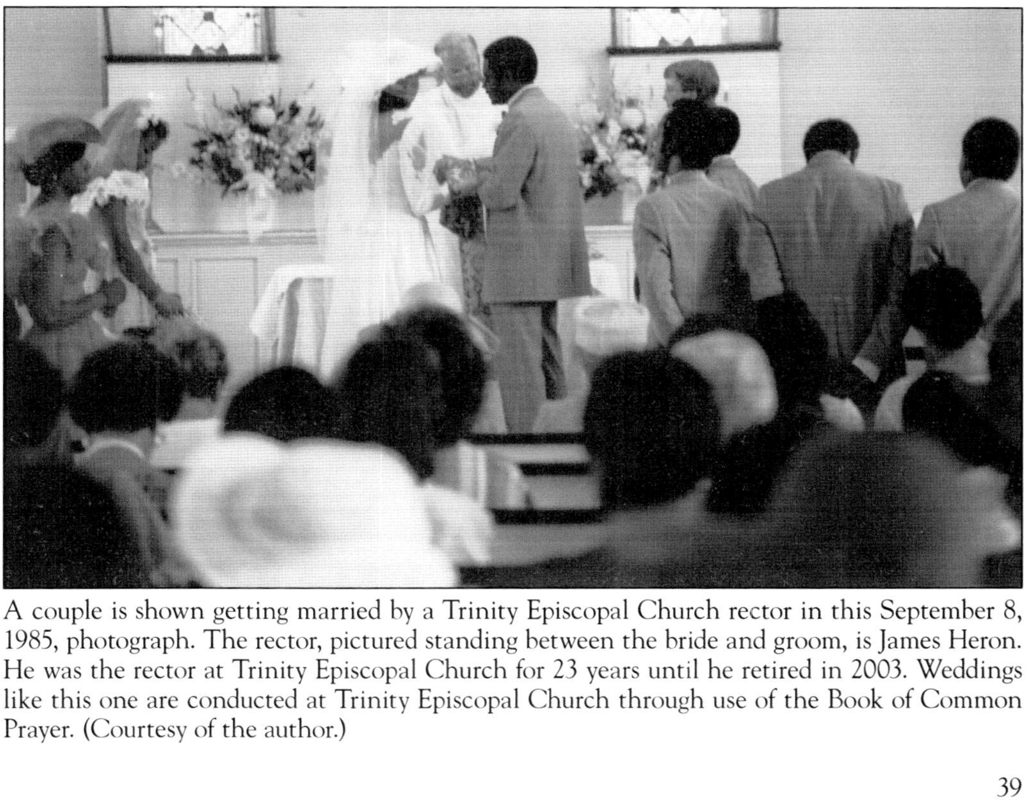

A couple is shown getting married by a Trinity Episcopal Church rector in this September 8, 1985, photograph. The rector, pictured standing between the bride and groom, is James Heron. He was the rector at Trinity Episcopal Church for 23 years until he retired in 2003. Weddings like this one are conducted at Trinity Episcopal Church through use of the Book of Common Prayer. (Courtesy of the author.)

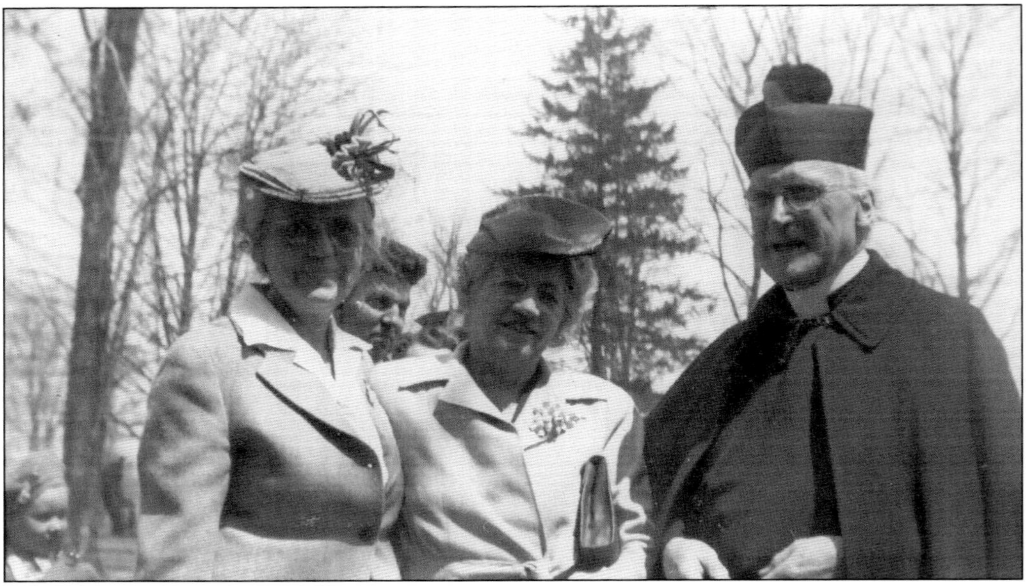

An older Rev. John B. Myers, his wife, and an unidentified woman stand in front of Trinity Episcopal Church on Easter Sunday, 1943. During the 1940s at Trinity Episcopal Church, an annual supper was held at the Hoose home. The supper was used to pay for operating expenses and also as part of the church missionary offerings. (Courtesy of Trinity Episcopal Church.)

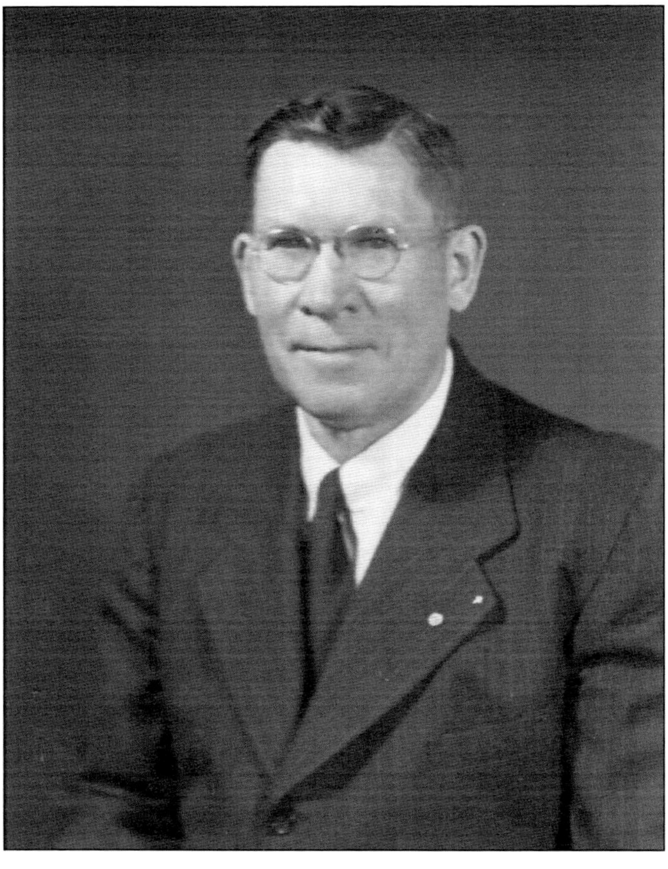

Arthur D. Hoose is depicted in a photograph from the 1950s. He was the superintendent of the Trinity Episcopal Church School. Every summer, the church school would have picnic, games, and swimming. It had events at various places such as Sekunna's Pool, Charlotte's Grove, Indian Point, Sylvan Lake, Tucker's Lake, Haight's Farm, Lake Walton, Snow Valley, and Wiccopee Grange Hall when it rained. (Courtesy of Trinity Episcopal Church.)

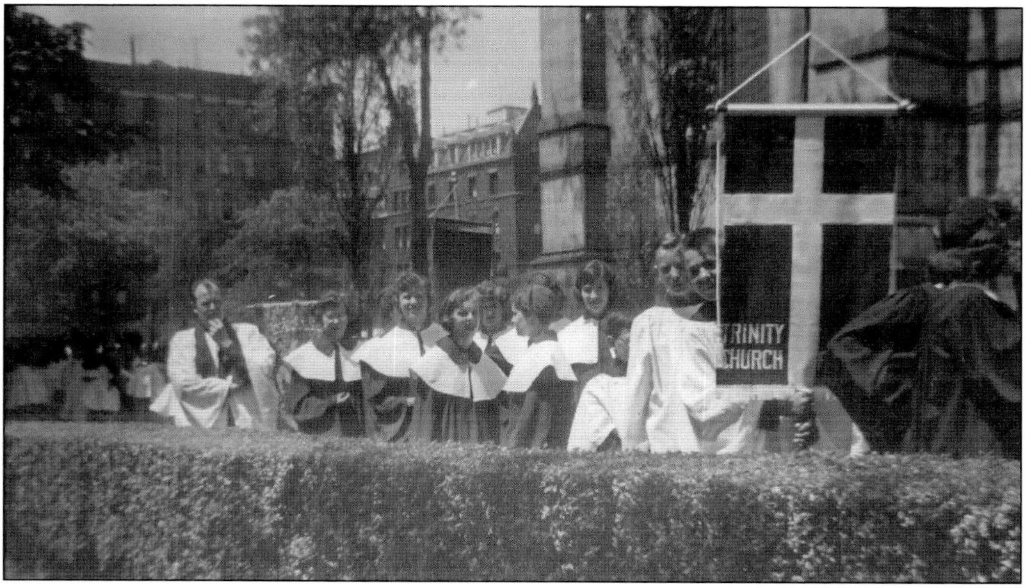

Delegates from Trinity Episcopal Church are shown in a processional at the Cathedral of St. John the Divine in a 1955 photograph. The Diocese of New York conducted an annual Presentation Service at the Cathedral of St. John the Divine, at which time the Sunday schools of the diocese presented their missionary offerings. The first attendance of Trinity Episcopal Church at this service was in 1934. (Courtesy of Trinity Episcopal Church.)

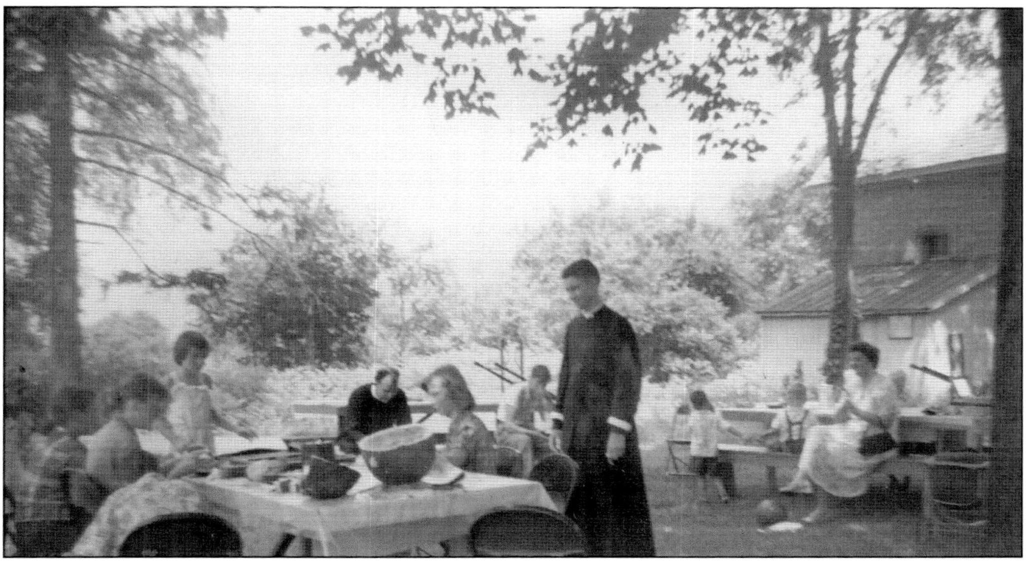

The rector and several parishioners celebrate the end of a summer session of vacation school in this 1953 photograph. The school was held under the direction of Rev. R. DeWitt Mallary and Rev. Otis Charles. A picnic was held following the session at St. Mark's Episcopal Church in nearby Chelsea for all who attended. (Courtesy of Trinity Episcopal Church.)

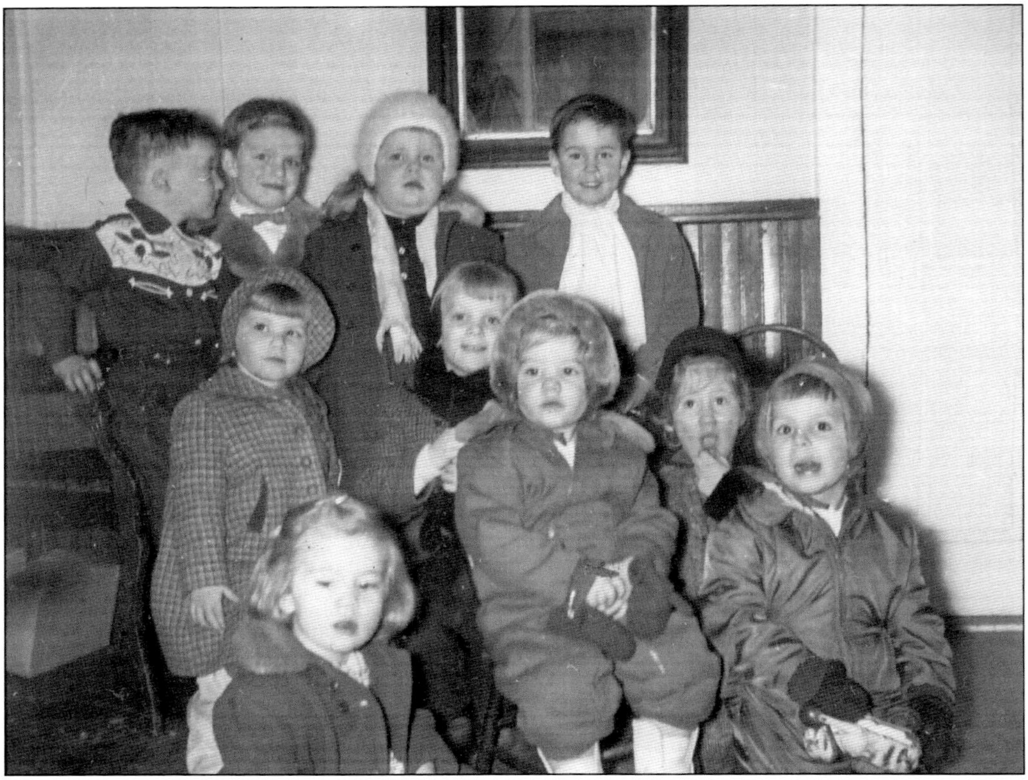

Several church school students are depicted in a photograph from the winter of 1955. They may have been attending the annual Children's Christmas Eve service that was held at 4:00 p.m. It was under the guidance of Father Mallary, and the children built the Nativity scene with white figurines in a crèche made by church workers. (Courtesy of Trinity Episcopal Church.)

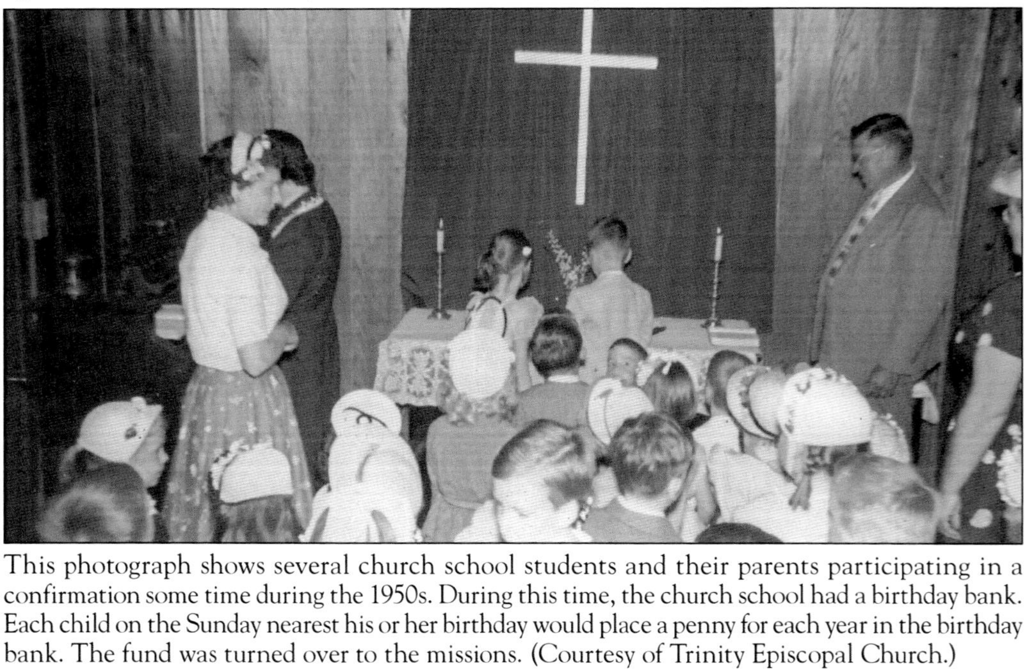

This photograph shows several church school students and their parents participating in a confirmation some time during the 1950s. During this time, the church school had a birthday bank. Each child on the Sunday nearest his or her birthday would place a penny for each year in the birthday bank. The fund was turned over to the missions. (Courtesy of Trinity Episcopal Church.)

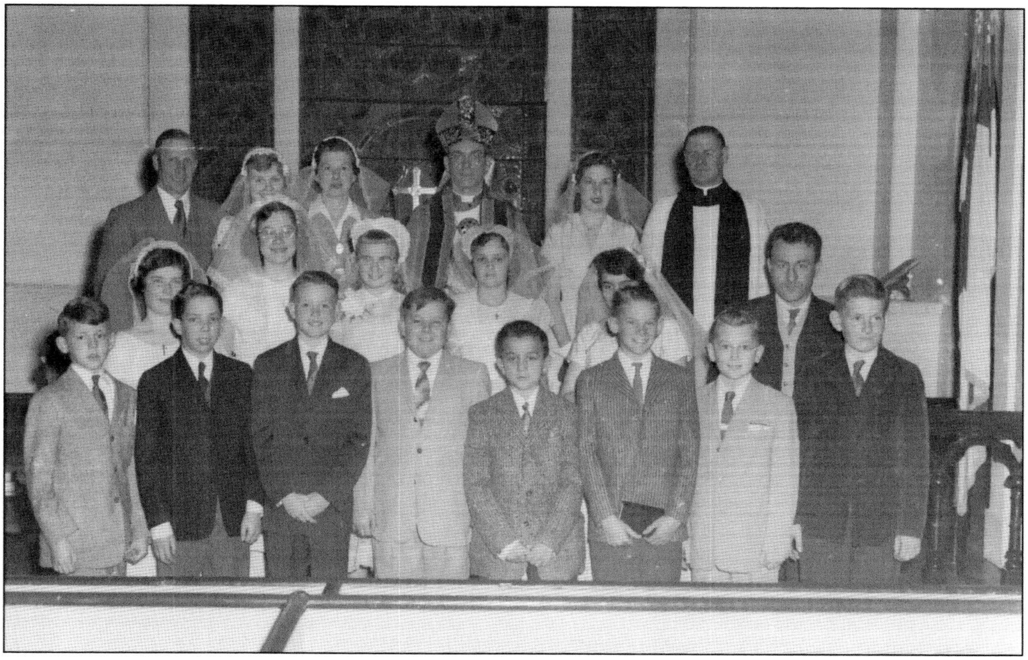

Another confirmation class is shown in a 1958 photograph inside Trinity Episcopal Church. Several of these children may have attended the Diocese of New York Presentation Service. The children who were chosen to go had high attendance records and were those who did the best Sunday school work. (Courtesy of Trinity Episcopal Church.)

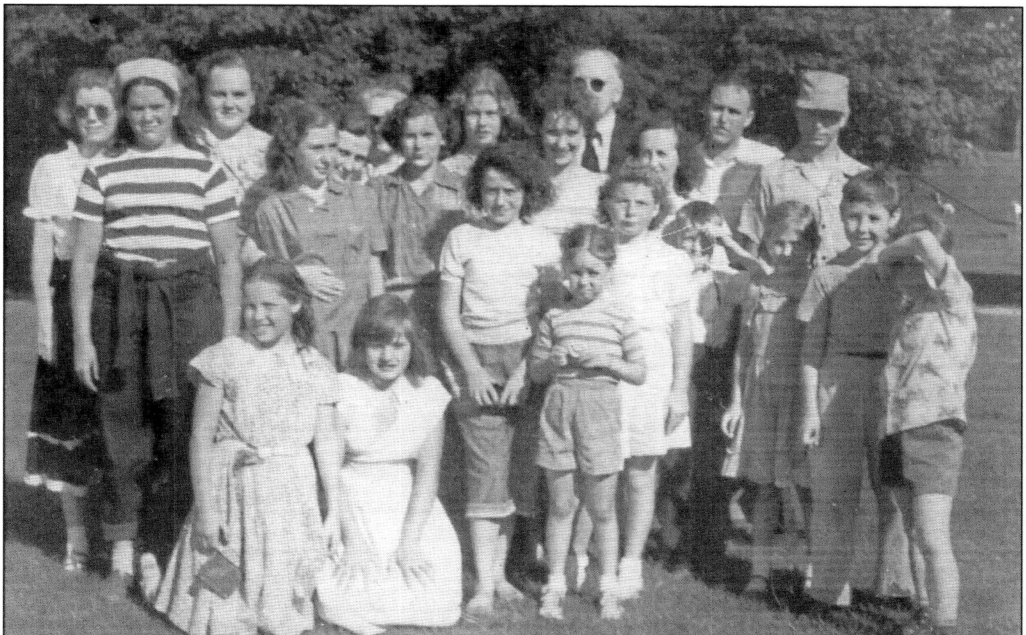

This is 1948 photograph of children from the Trinity Episcopal Church Sunday School at Indian Point. The group may have stopped at Indian Point on their way back from the presentation service. After the services, the group would visit places of interest in New York City and stop for picnics on the way back. (Courtesy of Trinity Episcopal Church.)

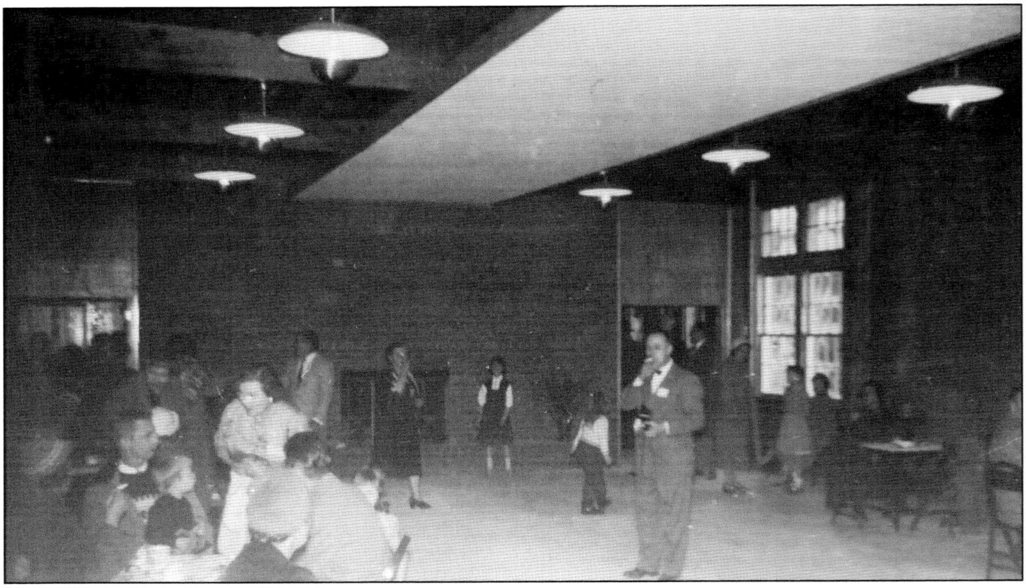

It took contributions from over 100 families in 1756 to erect an English church in Fishkill. Descendants of those families are shown here at the parish house in April 1955. Currently, the parish house is used for school classes, offices, and Coffee Hour. (Courtesy of Trinity Episcopal Church.)

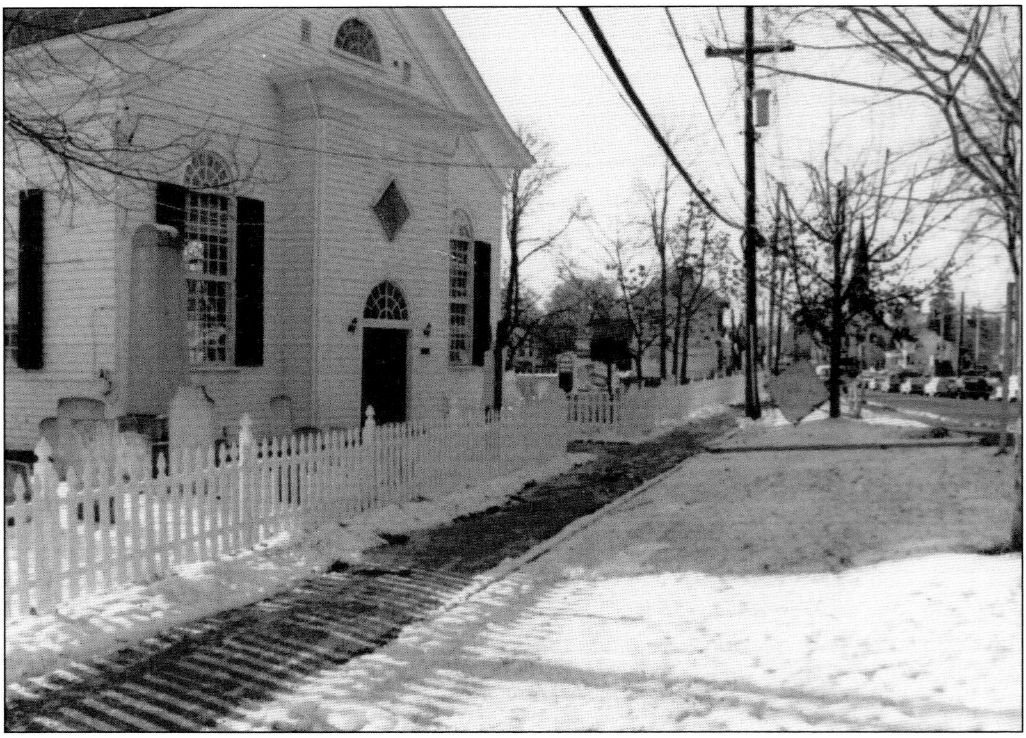

Trinity Episcopal Church stands in a photograph taken during the wintertime. The Verplanck family played significant roles as benefactors, wardens, and vestrymen throughout Trinity's history. In 1960, the last burial in the churchyard was for a member of the Verplanck family. A bit of the churchyard can be seen in this photograph. (Courtesy of Trinity Episcopal Church.)

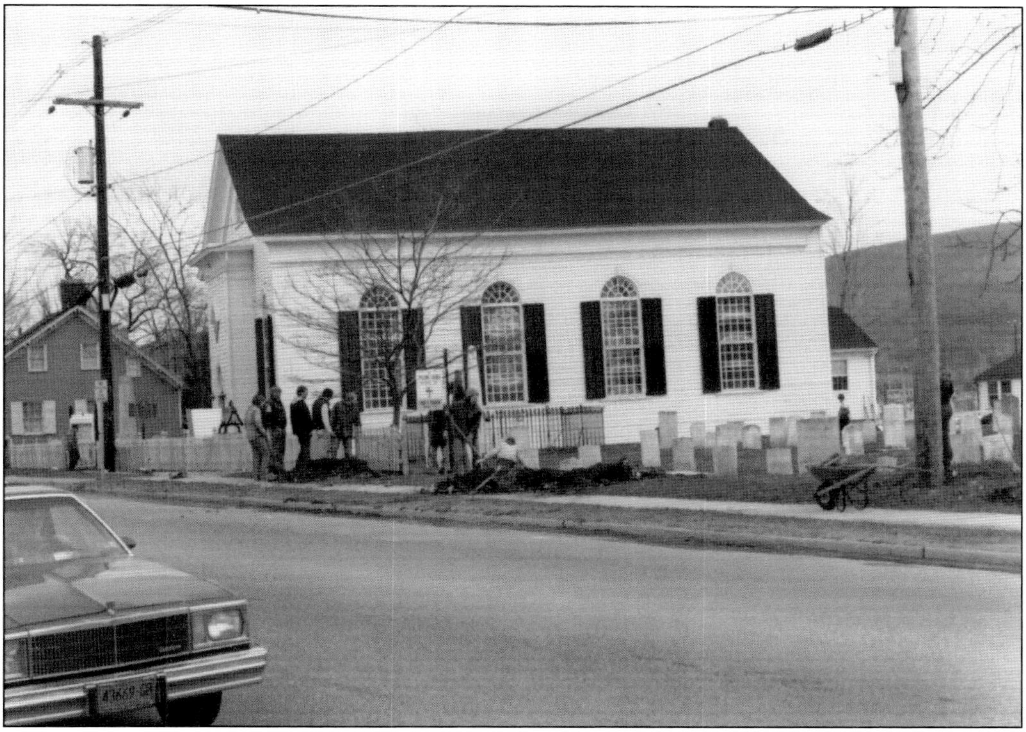

The photograph shows several men as they begin construction in the Trinity graveyard during the 1980s. According to the Trinity website, many patriots are buried in the churchyard, including Thomas Southard; Isaac Ter Boss; Sylvanus Pine and his sons John, Robert, and Thomas; Ezekiel Green; and Lt. William Alger. Other Trinity patriots include Philip Pine, Lt. James Cooper, and Jacobus Swartout. (Courtesy of Trinity Episcopal Church.)

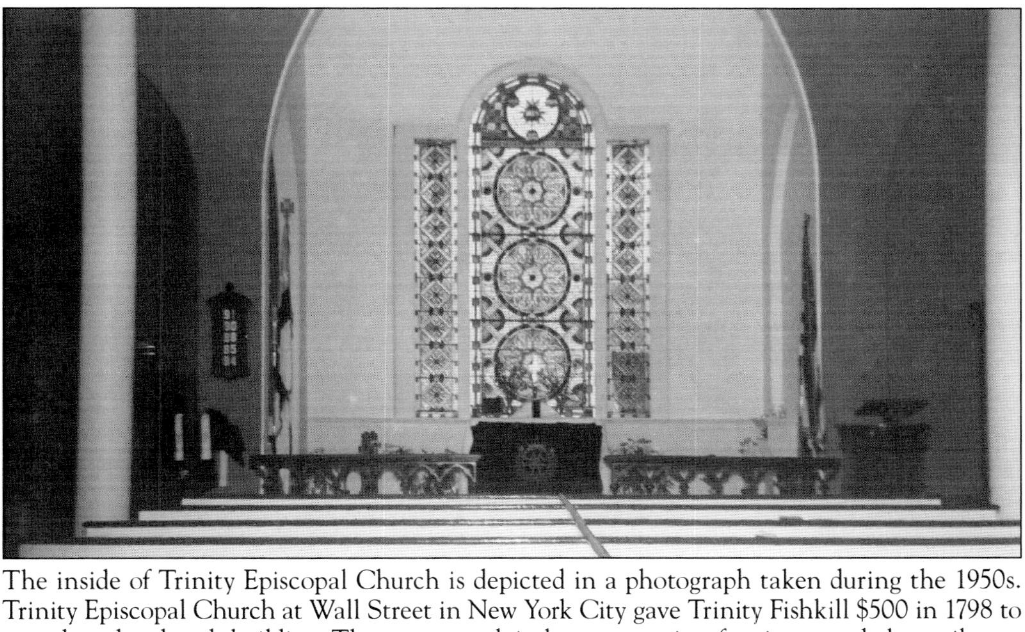

The inside of Trinity Episcopal Church is depicted in a photograph taken during the 1950s. Trinity Episcopal Church at Wall Street in New York City gave Trinity Fishkill $500 in 1798 to complete the church building. The current pulpit, lectern, sacristy furniture, and altar rail were installed during the 1960s. (Courtesy of Trinity Episcopal Church.)

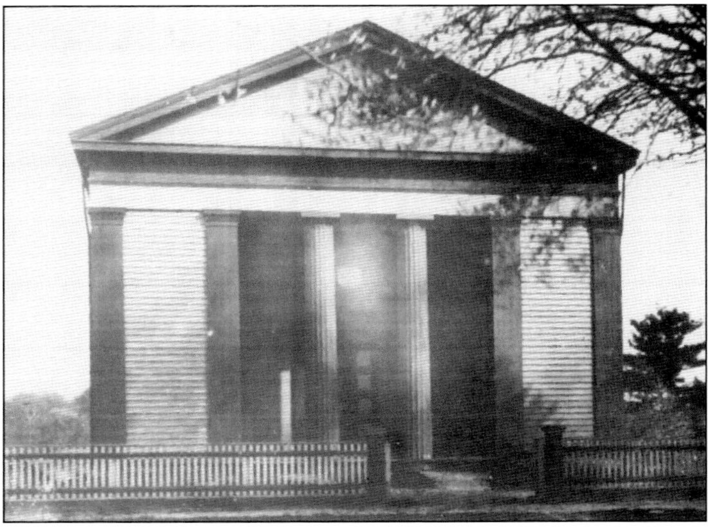

The Fishkill Methodist Church stands in a photograph taken some time during the late 19th or early 20th century. The Fishkill Methodist Church is located in the village of Fishkill on Broad Street. The structure exhibits the influence of the Greek Revival mode. The cornerstone was laid on October 17, 1838, and the building was completed on December 23, 1841. (Courtesy of the Fishkill Methodist Church.)

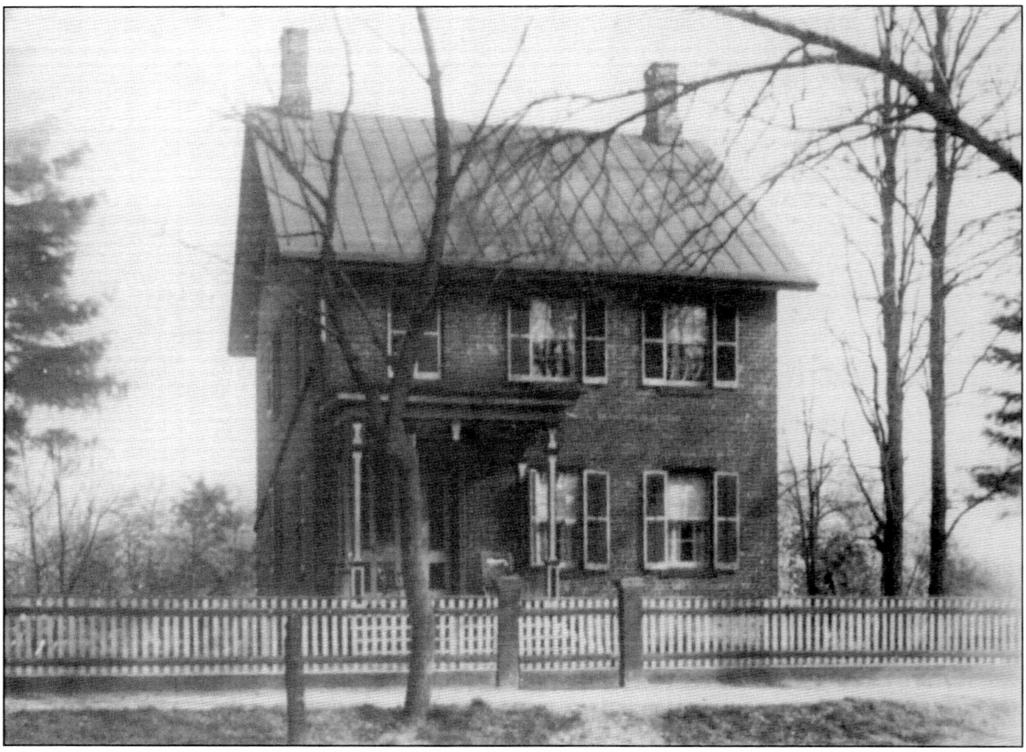

The brick parsonage next to the Fishkill Methodist Sanctuary is shown in this late-19th- or early-20th-century photograph. The building was constructed in 1865. It is no longer used as the parsonage and is now privately owned. The current parsonage was purchased in 1966 and allowed for more space. (Courtesy of the Fishkill Methodist Church.)

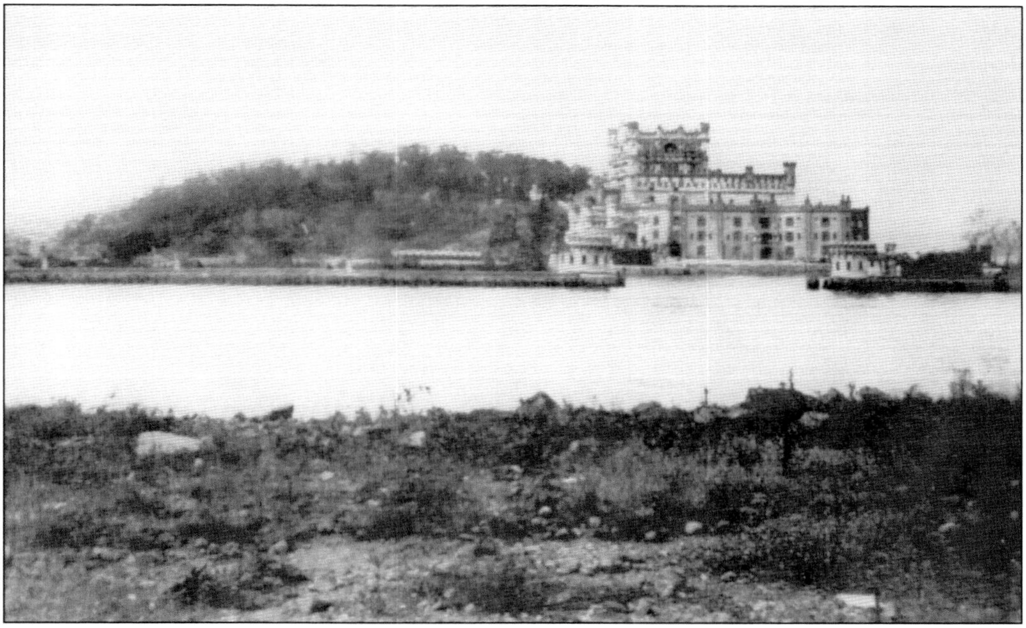

The Bannerman Island Arsenal is depicted in a photograph from around 1914. From left to right are the twin towers with the Bannerman residence above. From the center to the right is the arsenal with tower, harbor, and barges. Bannerman Castle was used in defense of the highlands from the British during the American Revolution. (Courtesy of the Churchill and Bannerman families, Bannerman Castle Trust.)

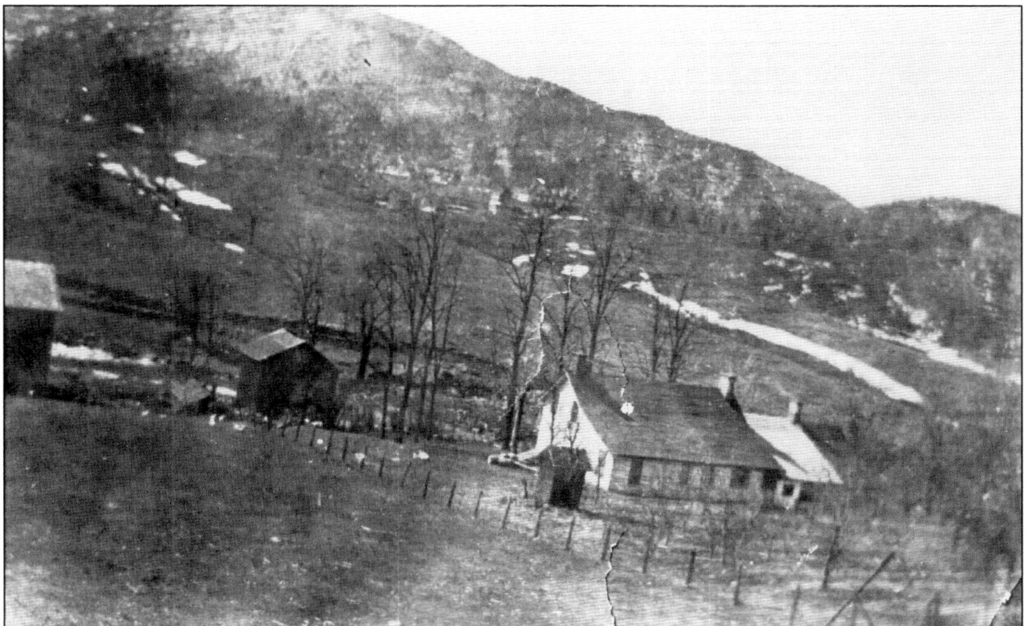

The home that would become the site of the Fishkill Historical Society is pictured during the mid-20th century. The home is known as the Van Wyck Homestead, and from the 1920s until the 1960s, the Snook family owned it. During this time, the area around the homestead was all farmland. (Courtesy of Betty Snook.)

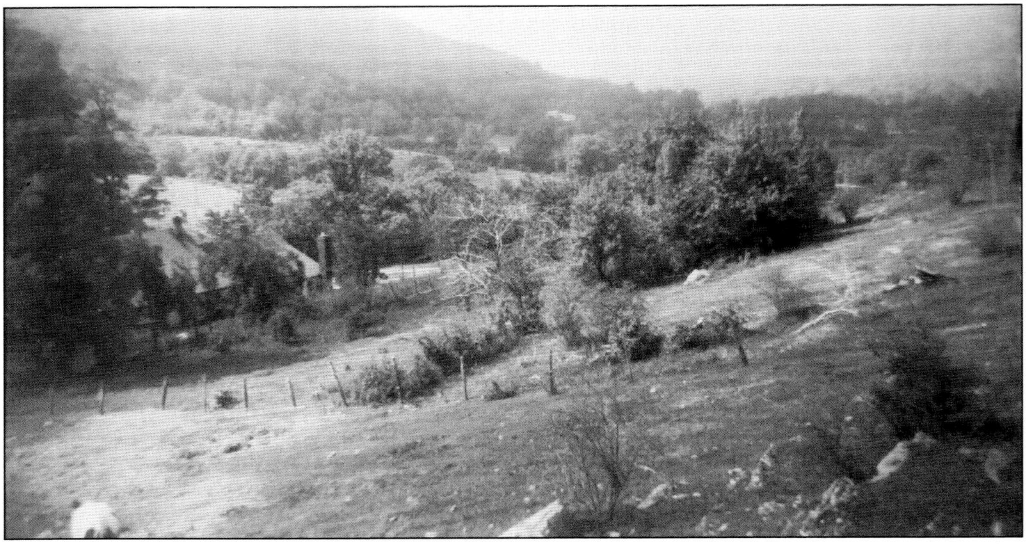

The back of the Van Wyck Homestead is depicted in a mid-20th century photograph. At this time, Route 9 was the main form of travel, yet it was not the major roadway it is today. During the mid-20th century, Route 9 was more of a scenic road. According to Betty Snook, at one point, the homestead had a wraparound porch as well as an addition. Once Interstate 84 was constructed not far from where the Van Wyck Homestead sits, Fishkill began to develop more. (Courtesy of Betty Snook.)

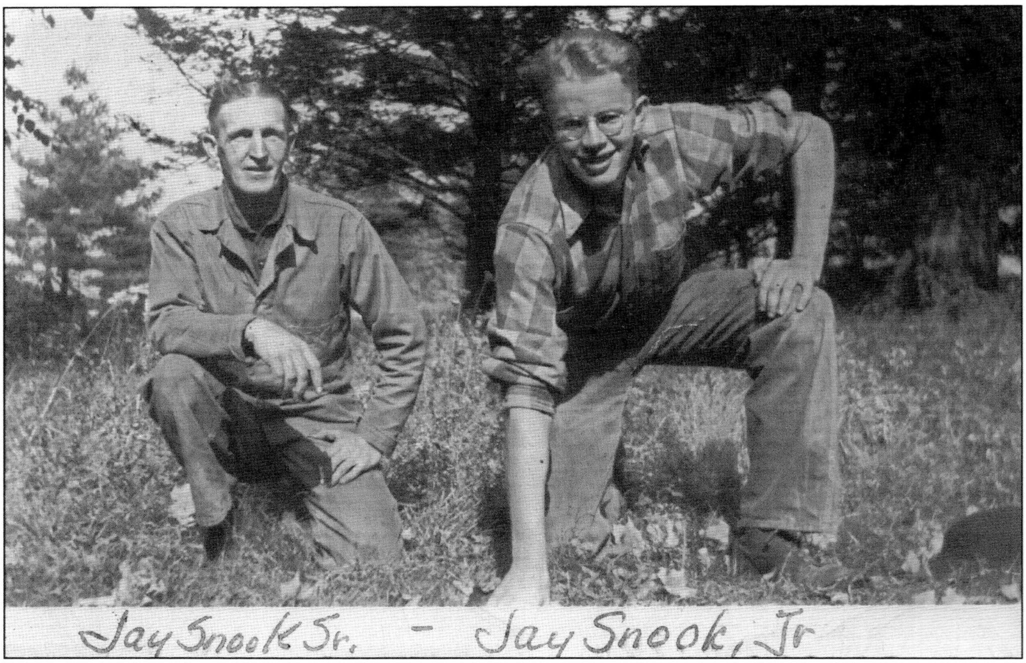

Jay Snook Sr. and Jay Snook Jr. are pictured during the mid-20th century. The Snook family lived at the Van Wyck Homestead for several generations and decades. However, during the early 1960s, construction of Interstate Highway 84 threatened the homestead. As a result, the Snook family donated the house and an acre of land to the Fishkill Historical Society. The Fishkill Historical Society was founded in 1962 in order to preserve the house from demolition. (Courtesy of Betty Snook.)

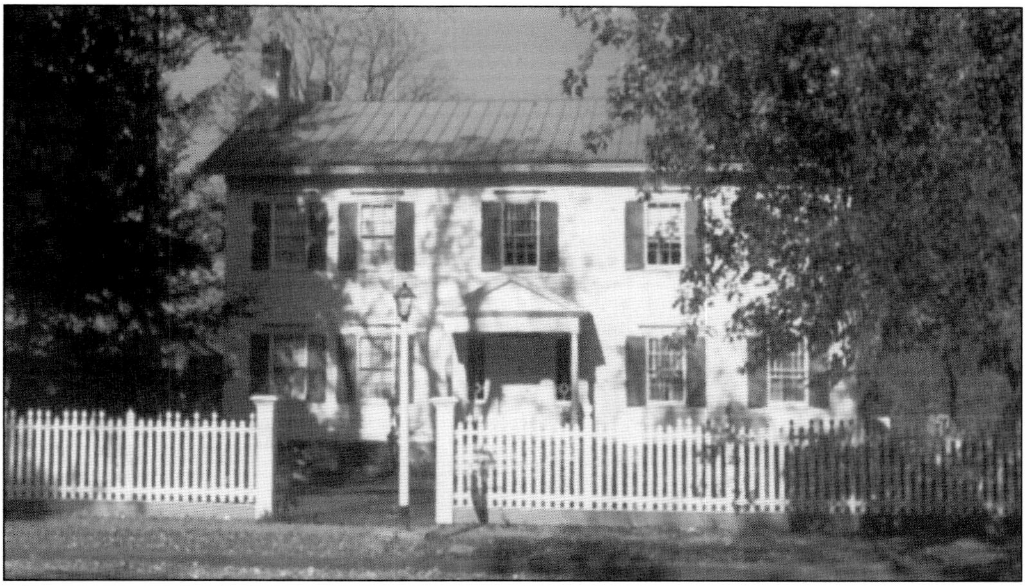

This is a copy of a slide taken in October 1952 of the home once known as Shillelagh. James Givens built the home in 1812 in the Federal style. He came to Fishkill from Ireland and was active in the Dutch Reformed Church. The slide was taken by Frederick J. Villforth. He lived in Fishkill for many years and worked at Texaco Research Center. Today, Shillelagh is the site of McHoul Funeral Home. (Courtesy of Frederick Vilforth.)

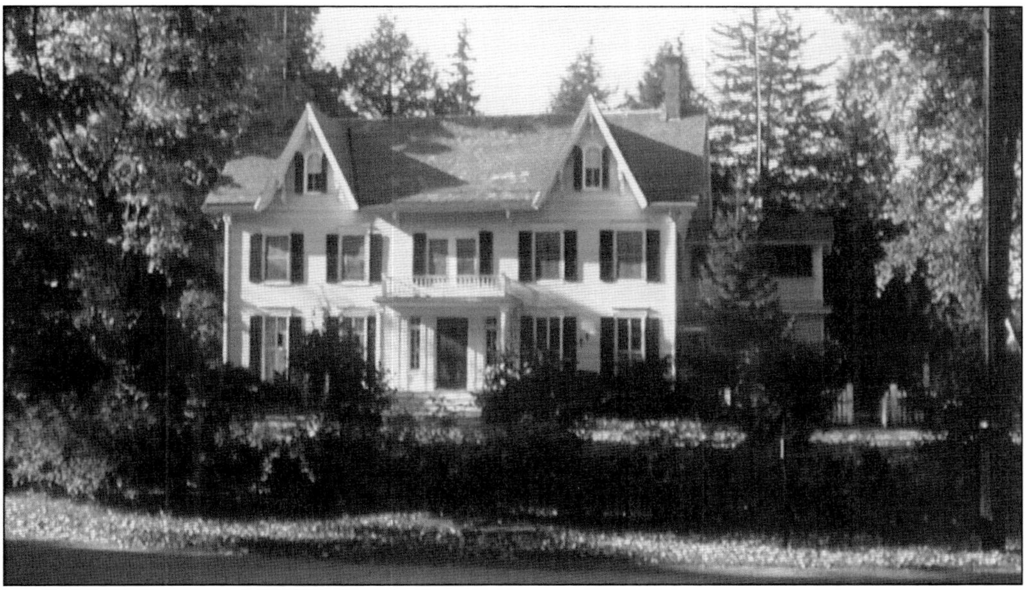

The Mid Hudson Medical Building is depicted in a copy of a slide taken during the 1950s. Evert Swart built the house in 1741. James Weeks had a tavern located on this property during the American Revolution. The tavern was located at the old Albany Post Road and the road leading to the Hudson River and was a stopping point for travelers during the 18th century. Judge Joseph Jackson used the home as a residence in 1829. He was a lawyer and the first secretary of the Fishkill Fire Department. In 1900, the house was turned into the Colonial Inn. The Mid Hudson Medical Group moved from this home on Jackson Street during the mid-2000s. (Courtesy of Frederick Vilforth.)

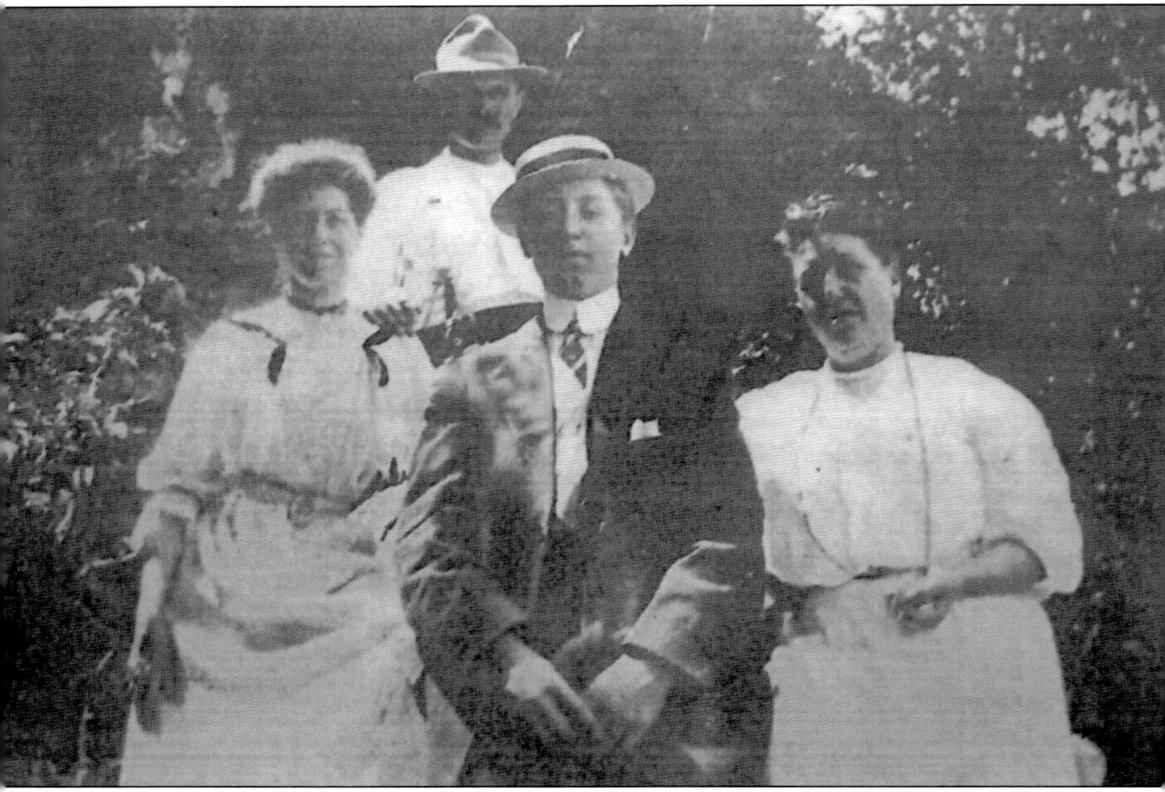

Fishkill resident William Bastian and his family are depicted in a 1905 family photograph. He would often work with Albert Knapp on Albert Knapp's farm located on the Moog farm site. He was a member of the Fishkill Historical Society, served in Europe in the US Army during World War I, and worked in banking. (Courtesy of Town of Fishkill Archives, William Bastian Estate.)

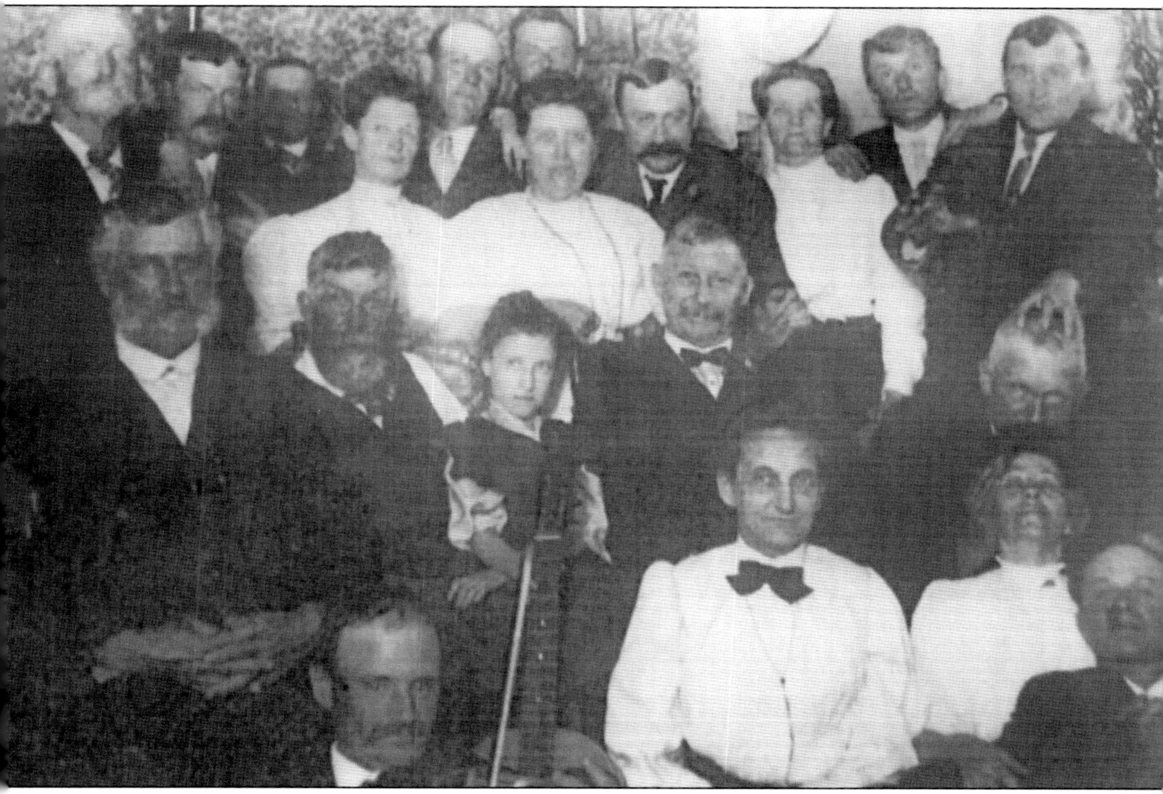

Members of the Albert Knapp family are pictured as they celebrate Albert Knapp's 71st birthday in 1908. He was featured feeding his chickens in the 1996 *Around Fishkill*. There are several roads and communities that bare the Knapp name. A subdivision in East Fishkill is named Knapp Subdivision. (Courtesy of Willa Skinner.)

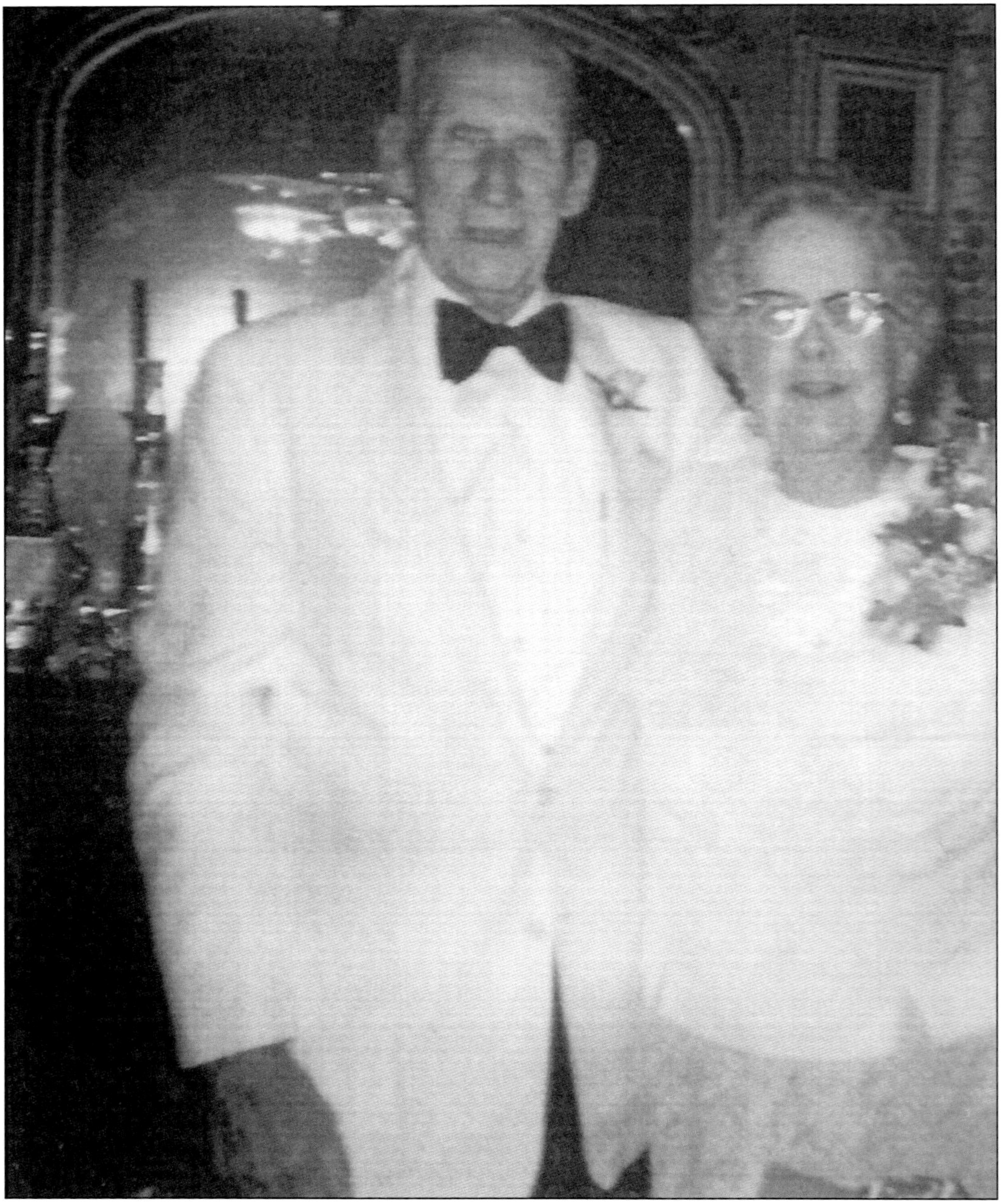

Royal and Robin Gay are pictured at their 50th wedding anniversary in 1975. The anniversary party was held at Dutchess Manor in Beacon. At the time, Royal Gay was retired from the New York State police force. Robin Gay's birth name was Helena White Gay, and she was the daughter of Doctor Howell White. (Courtesy of Willa Skinner.)

Three

STORIES FROM MOUNT GULIAN

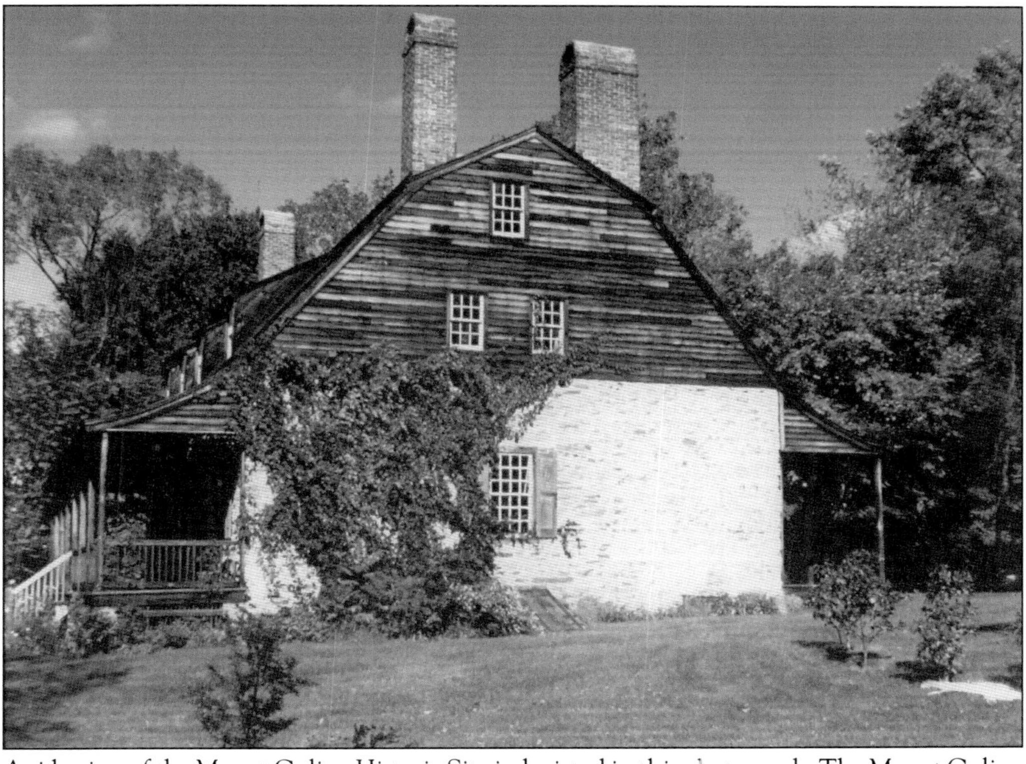

A side view of the Mount Gulian Historic Site is depicted in this photograph. The Mount Gulian Historic Site is located between Fishkill and Beacon. The Verplanck family owned the homestead. Before the Dutch came, the Wappinger Indians, who were closely related to the Lenape people or Delaware Indians, settled the land. James F. Brown worked for the Verplanck family after escaping slavery in Maryland. He kept a seven-volume journal over several decades, from 1829 to 1866. That journal is one of the only lasting accounts of life for a free black person or anyone in general living in the Hudson Valley. (Courtesy of Mount Gulian Historic Site.)

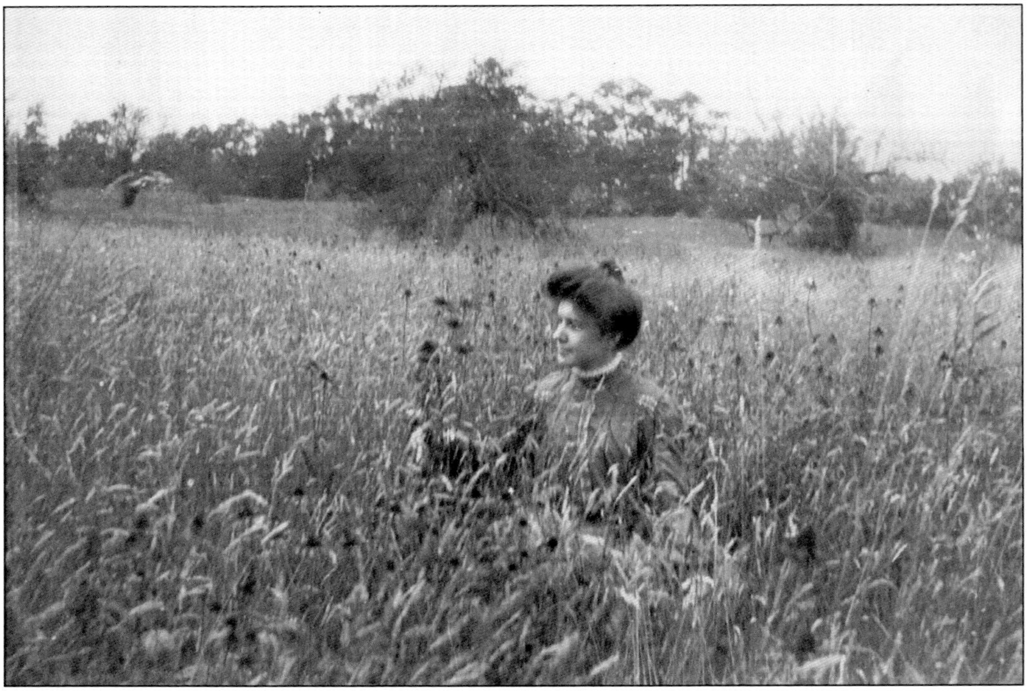

Virginia Eliza Everett Verplanck is pictured sitting among yellow daises at the Mount Gulian Historic Site. She was the daughter of Rev. Henry Darby and was born in 1856. She also wrote the book *Every Day in May Garden* in 1913 about the gardens at the Mount Gulian Historic Site. (Courtesy of Mount Gulian Historic Site.)

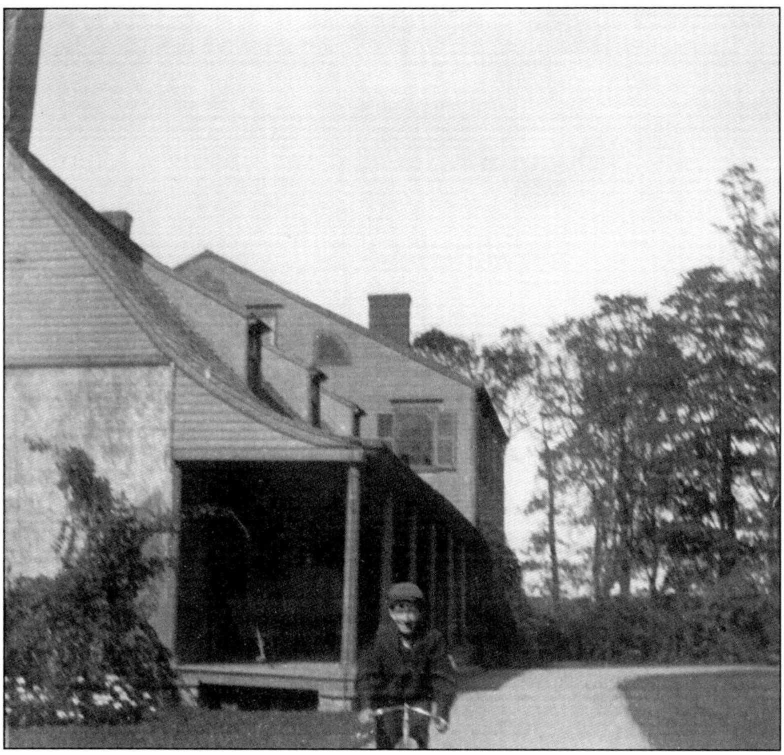

A boy is shown playing on a bicycle outside Mount Gulian Historic Site around the early 1900s. This photograph is most likely of William Everett Verplanck or his brother Edward Verplanck. Both boys were the children of William Edward and Virginia Eliza Everett Verplanck, and they were born in 1880 and 1890 respectively. (Courtesy of Mount Gulian Historic Site.)

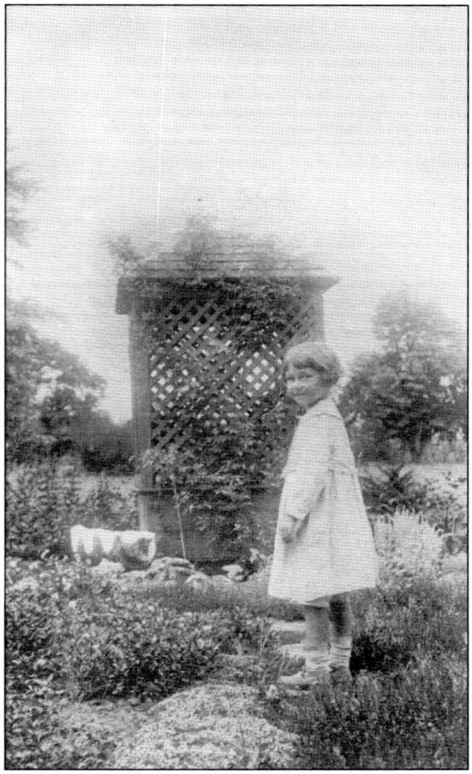

Virginia Darby Verplanck is depicted standing in the garden around the 1900s. She was the only daughter of William Edward Verplanck and Virginia Eliza Everett Verplanck. She was born on June 11, 1883. (Courtesy of Mount Gulian Historic Site.)

Edward Verplanck is caught playing at Mount Gulian Historic Site in 1894. He was born on November 5, 1890. He was the youngest son of William Edward Verplanck and Virginia Eliza Everett Verplanck. (Courtesy of Mount Gulian Historic Site.)

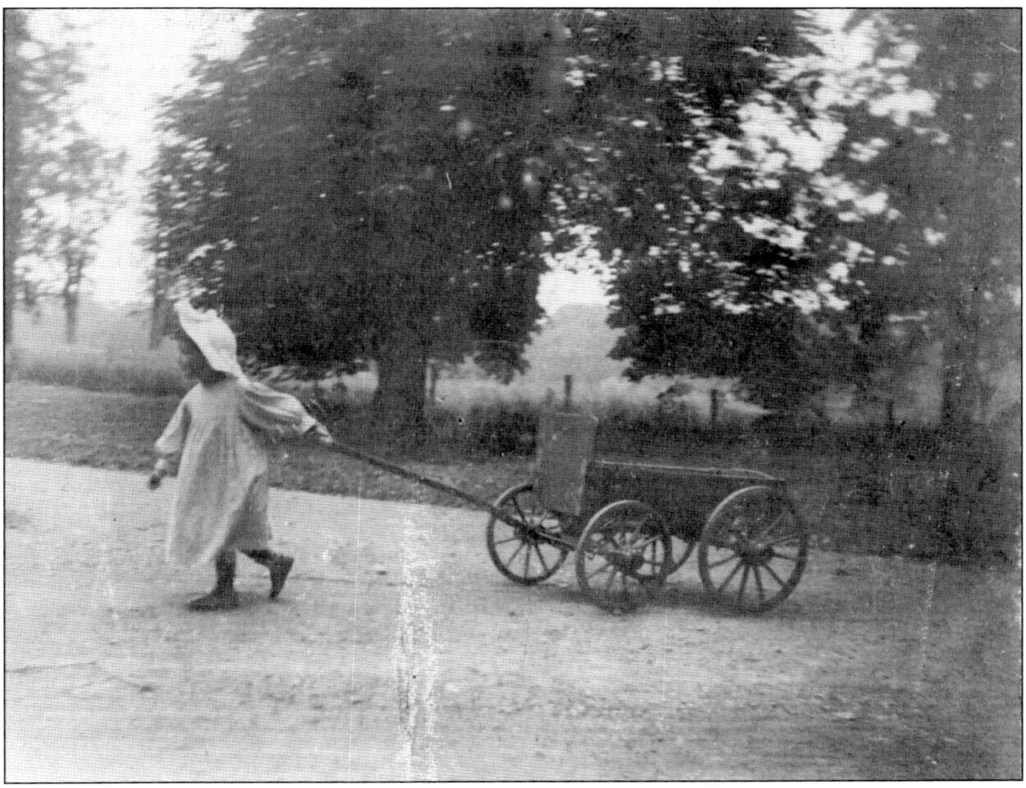

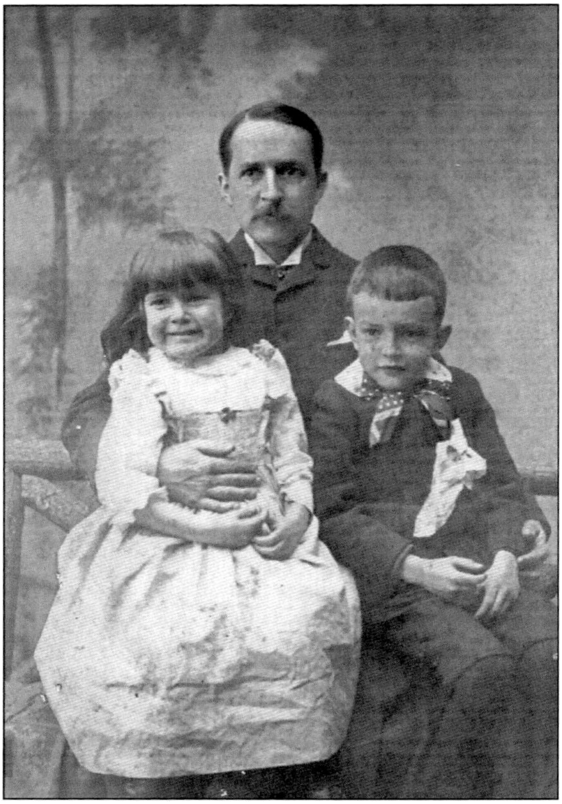

A family photograph shows William Edward Verplanck with two of his children. William was born on April 8, 1856, and married Virginia (Darby) Everett on January 6, 1890. The Verplancks had four children, William Everett, Virginia, Edward Fenno (1886–1887) and Edward. (Courtesy of Mount Gulian Historic Site.)

This image is of the front of a postcard sent from William Edward Verplanck to a friend in Washington, DC. The postcard is stamped December 23, 7:00 a.m., Fishkill-on-Hudson. The postage cost 1¢. The postcard depicts Mount Gulian Historic Site and Verplanck Homestead. (Courtesy of Mount Gulian Historic Site.)

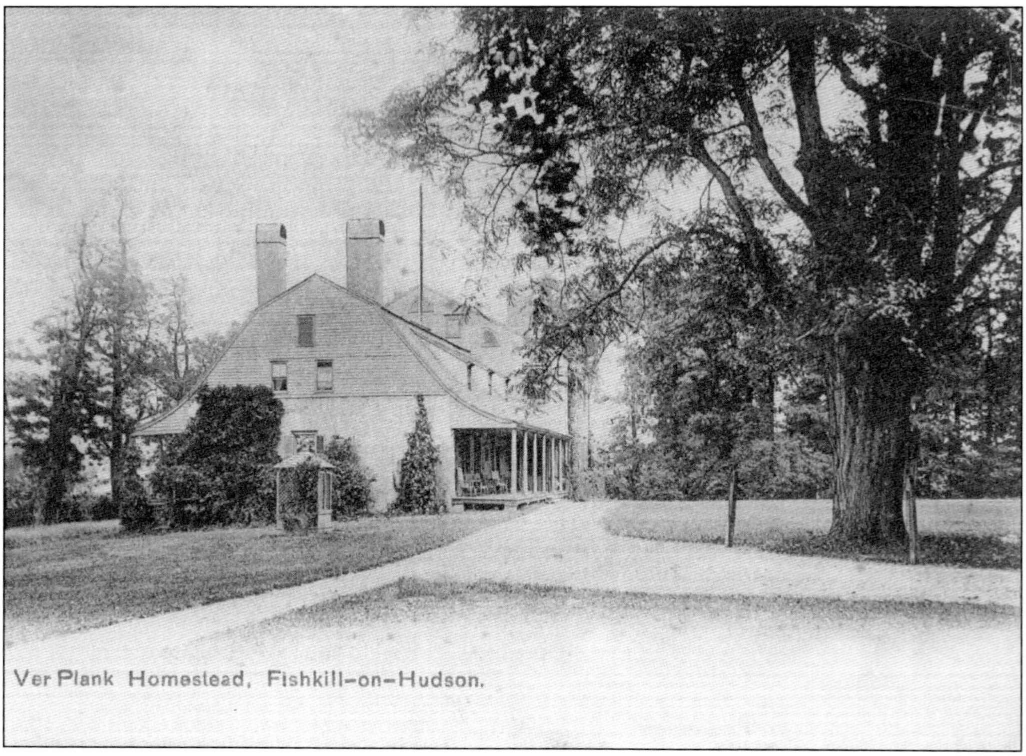

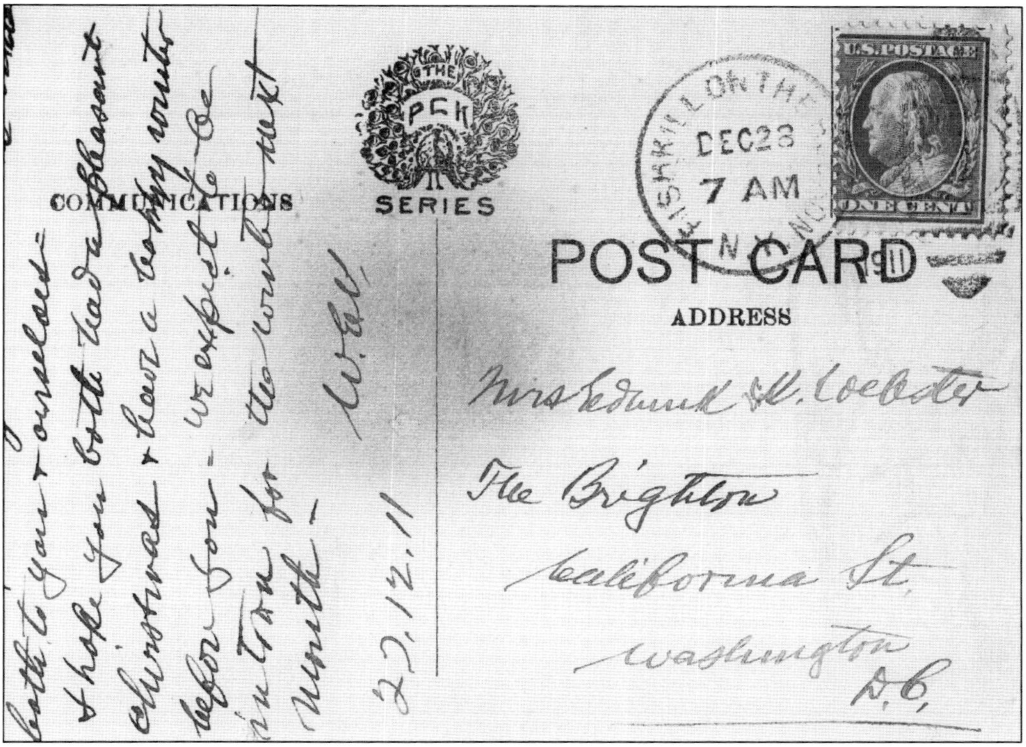

William Edward Verplanck wrote the words shown on the back of this postcard. He writes, "I hope you both had a pleasant Christmas and have a happy winter before you. We expect to be south for the winter next month." (Courtesy of Mount Gulian Historic Site.)

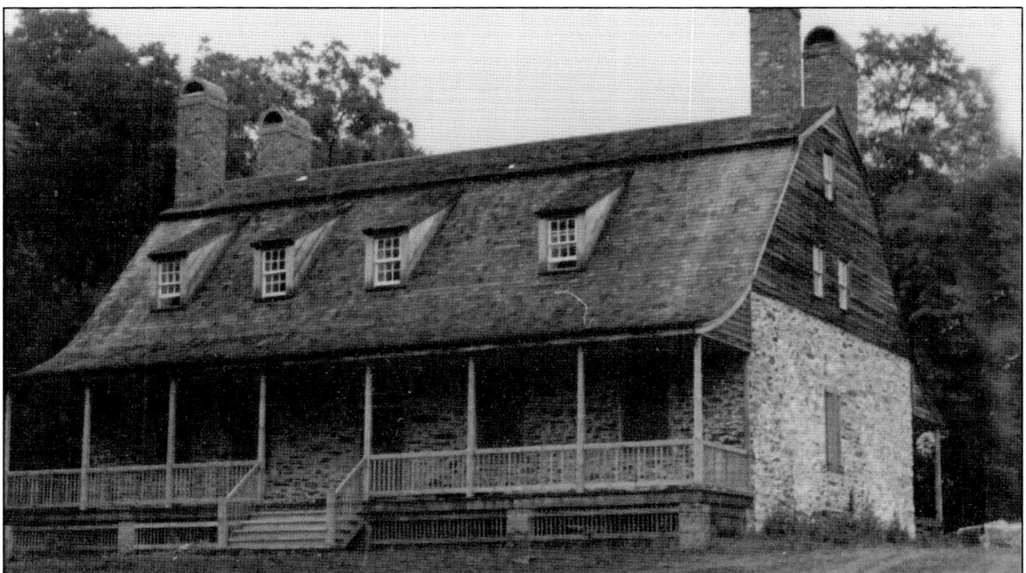

Mount Gulian Historic Site stood on a hill above the Hudson River for almost 200 years. However, in 1931, a fire destroyed the home, leaving it in ruins with just stonework remaining. In 1967, restoration began to reconstruct the homestead. This photograph depicts the completed structure in 1972. (Courtesy of Mount Gulian Historic Site.)

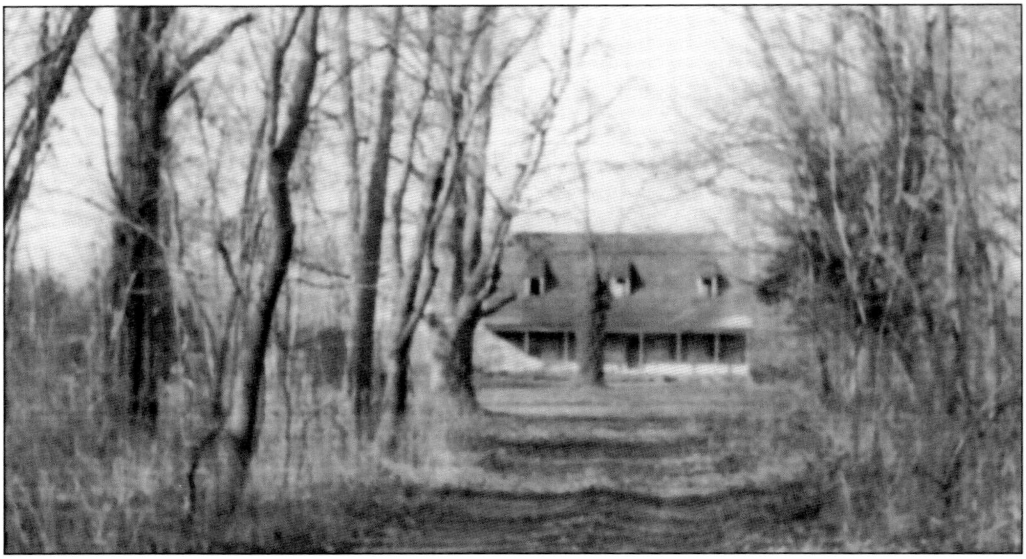

This is an early-20th-century photograph of the Mount Gulian Historic Site from the road. When Gulian Verplanck II inherited the property between 1730 and 1740, he built the Mount Gulian Historic Site on 400 acres of land. (Courtesy of Mount Gulian Historic Site.)

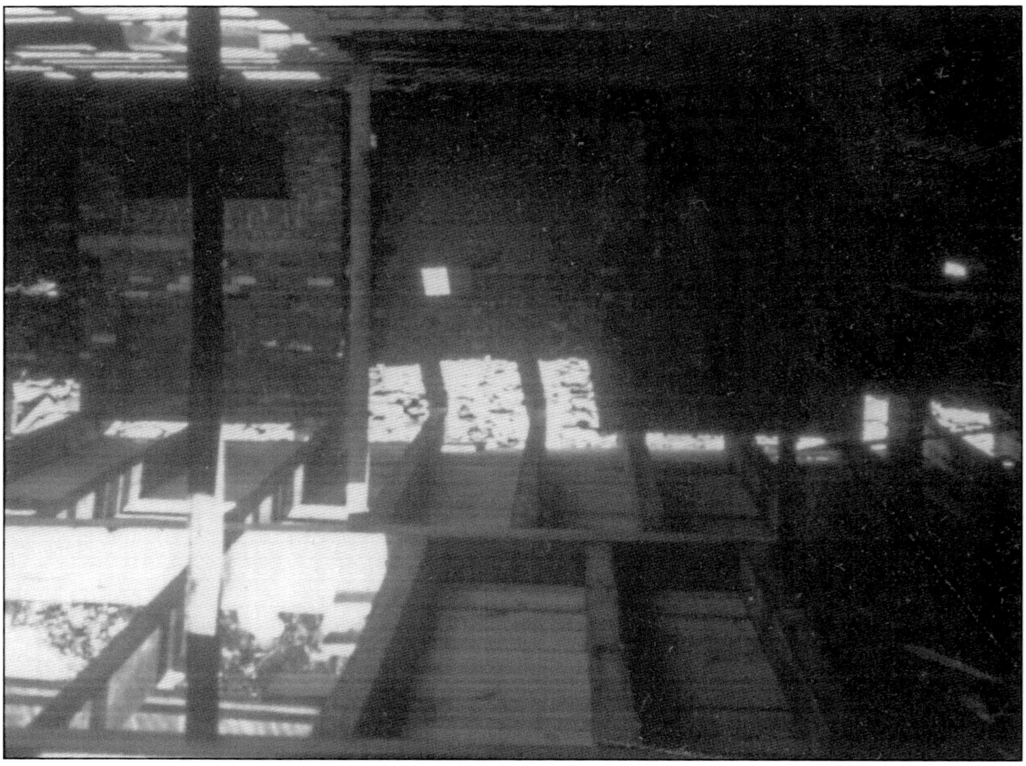

Kenneth Clinton, an architect, approached Bache Bleecker, a Verplanck descendant, about rebuilding the Mount Gulian Historic Site across the river in New Windsor. Instead, Mr. Bleecker decided to give 10 acres of the land to the Mount Gulian Historic Site Society to rebuild on its original site. The Mount Gulian Historic Site Society was founded in 1966. (Courtesy of Mount Gulian Historic Site.)

Mount Gulian Historic Site remained in ruins for 34 years. An apartment complex hoped to be placed on the property in 1965. This photograph shows the reconstruction of Mount Gulian Historic Site, beginning with the existing foundation. (Courtesy of Mount Gulian Historic Site.)

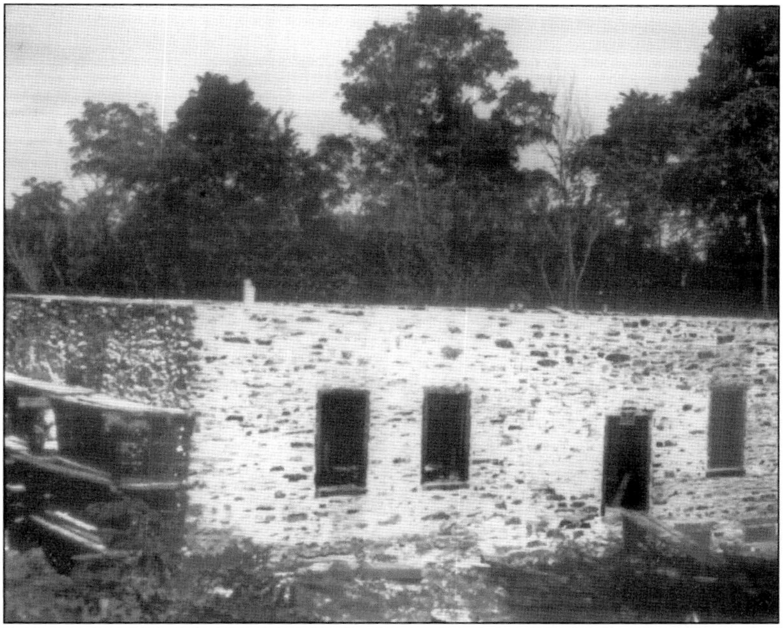

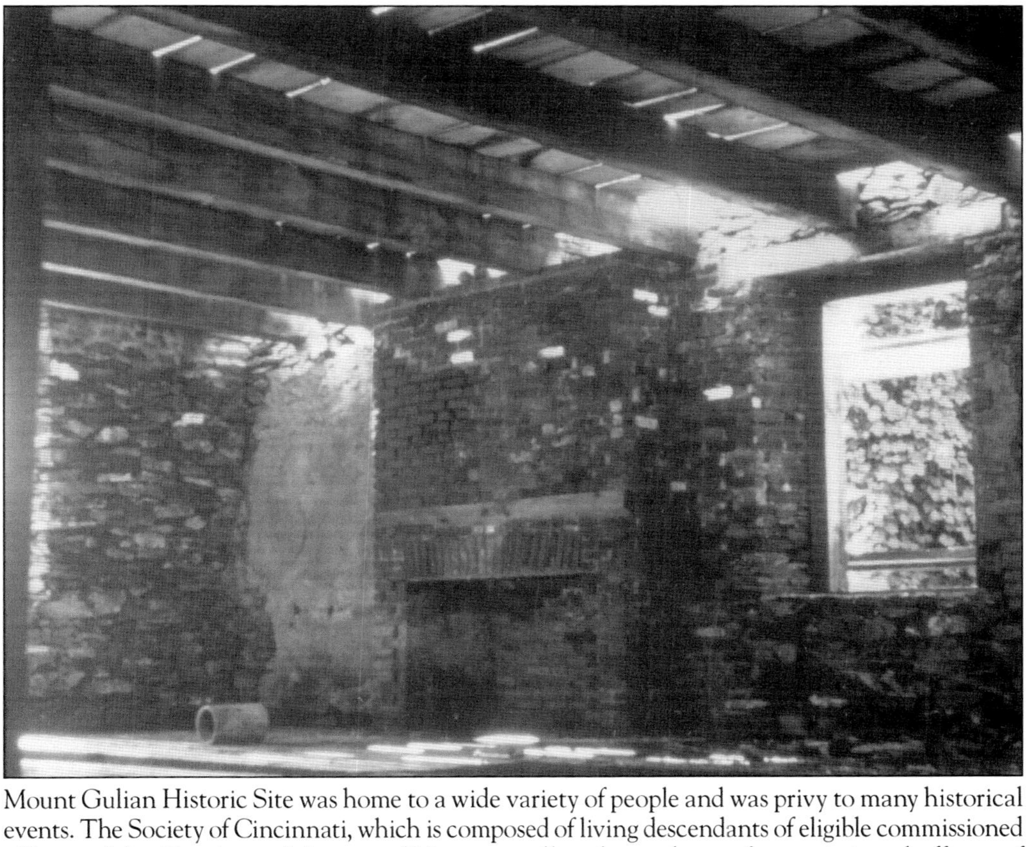

Mount Gulian Historic Site was home to a wide variety of people and was privy to many historical events. The Society of Cincinnati, which is composed of living descendants of eligible commissioned officers of the Continental Army and Navy, as well as descendants of commissioned officers of the French Army and Navy who served during the Revolutionary War, was formed at the Mount Gulian Historic Site in 1783. (Courtesy of Mount Gulian Historic Site.)

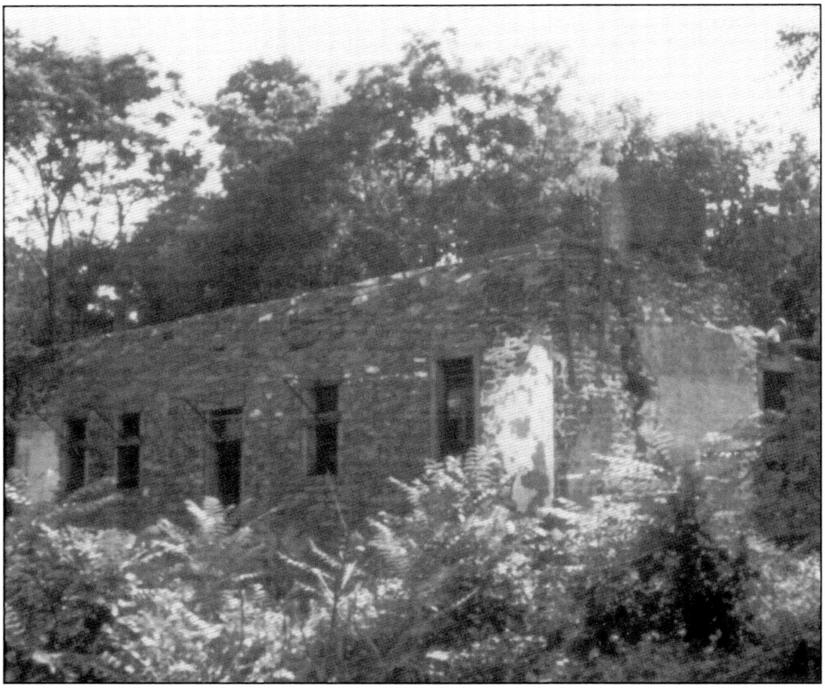

After the 1930s fire that destroyed most of Mount Gulian, all that remained was a cellar filled with weeds and the remains of handmade bricks and cut native sandstone. Stone walls, fireplaces, and the chimneys also survived. (Courtesy of Mount Gulian Historic Site.)

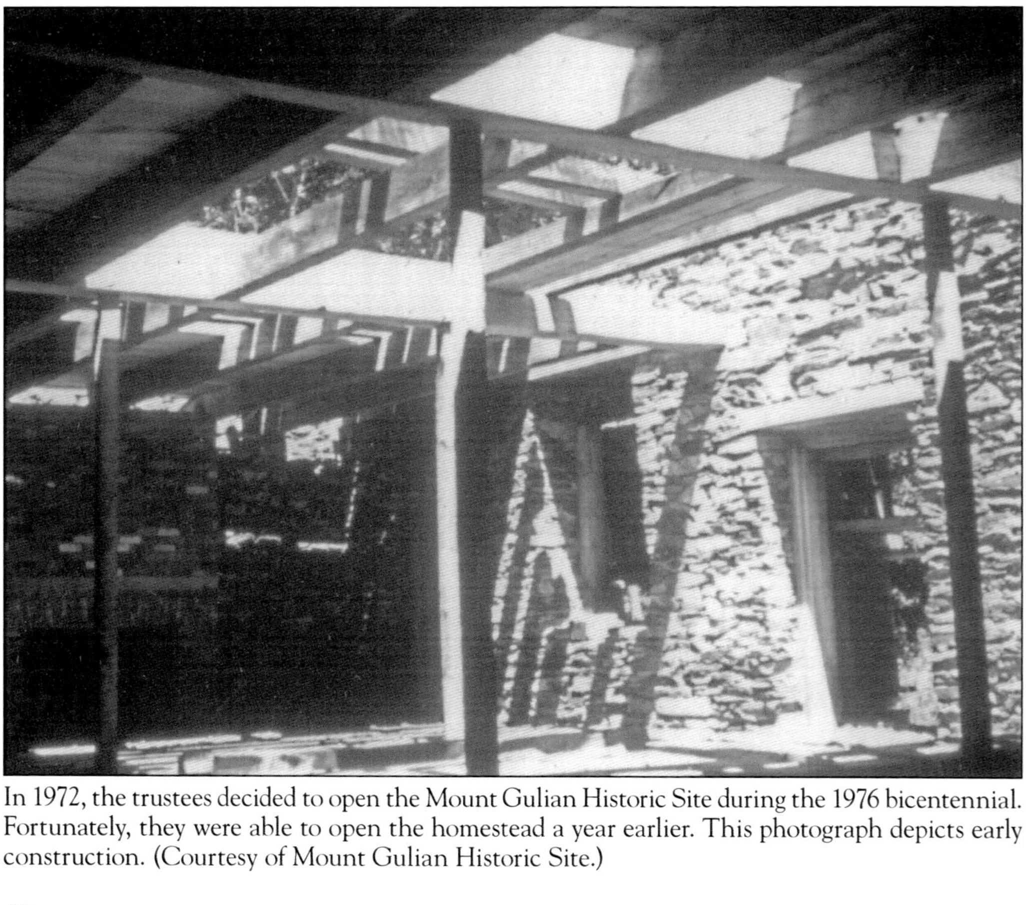

In 1972, the trustees decided to open the Mount Gulian Historic Site during the 1976 bicentennial. Fortunately, they were able to open the homestead a year earlier. This photograph depicts early construction. (Courtesy of Mount Gulian Historic Site.)

The Mount Gulian Historic Site is photographed in 1972 in the final stages of the reconstruction. Since the Mount Gulian Historic Site has been open to the public, the site has conducted various workshops, reenactments, living history, and educational programs for schools in the area. (Courtesy of Mount Gulian Historic Site.)

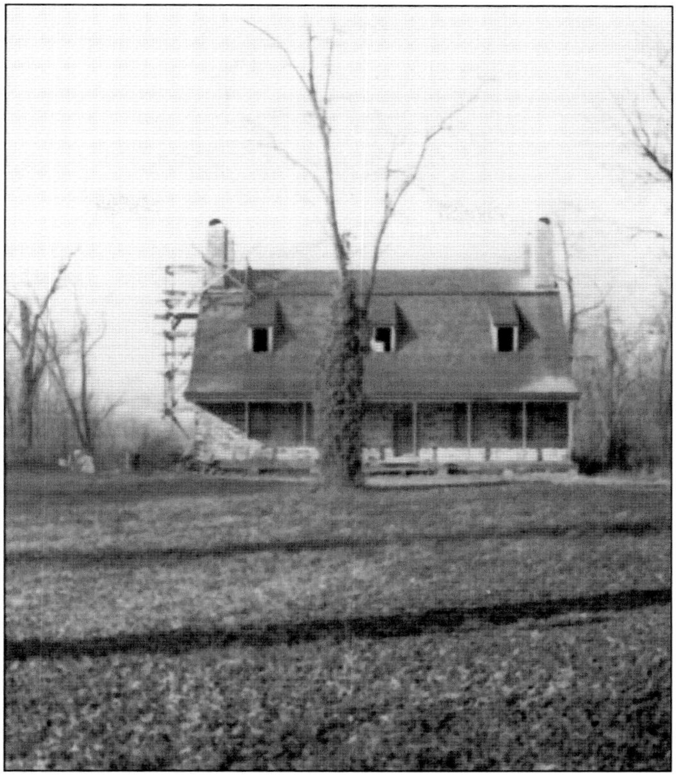

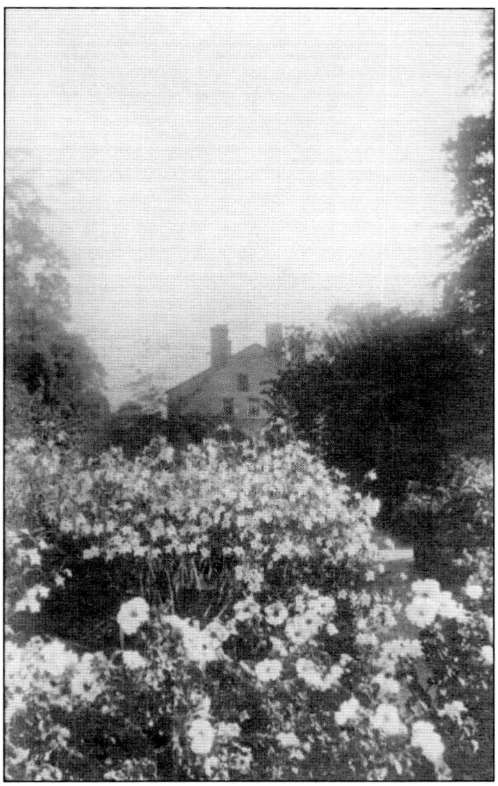

This photograph depicts a view of the Mount Gulian Historic Site from the Victorian garden in full bloom. Virginia Verplanck kept the garden in meticulous condition. Her 1912 map is considered to be one of the best documentations of an early American garden. (Courtesy of Mount Gulian Historic Site.)

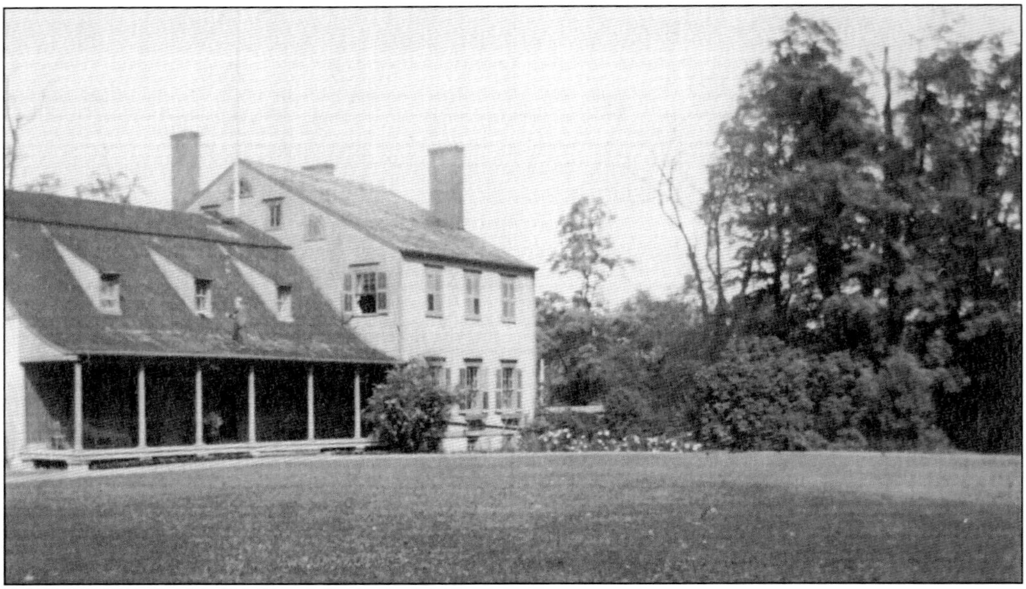

In 1804, Daniel Crommelin Verplanck built an addition to the house and garden located to the right of this photograph. General Lafayette once stayed in a room in the addition and planted a rosebush in the garden. (Courtesy of Mount Gulian Historic Site.)

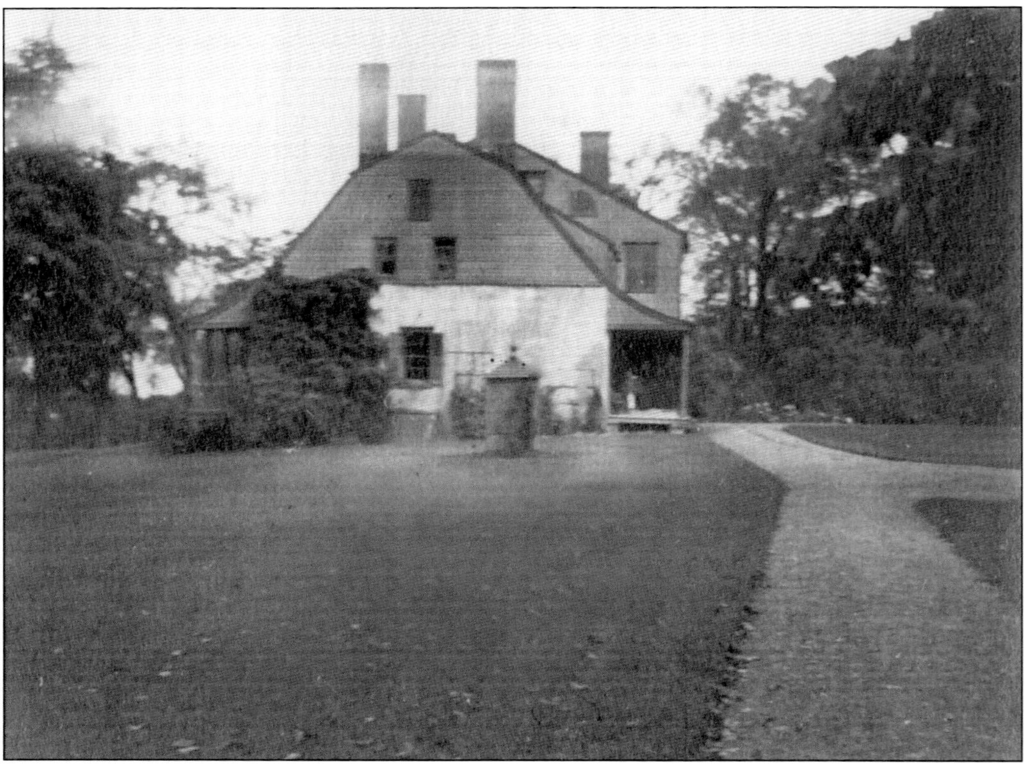

The Mount Gulian Society decided not to rebuild the 1804 edition depicted in the back of this photograph. They agreed to restore the home to its 1783 state, which was when General von Steuben used it as his headquarters. Mount Gulian is also the site of where the Society of Cincinnati was formed. (Courtesy of Mount Gulian Historic Site.)

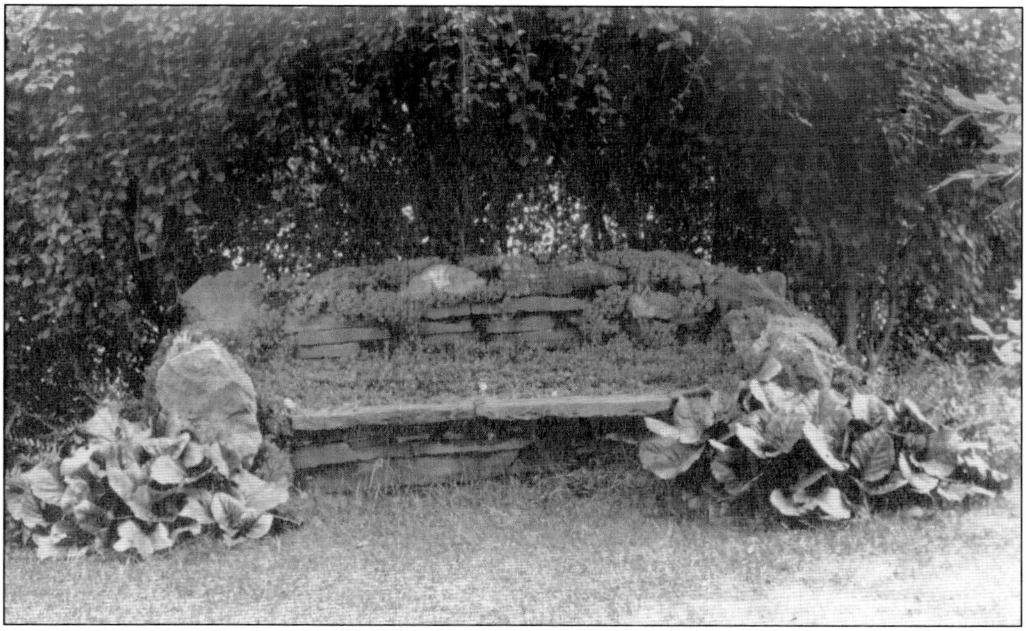

This is a stone bench that was located in the formal part of the garden. Using pieces from the original bench depicted in this photograph, volunteers reconstructed the garden back to its former glory in 1995. (Courtesy of Mount Gulian Historic Site.)

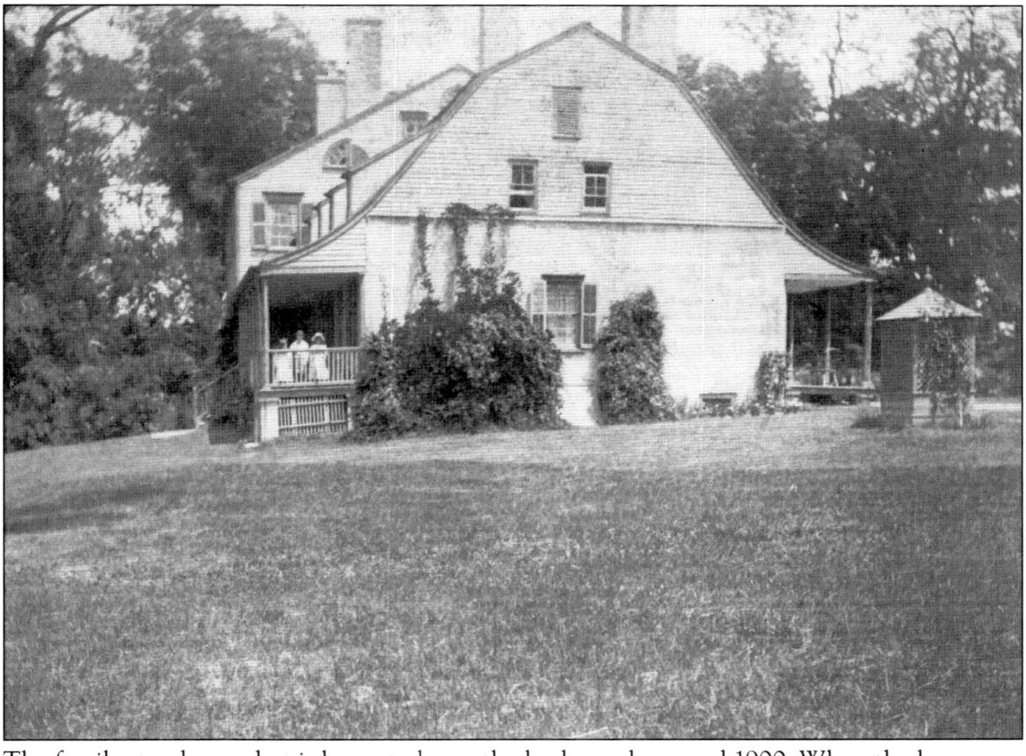

The family stands on what is know today as the back porch around 1900. When the home was built in 1731, the back door was originally the front door. This was because the house was oriented to face the Hudson River. (Courtesy of Mount Gulian Historic.)

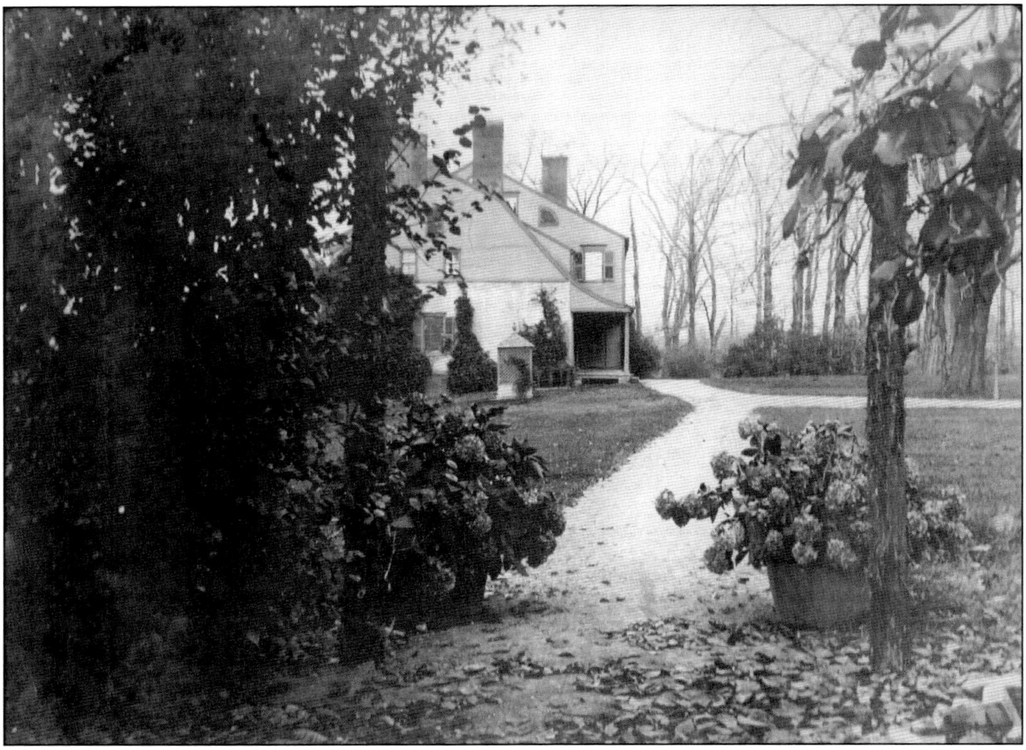

This image shows fall at Mount Gulian Historic Site around 1906. Virginia Eliza Everett Verplanck stated, "Our old garden has been a joy to the wives of the Verplancks since the beginning of the last century." (Courtesy of the Mount Gulian Historic Site Society's 35th Anniversary.)

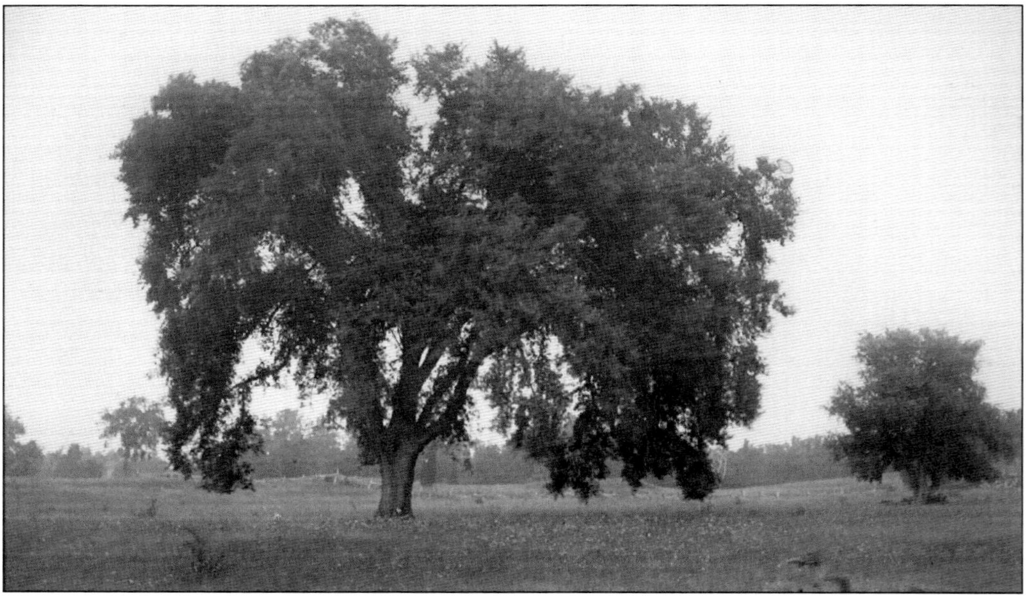

This is a photograph of the property around Mount Gulian Historic Site in the 20th century. The Verplancks had several tenant farmers working on their land throughout the years. This photograph shows one of the old trees that grew at Mount Gulian Historic Site. It still stands today. (Courtesy of Mount Gulian Historic Site.)

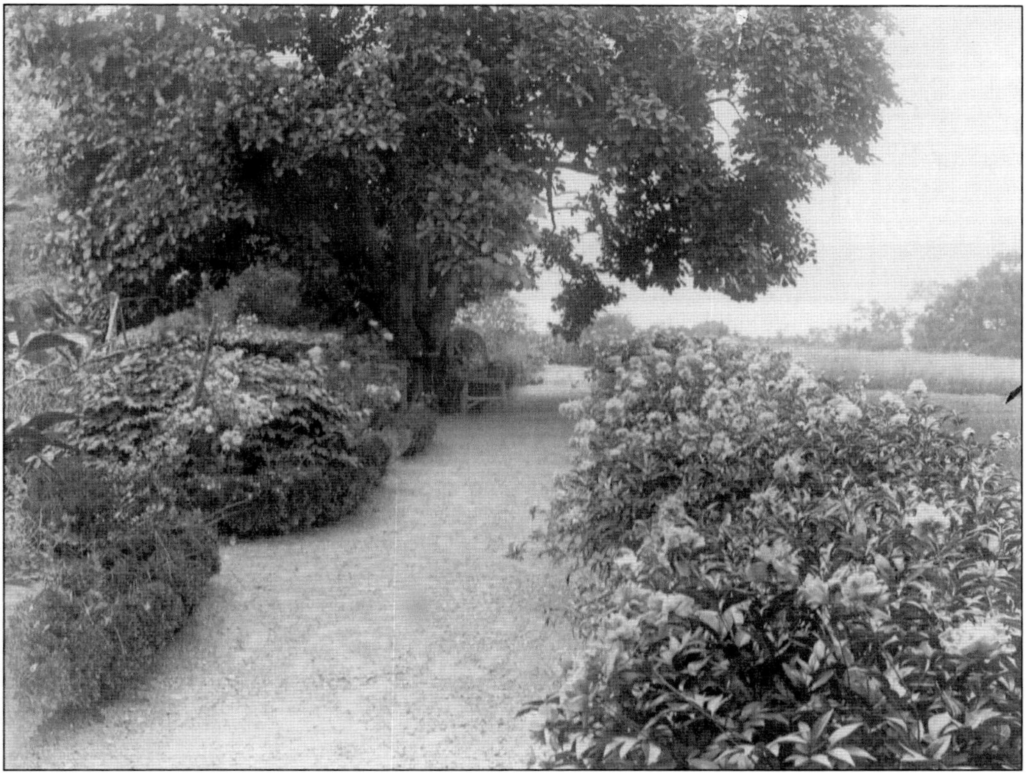

According to various sources such as Virginia Eliza Everett Verplanck's books, the 1912 map, and James F. Brown's diary, the garden had 140 roses, including Harrison's Yellow, Maiden's Blush, and Rose of Catile. Other flowers were delphiniums, hollyhocks, irises, oriental poppies, sweet Williams, and peonies. (Courtesy of Mount Gulian Historic Site.)

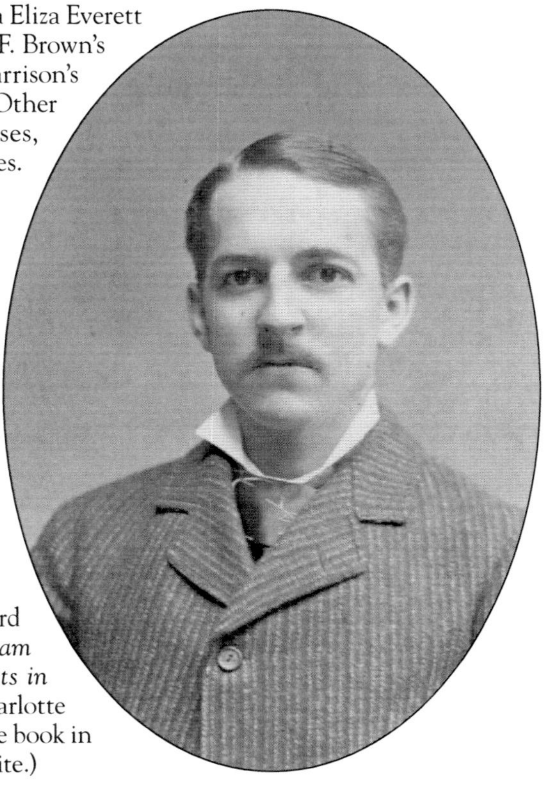

This photograph is a portrait of William Edward Verplanck. He wrote *The History of Abraham Isaacse Ver Planck and his Male Descendants in America* in 1892. His great-granddaughter Charlotte VerPlanck Willman added an addendum to the book in 1998. (Courtesy of Mount Gulian Historic Site.)

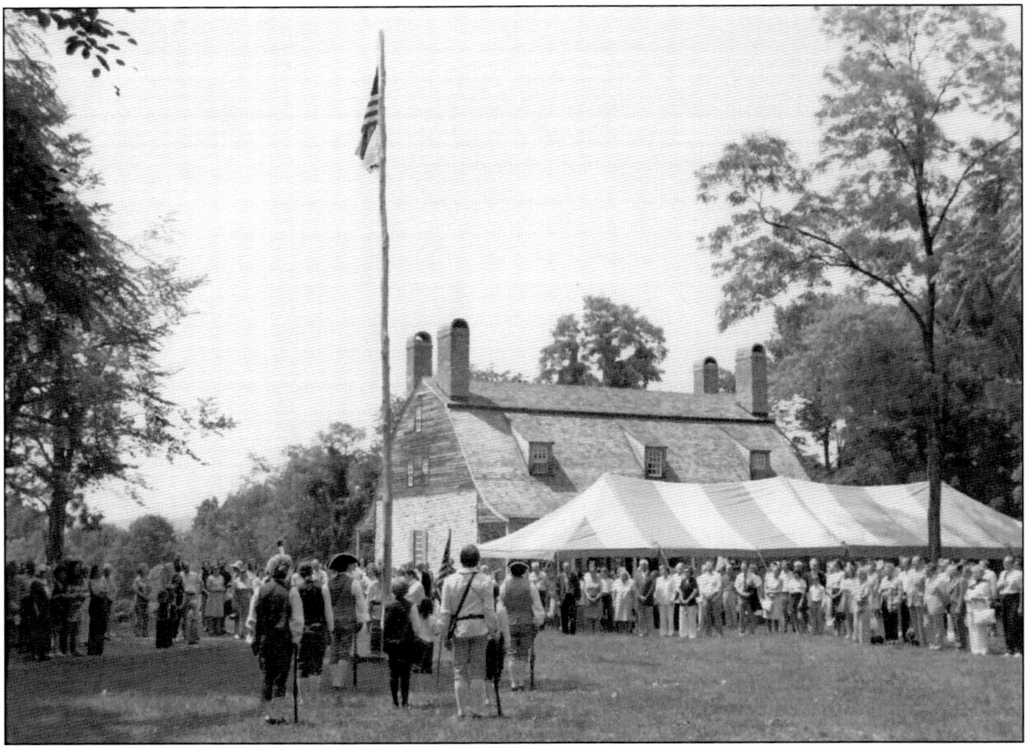

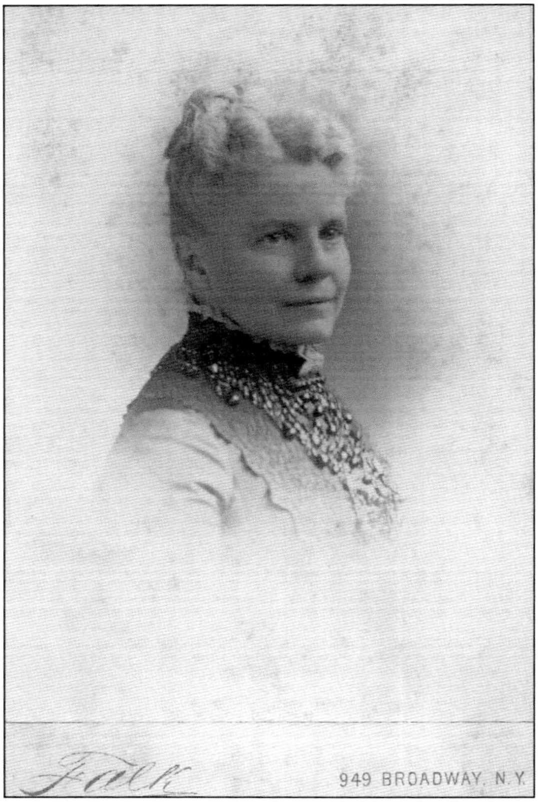

Two hundred guests celebrate the opening and dedication of the Mount Gulian Historic Site in this 1975 photograph. A color guard of members of the Fishkill Historical Society and the Fourth Dutchess Militia Revolutionary War reenactors in tricornered hats and britches participated in a flag raising. (Courtesy of Mount Gulian Historic Site, photograph by Henry Reichert Photography.)

This is a portrait of Josephine Kirby taken in 1886. The Kirbys had close connections to the Verplancks. Both families are descendants of Gen. George Brown, who was born in 1643 in Leicester, England. (Courtesy of Mount Gulian Historic Site.)

This is a portrait of William Elias Everett of the US Navy. He died in 1881 at Saratoga and is buried at Brownville, New York, beside his wife, Pamela Everett. He was a relative of Virginia Darby, wife of William Everett Verplanck. (Courtesy of Mount Gulian Historic Site.)

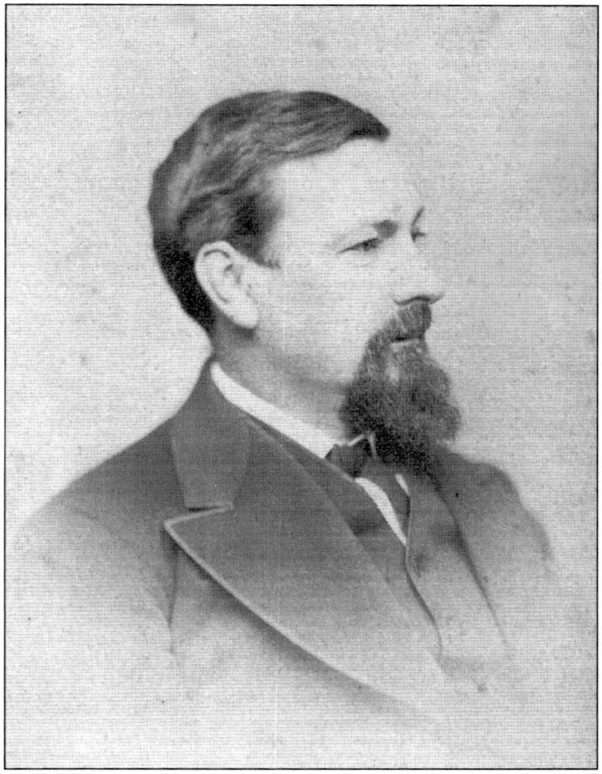

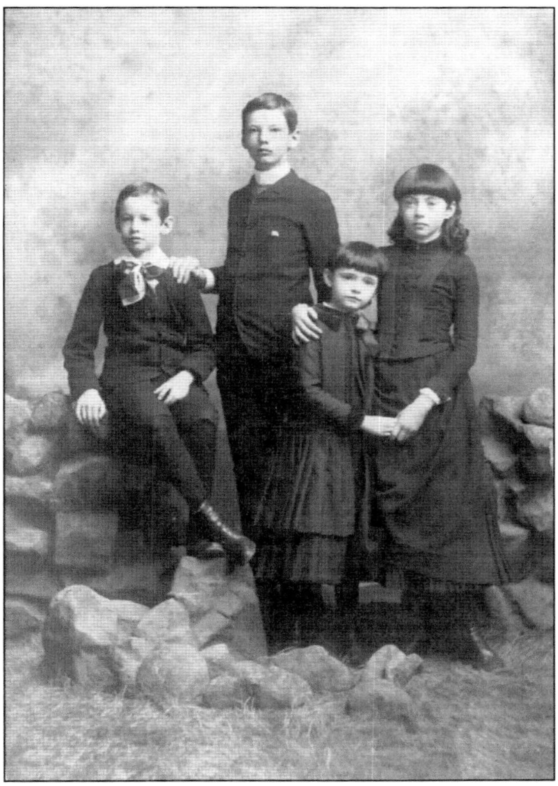

Some Kirby children are depicted as they pose for a photograph in 1888. The photograph was printed by Stone's Great Northern Photo and Copying House in nearby Potsdam, New York. (Courtesy of Mount Gulian Historic Site.)

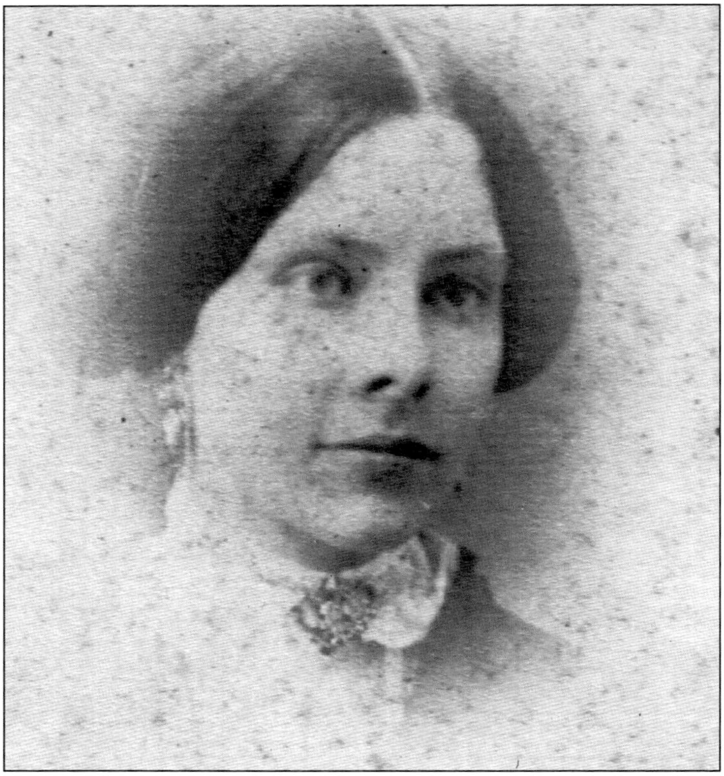

This is a daguerreotype of Virginia (Darby) Everett Verplanck's "Aunt Minnie." Daguerreotypes were the earliest non-film, non-paper photographs. They were made between 1839 and 1860. (Courtesy of Mount Gulian Historic Site.)

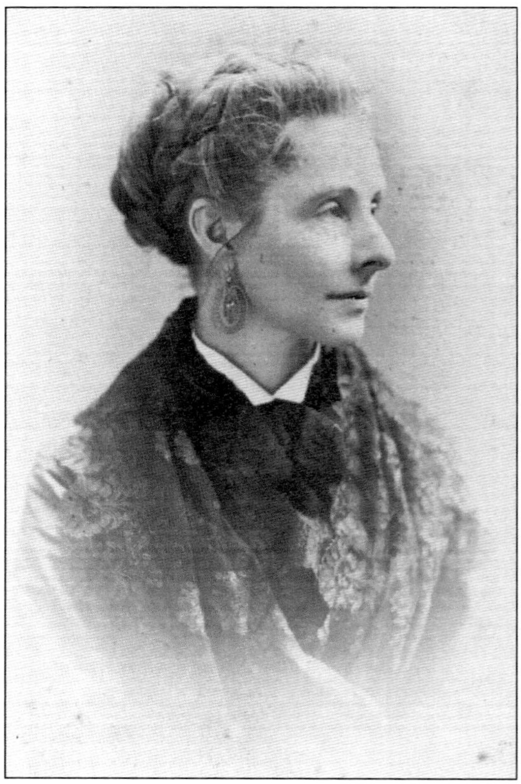

Pictured here is "Aunt Minnie" in her later years. Her name was Pamela Williams, and she was the daughter of Edmund Kirby and the wife of William Elias Everett. She was born at Brownville, New York, and died in 1878. (Courtesy of Mount Gulian Historic Site.)

Albert K. Fairfax is shown posing for this photograph, taken in August 1888 in Matteawan, New York. He was an American-born Scottish representative peer in the British House of Lords. He later became the 12th Lord Fairfax of Cameron after the family discovered the title during the early 1900s. His mother was Mary Brown Kirby. (Courtesy of Mount Gulian Historic Site.)

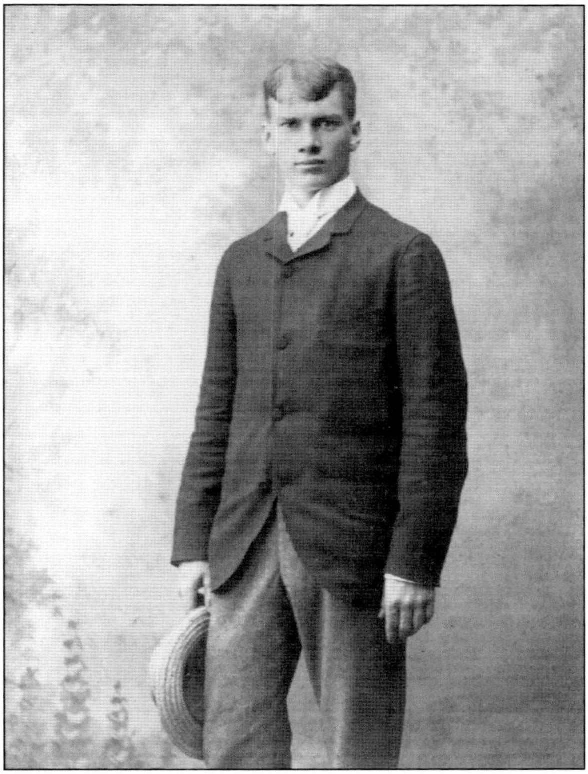

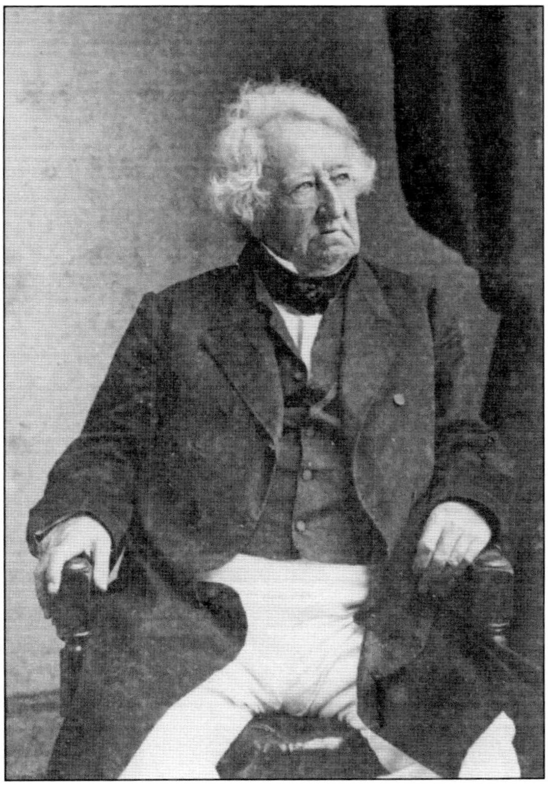

This is Brady's photograph of Gulian Crommelin Verplanck. He was born in 1786 and died at 84 years old in 1870. In 1811, he married Eliza Fenno, and together they had two children, William Samuel Verplanck and Gulian Verplanck. He took a great interest in politics, having sat on the New York State Senate and the US House of Representatives and also made an unsuccessful run for mayor of New York City. He was said to be a great lover of art and poetry and very affectionate with his grandchildren. (Courtesy of Mount Gulian Historic Site.)

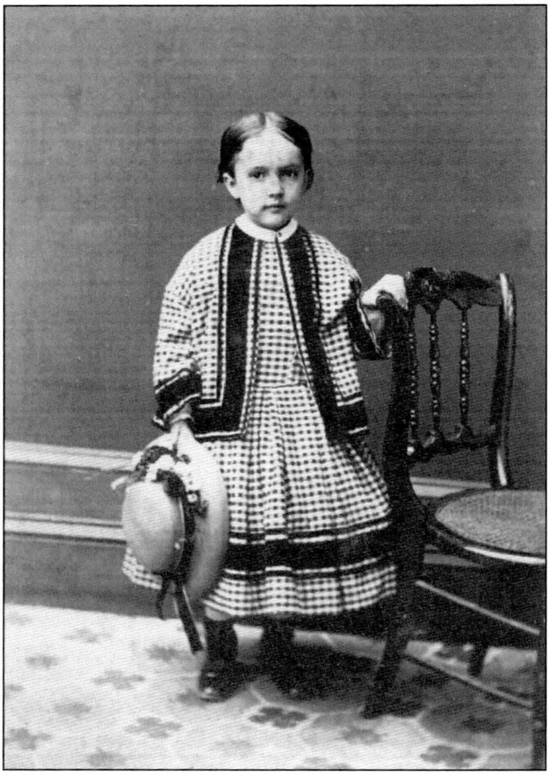

These images show Virginia Eliza Everett Verplanck between the ages of four and 14. Virginia married into the Verplanck family on January 6, 1880. She was the daughter of Rev. Henry Darby, but several years prior to her marriage she was "adopted" by William E. Everett, who had married her aunt Pamela W. Kirby. Several drawings and painting of Virginia by her father are at Mount Gulian Historic Site. One of her father's paintings, *The Reverend John Atwood and His Family*, currently resides at the Museum of Fine Arts in Boston. Letters Henry F. Darby wrote to his daughter, Virginia, are preserved at the Oneida Historical Society in New York. (Both, courtesy of Mount Gulian Historic Site.)

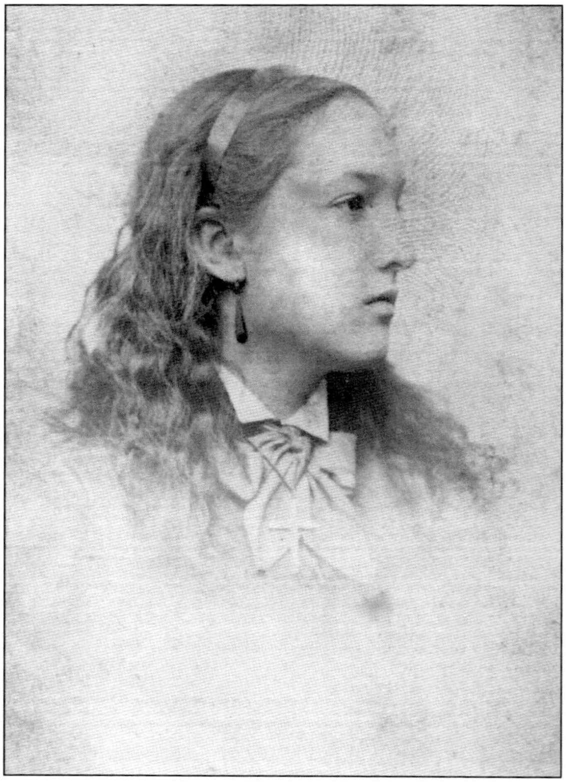

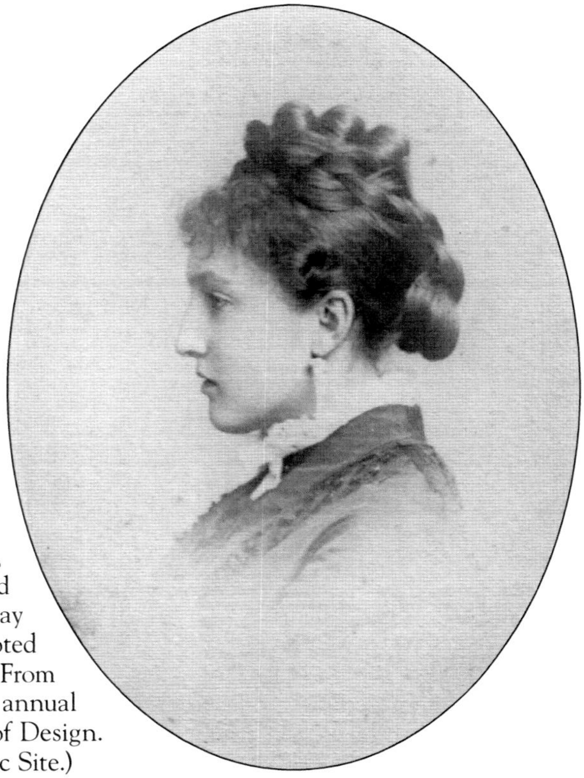

These are two photographs of Virginia Eliza Everett Verplanck taken in 1879 by William Klauser Photography. The photographer was located on Sixth Avenue in New York City. Verplanck is about 23 years old in these photographs and is dressed in her evening best. As mentioned, her father, Henry F. Darby, was an accomplished painter. He crafted an oil-on-canvas painting of Henry Clay around 1848. He shared a studio with noted painter Samuel Colman in the late 1850s. From 1853 to 1860, he displayed portraits at the annual exhibitions of the National Academy of Design. (Both, courtesy of Mount Gulian Historic Site.)

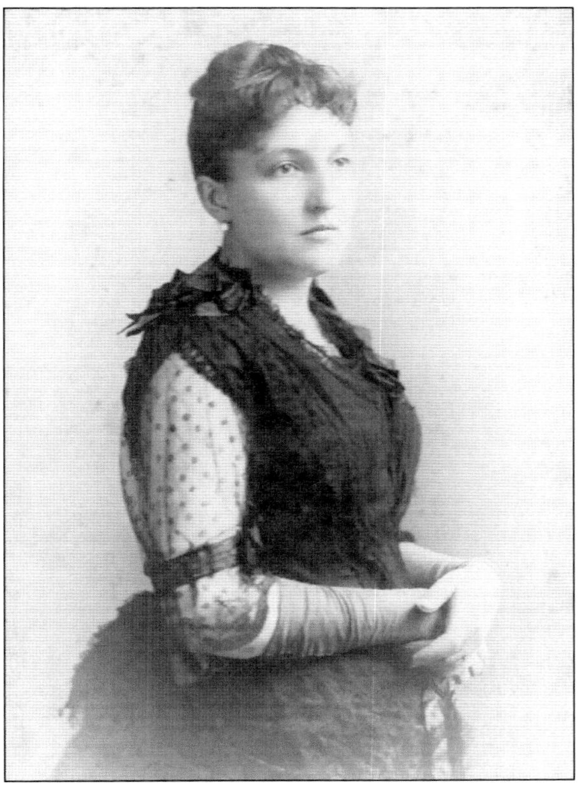

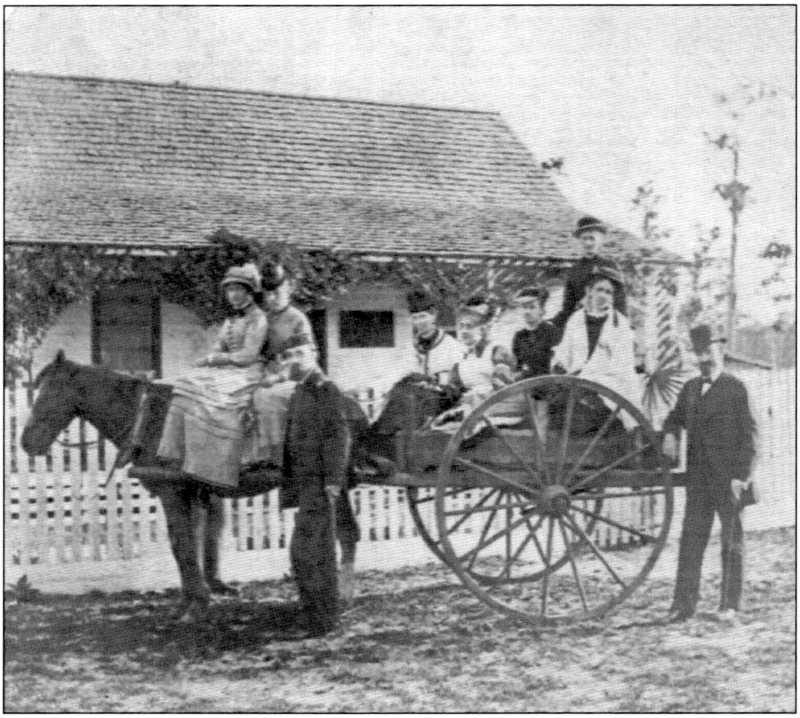

This is a photograph taken of Virginia Eliza Everett Verplanck on vacation in Florida in 1875. Depicted in the photograph are William, Captain Ramsey, Minnie Everett, Captain Ramsey's wife (front seat), Anna, Bessie Stillmore (back seat), Clara Stillmore (standing), and Virginia Everett (on the right in back). (Courtesy of Mount Gulian Historic Site.)

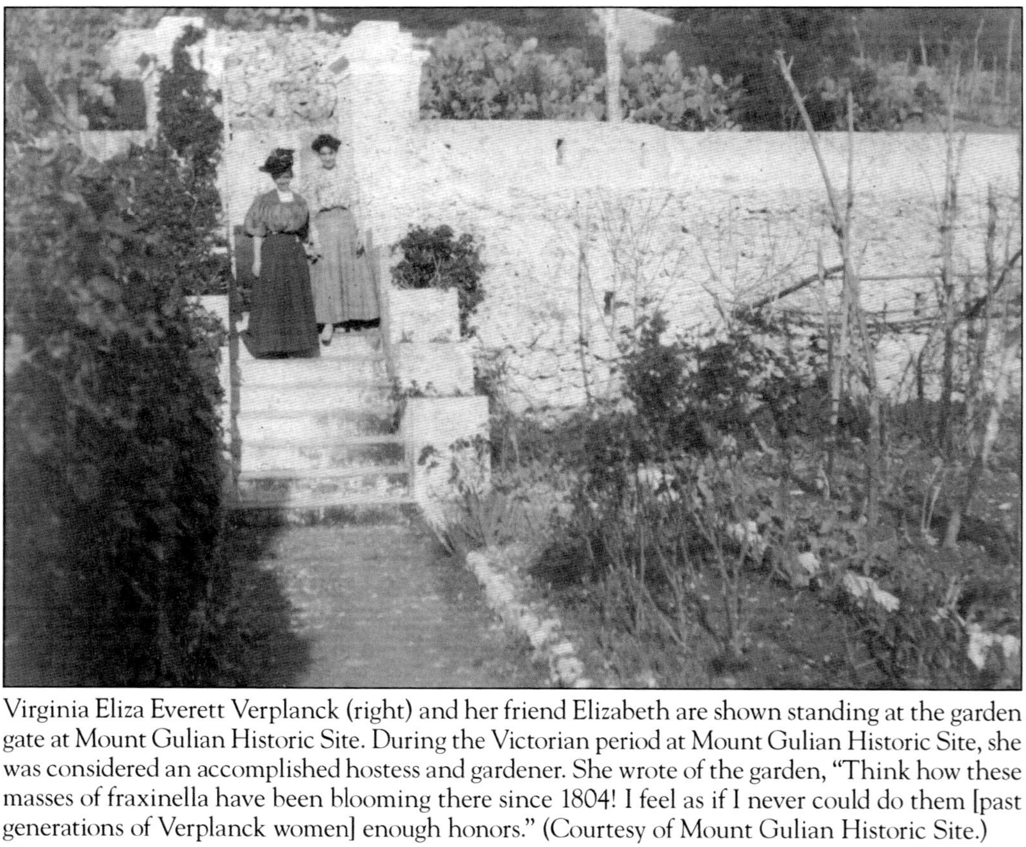

Virginia Eliza Everett Verplanck (right) and her friend Elizabeth are shown standing at the garden gate at Mount Gulian Historic Site. During the Victorian period at Mount Gulian Historic Site, she was considered an accomplished hostess and gardener. She wrote of the garden, "Think how these masses of fraxinella have been blooming there since 1804! I feel as if I never could do them [past generations of Verplanck women] enough honors." (Courtesy of Mount Gulian Historic Site.)

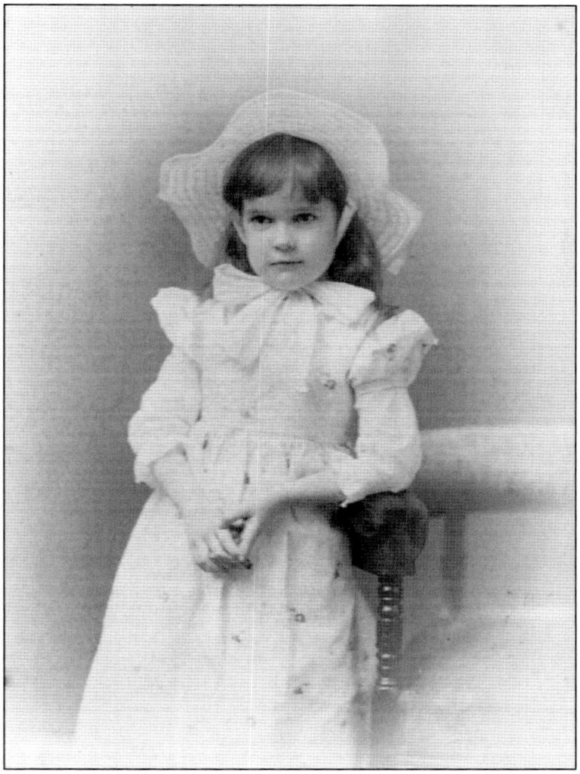

These photographs show Virginia Darby Verplanck, who was born in 1883, between the ages of four and 12. In the photographs, she looks similar to her mother, Virginia Eliza Everett Verplanck. Her grandfather Henry F. Darby painted several significant pieces of art before his death in 1897. He also taught at the South Carolina Female College in Barhamville. He was married briefly to Virginia Darby Verplanck's grandmother, and after she died, he traveled across the country and the Atlantic Ocean frequently. He spent some time in an English seminary, New York City, South Carolina, Connecticut, and upstate New York. (Both, courtesy of Mount Gulian Historic Site.)

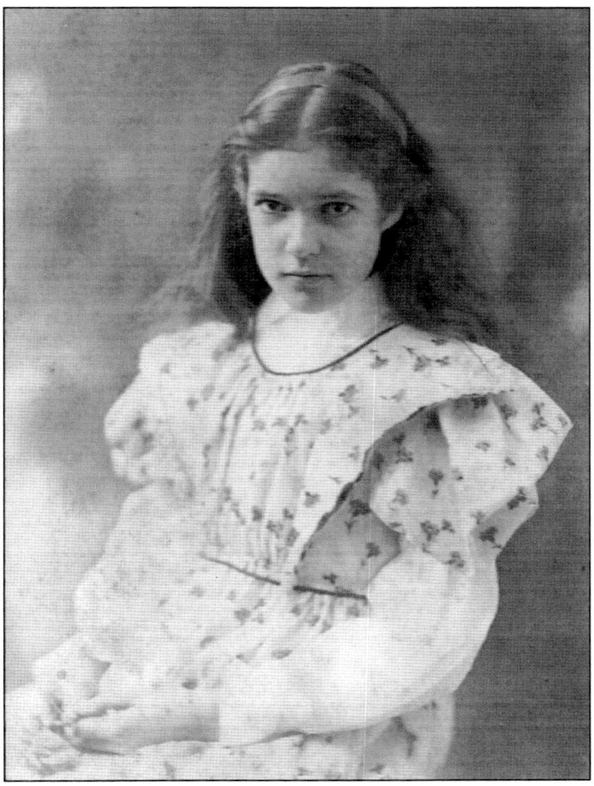

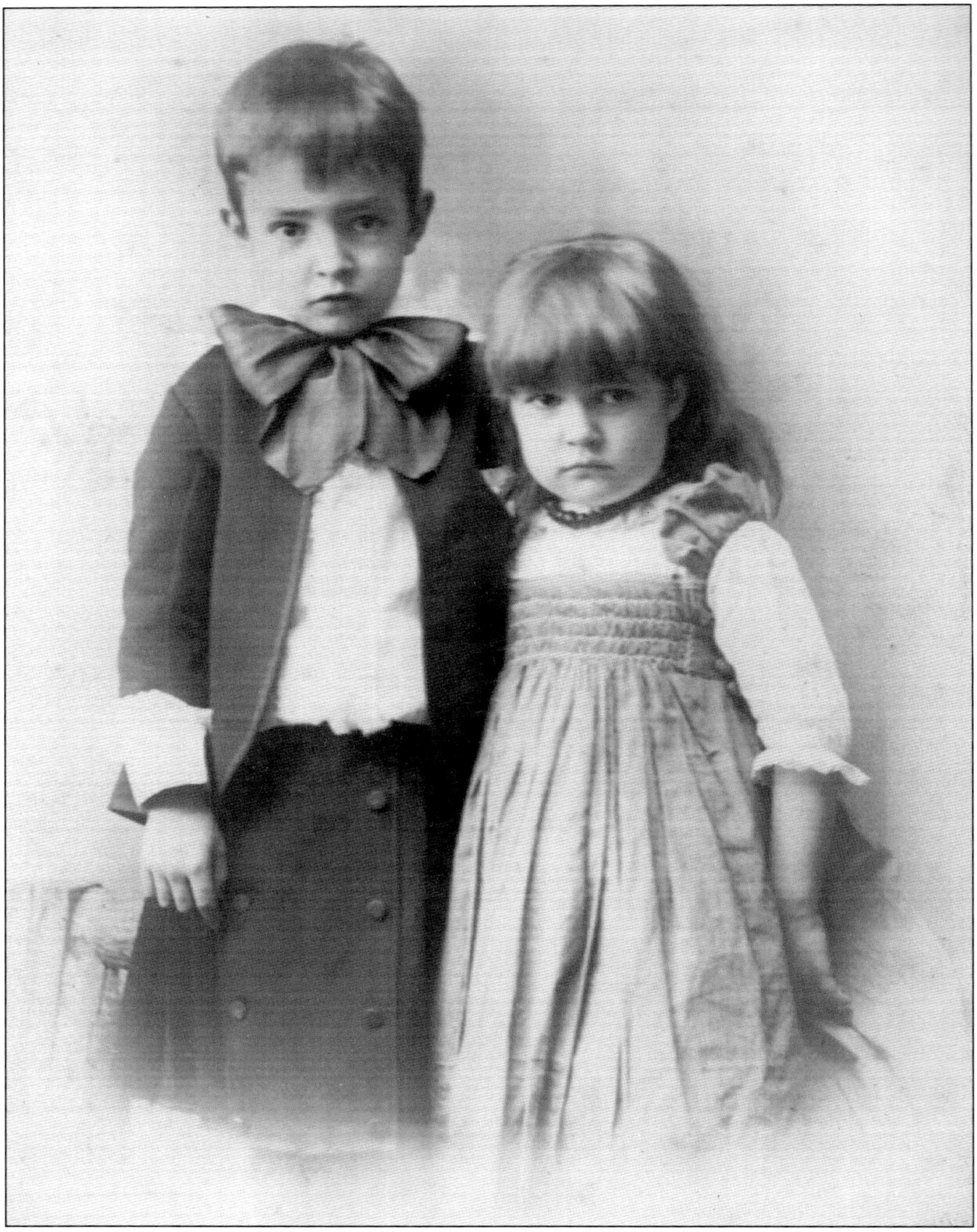

This is a photograph of William Everett Verplanck and Virginia Darby Verplanck. On the back of the photograph it reads "For dear Aunt Kim–William Everett Verplanck and Virginia Darby Verplanck 1887." William Verplanck and Virginia Verplanck are seven and four years old in this photograph. William Verplanck's son, Warburton King Verplanck, wrote about his trips to Mount Gulian Historic Site during the 1920s and 1930s in *Boyhood Visits to My Grandparents at Mount Gulian Historic Site*, which was edited by his daughter Charlotte Verplanck Willman. (Courtesy of Mount Gulian Historic Site.)

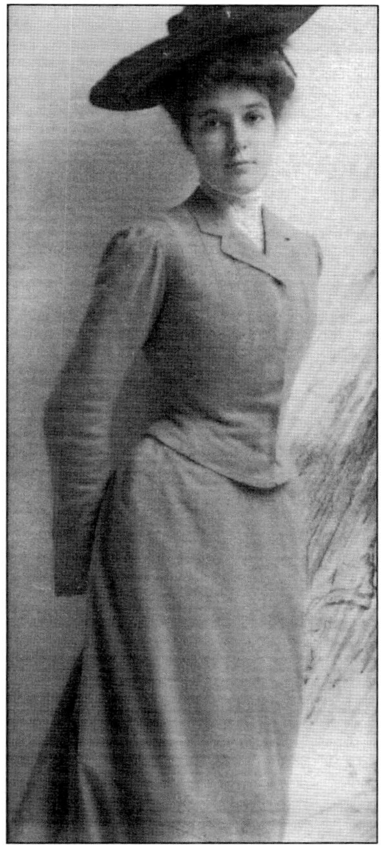

These are two photographs of Virginia Darby Verplanck in two different states of dress. In the photograph at right, taken by Rose and Bickler of 50 West Twenty-second Street in New York, Virginia is around 20 years old. The other photograph (below) is of her in her great-great-great grandmother's dress in the spring of 1901. She is 18 years old. The dress is fashioned after the Colonial period, perhaps in celebration of the Fourth of July. (Both, courtesy of Mount Gulian Historic Site.)

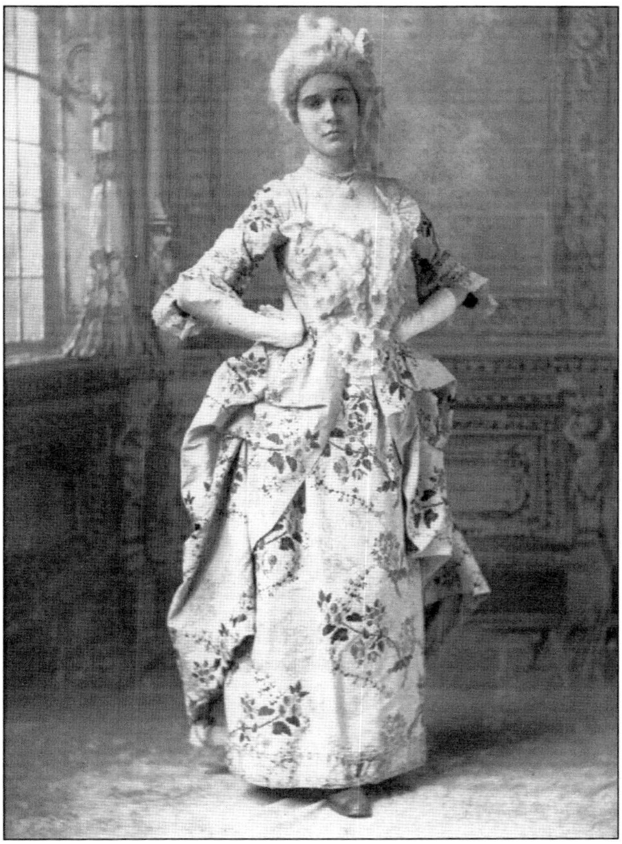

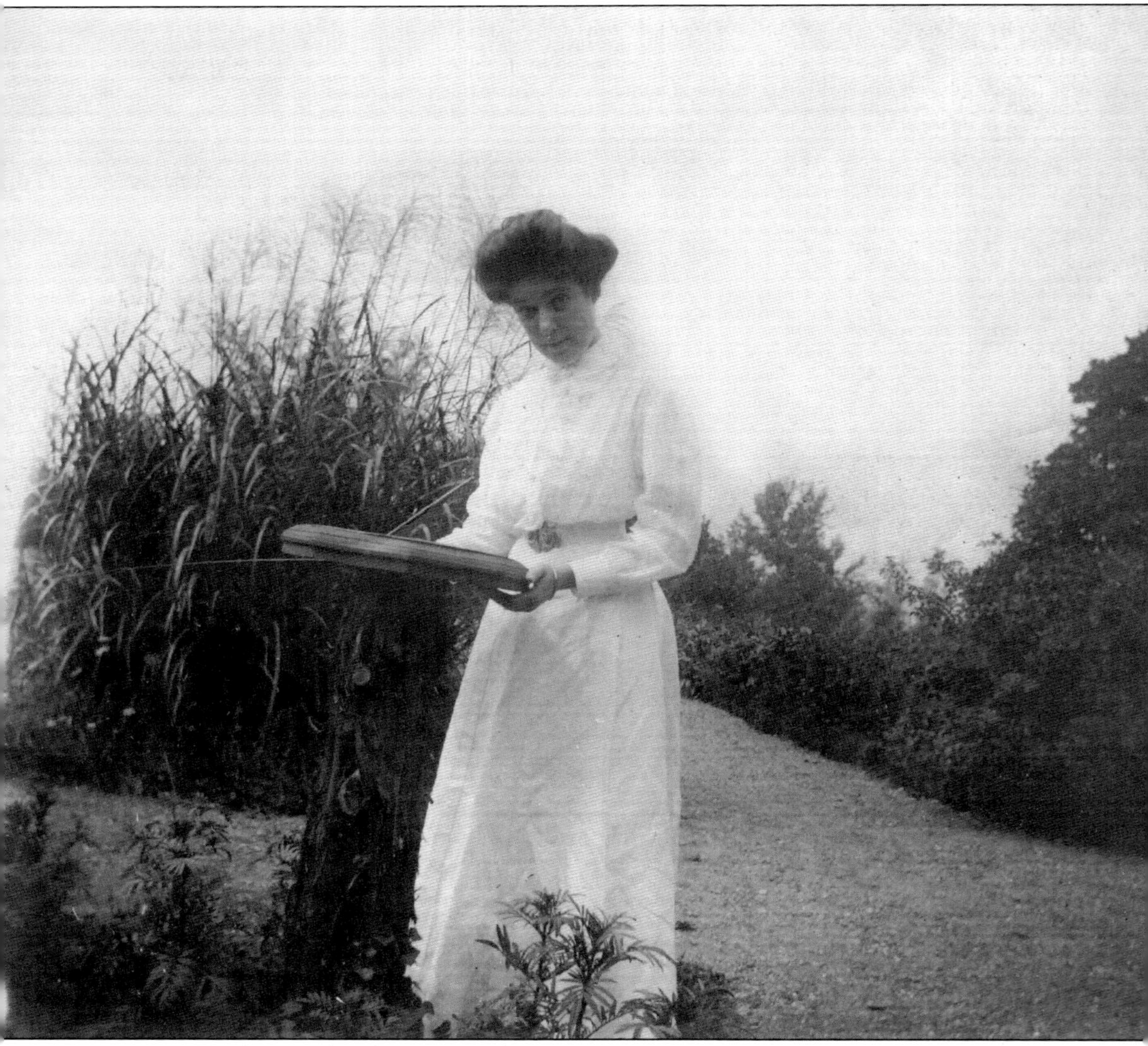

Virginia Darby Verplanck is pictured in the Mount Gulian Historic Site garden standing in front of a sundial. A replica sundial was donated and placed at Mount Gulian Historic Site in the same spot that is depicted in this photograph during the 2000s. (Courtesy of Mount Gulian Historic Site.)

These are two photographs of Verplanck family members, William Everett Verplanck (right) and Virginia Darby Verplanck. William Everett Verplanck is pictured at 17 months, and E.K. and S.E. Hough at 487 Eighth Avenue in New York City printed the photograph of him. His son Warburton wrote "My parents enjoyed automobile trips and took their four children with them . . . one of the trips each summer was to Fishkill, New York, to visit my father's parents in the family homestead, Mount Gulian Historic Site on the east side of the Hudson River just above Beacon and across the river from Newburgh." Virginia Darby Verplanck (below) is dressed in costume during the Gilded Age. (Both, courtesy of Mount Gulian Historic Site.)

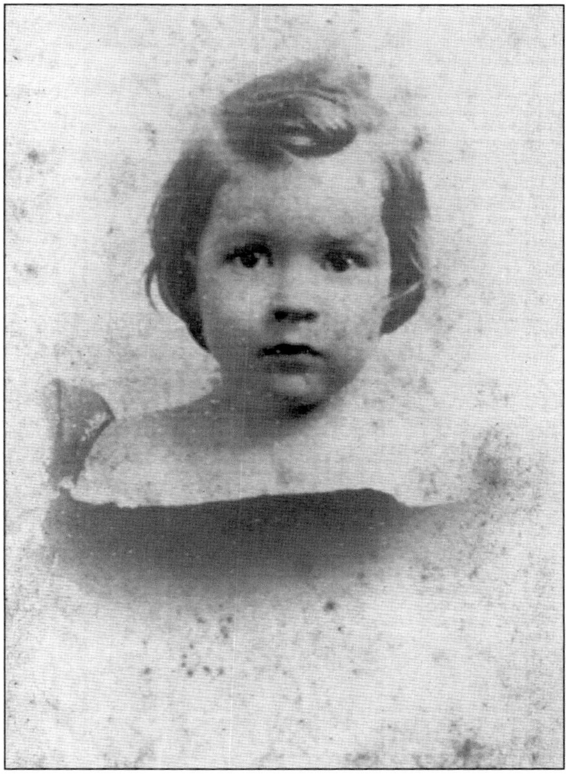

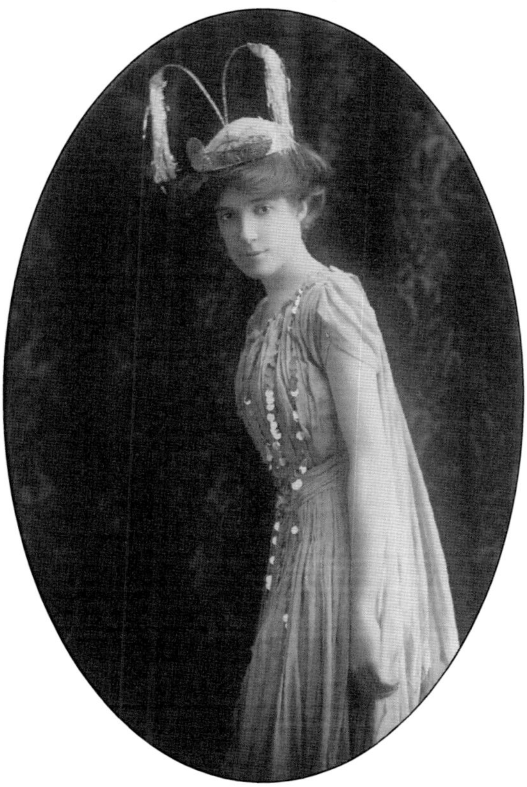

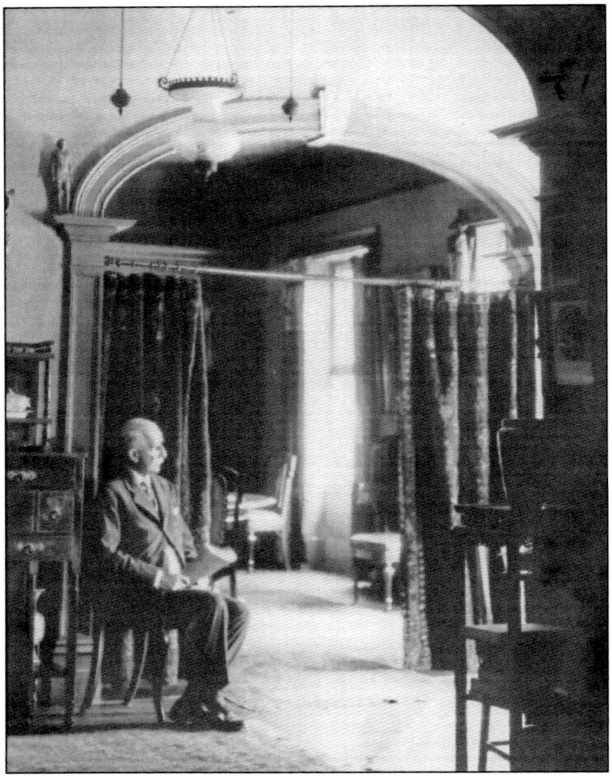

This is a photograph of William Everett Verplanck in later years, sitting in one of the rooms at Mount Gulian Historic Site. The inscription on the back of the photograph reads: "Mount Gulian Historic Site, Papa's father, William Everett Verplanck." (Courtesy of Mount Gulian Historic Site.)

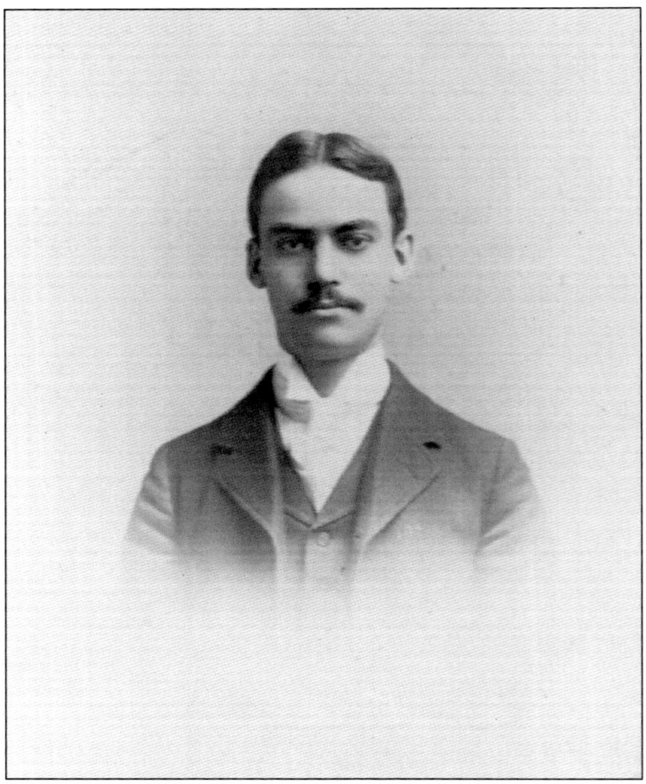

Charles Bleecker sits for a photograph that was printed in New York City by Hargrave. He was the brother of T. Bache Bleecker, who married Virginia Darby Verplanck. The son of Virginia and T. Bache, Bache Bleecker, was born in 1926 and led the effort to have Mount Gulian Historic Site restored to its Colonial state. (Courtesy of Mount Gulian Historic Site.)

This is a photograph of Theophylact Bache Bleecker printed by Otto J. Frank of the southwest corner of 125th street and Third Avenue New York City. T. Bache Bleecker was the husband of Virginia Darby Verplanck. He was born on December 8, 1870. They were married on November 9, 1909, and he died on December 7, 1951. (Courtesy of Mount Gulian Historic Site.)

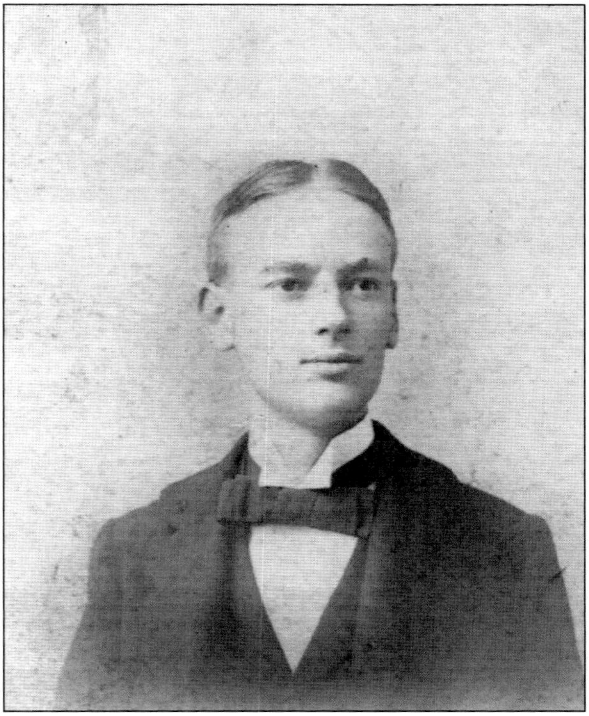

This is a photograph of the barn at Mount Gulian Historic Site. It was acquired in 1974 from a former Verplanck family farm in Hopewell Junction. The barn is one of the oldest lasting examples of a Dutch barn in New York State. Interesting parts of the barn are that it has martin holes that allow for insect-eating birds to enter and low gables on each side. (Courtesy of Mount Gulian Historic Site.)

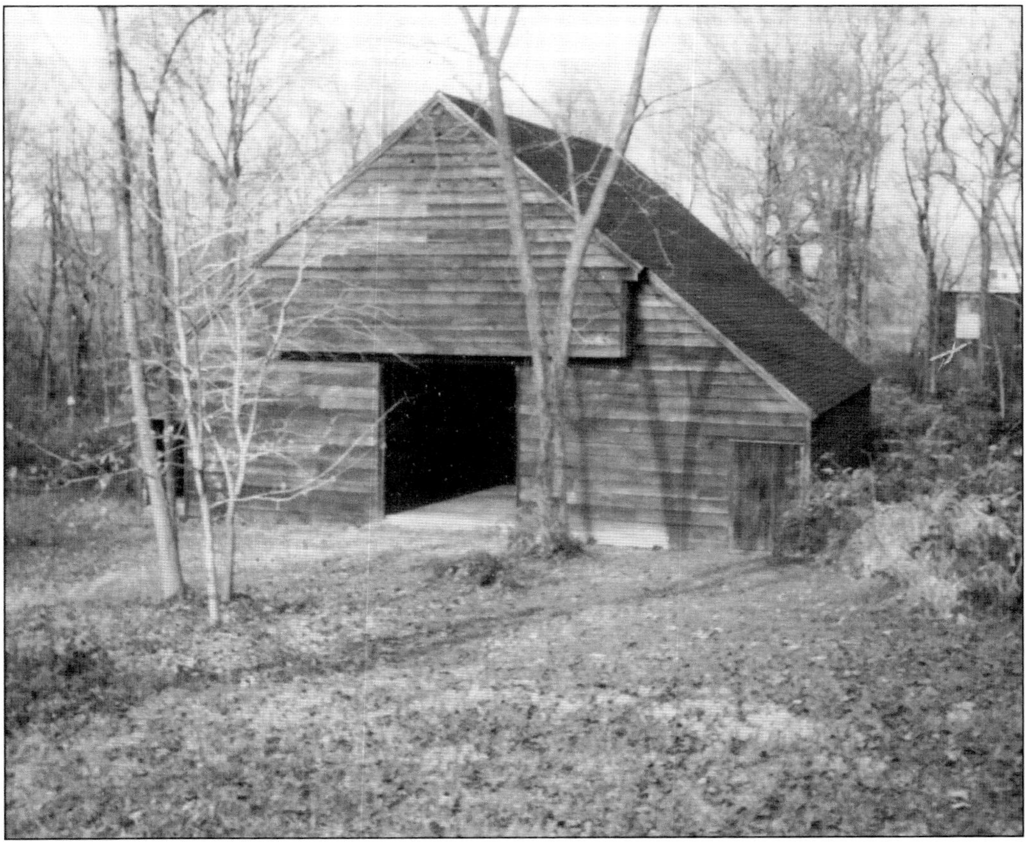

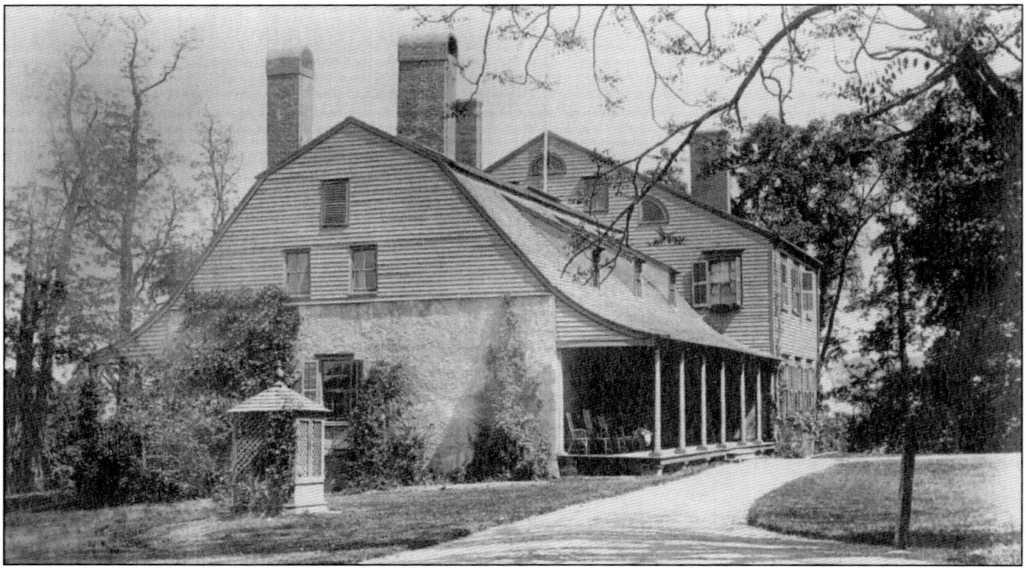

Mount Gulian Historic Site is depicted in this early-20th-century photograph. William Samuel Verplanck lived at Mount Gulian Historic Site. He was the oldest son of Gulian Crommelin Verplanck and Eliza Fenno and was born in 1812. His baptism is in the records of Trinity Episcopal Church in Fishkill. He had eight children: Eliza, Mary, Robert, Daniel, Anna, Jeannette, Gelyna, and William Edward. Like his father, William enjoyed reading and had a very good memory. He was also fond of hunting. A portrait of William Samuel Verplanck that was painted by Rev. Henry F. Darby hangs at Mount Gulian Historic Site. (Courtesy of Mount Gulian Historic Site.)

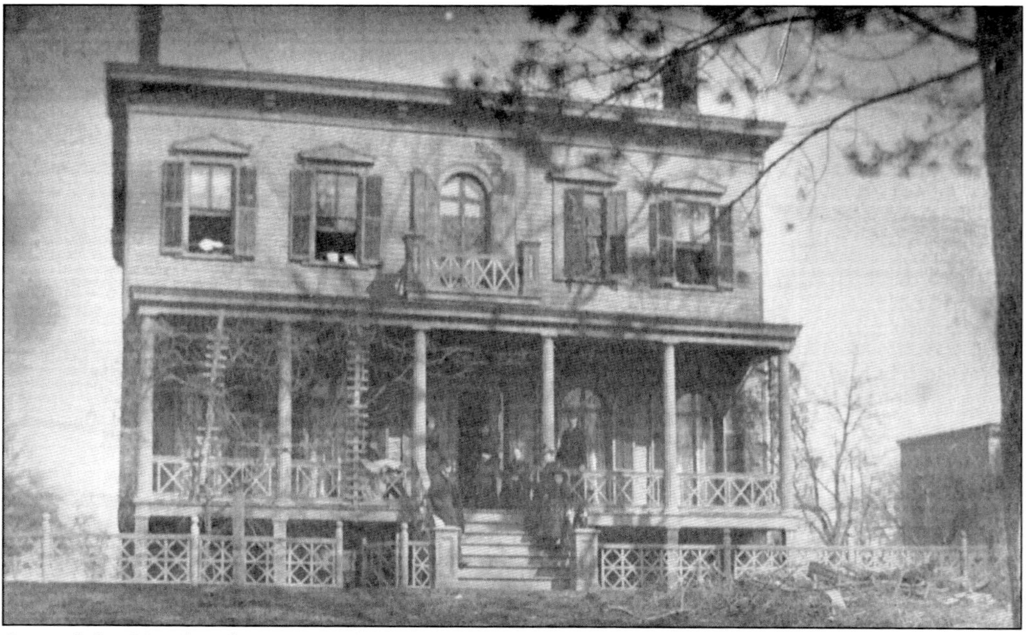

One of the Verplancks' various homes in the area may be depicted in this early-19th-century photograph. William Samuel Verplanck had a home in the Fishkill area called New Place. At both Mount Gulian and New Place, the Verplancks hosted an open house in both winter and summer. During this time, they entertained their many children and friends. (Courtesy of Mount Gulian Historic Site.)

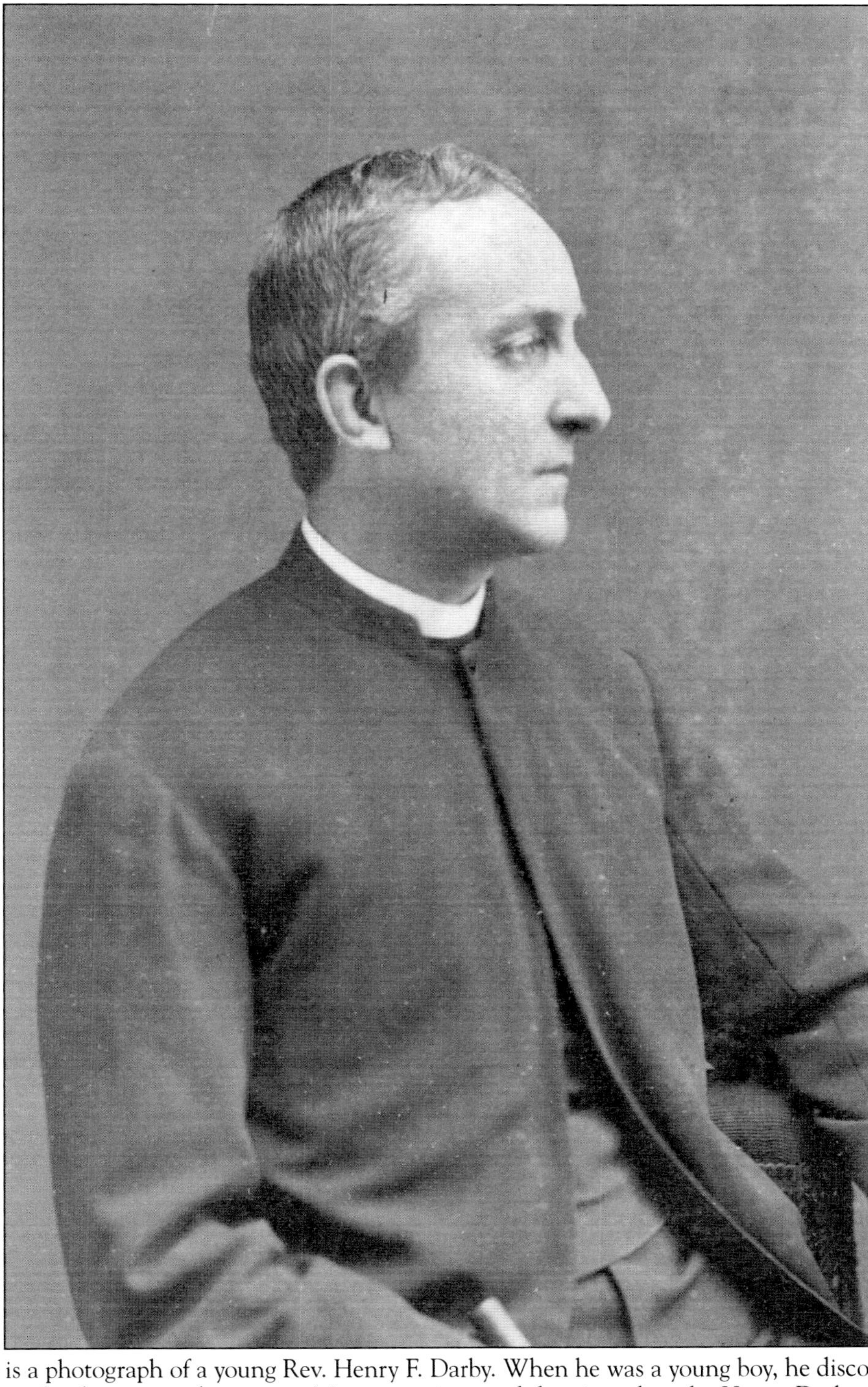

This is a photograph of a young Rev. Henry F. Darby. When he was a young boy, he discovered a talent for drawing and painting. Many paintings and drawings done by Henry Darby reside at Mount Gulian Historic Site, especially of his daughter Virginia Eliza Everett Verplanck. His wife died only three years into his marriage, and this caused him to study for the ministry in the Protestant Episcopal Church. (Courtesy of Mount Gulian Historic Site.)

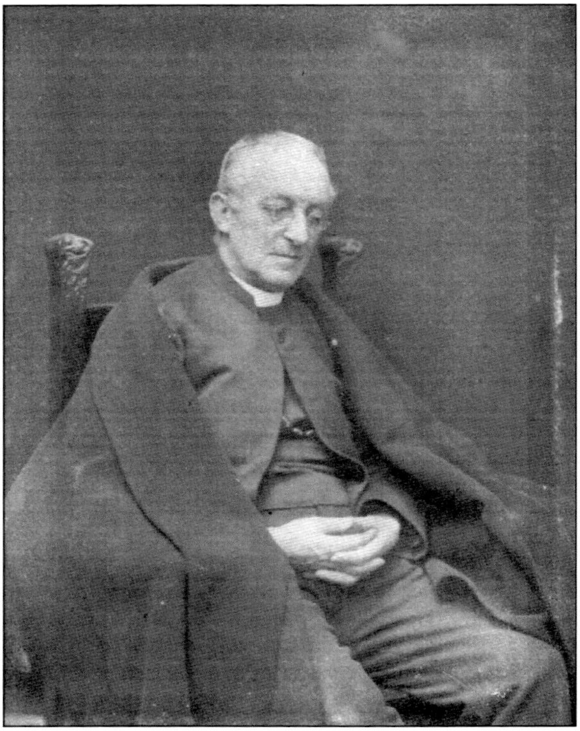

Rev. Henry Darby is pictured posing for the camera in his later years. He pursued becoming a clergyman in the Episcopal Church and even went to England in pursuit of this goal. While in England, he spent a lot of his time working on religious painting and designs for church embroidery. Around 1890, he came back to live with Virginia Eliza Everett Verplanck in Fishkill. (Courtesy of Mount Gulian Historic Site.)

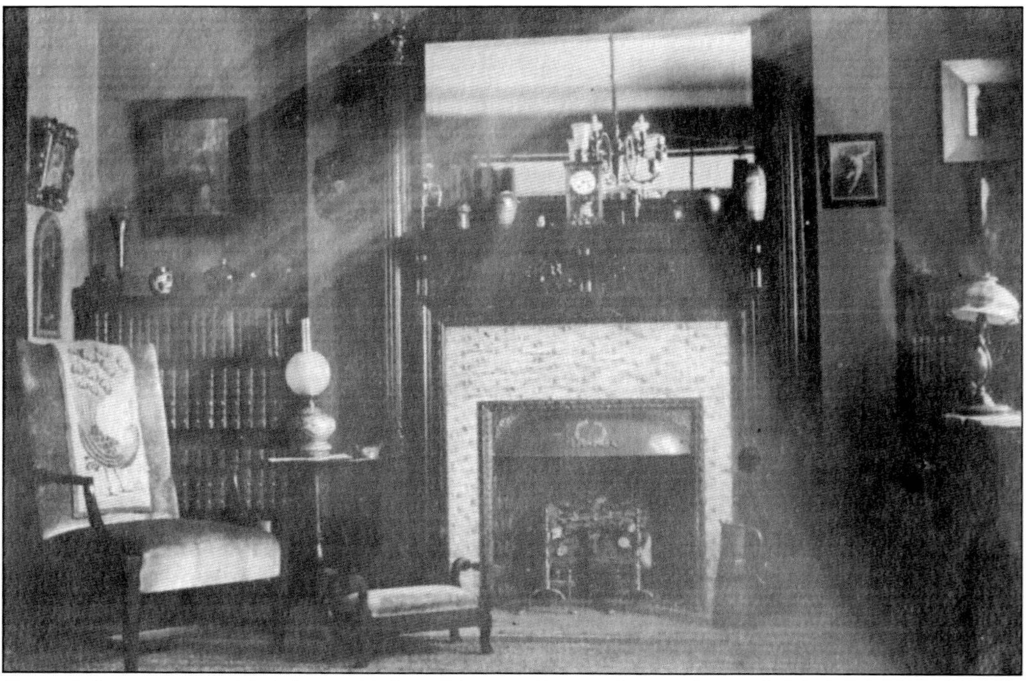

One of the rooms inside Mount Gulian Historic Site is depicted in a Gilded Age photograph. Several generations of Verplancks lived at Mount Gulian Historic Site. One Verplanck who lived at the homestead is Robert Newlin Verplanck. He served in the Union army in the Civil War. He wrote to his mother about the death of President Lincoln, "The death of the President has had a most depression effect on the army." (Courtesy of Mount Gulian Historic Site.)

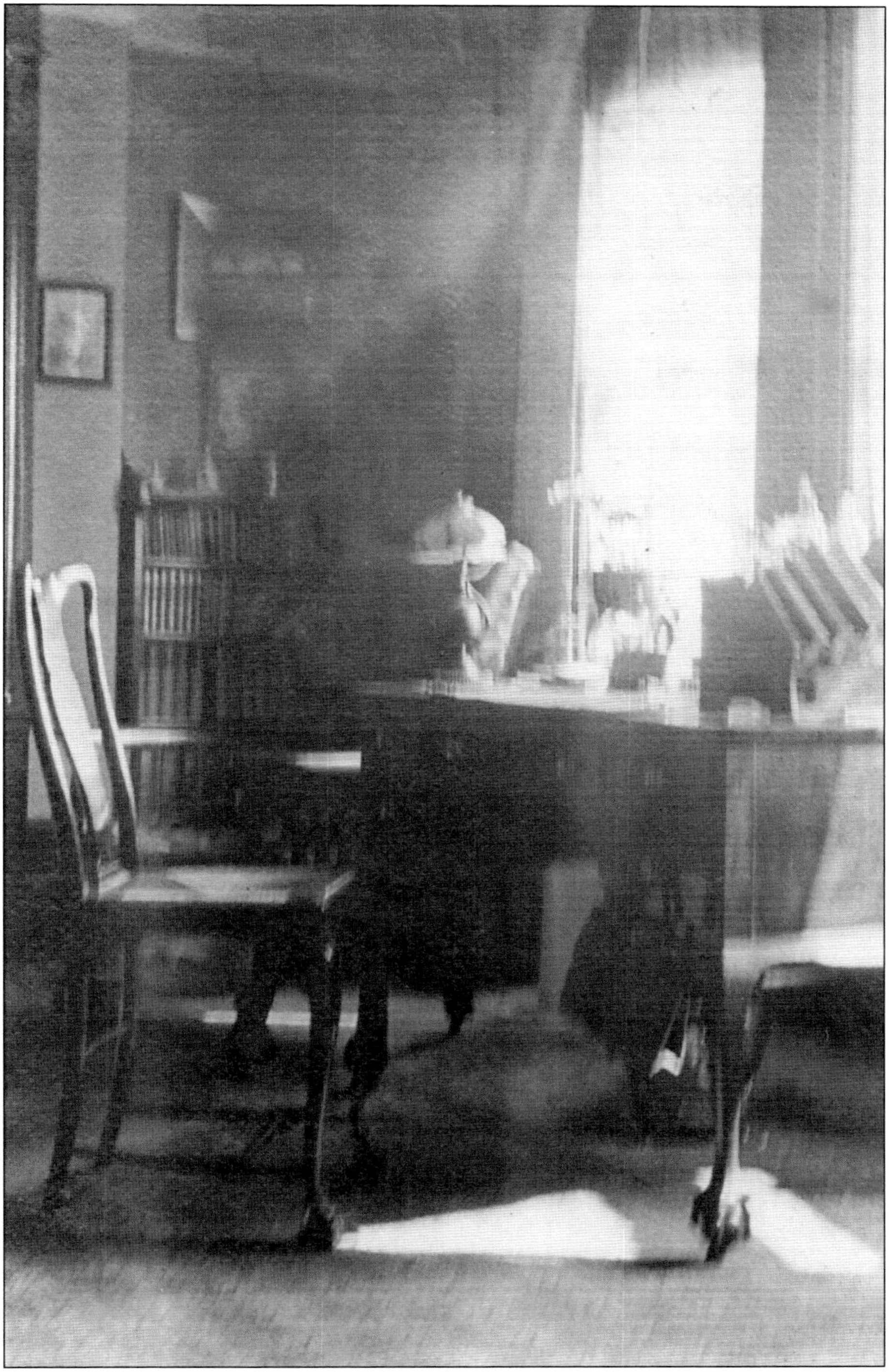

This photograph is of another room inside the Mount Gulian Historic Site homestead. It may be of what is now known as the Robert Newlin Verplanck room. This room contains various artifacts, books, and other parts of the Mount Gulian Historic Site archive. One item of note in the room is a Native American peace pipe. Local Native Americans used the land Mount Gulian Historic Site sits on as a summer hunting ground. (Courtesy of Mount Gulian Historic Site.)

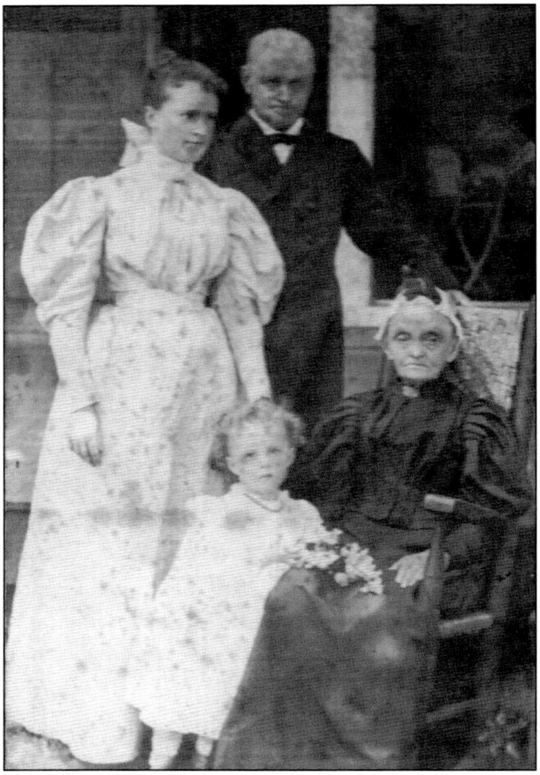

Lawrence Knevels is photographed (below) in uniform in December 1886. He was a cousin to the Verplancks. William Samuel Verplanck and his brother Gulian Verplanck discuss the Knevel family frequently in their letters to each other. Gulian Verplanck was born on April 19, 1815. He was a shy boy and eventually became a whaler. James F. Brown notes in his diary that Gulian Verplanck wrecked of Hatteras in 1840. On another sea voyage he became ill and was sent home to Mount Gulian Historic Site. He died at the age of 31 and is buried at Trinity Episcopal Church. From left to right, Caroline Eliza, John Fairfax, Josephine Fairfax Smith, and Josephine Smith are depicted (left) in an 1896 photograph. There is a Fairfax Road located around Brinckerhoff in Fishkill. (Both, courtesy of Mount Gulian Historic Site.)

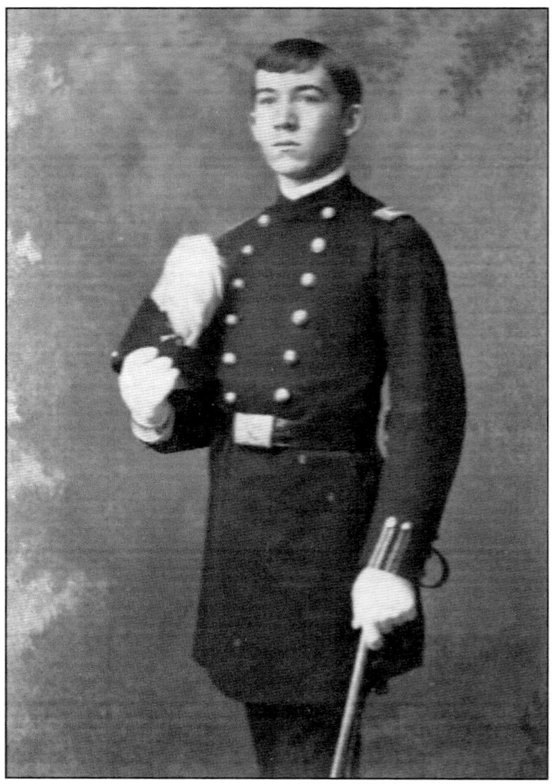

Henry Morgan is depicted in an 1897 photograph with his grandchildren Eunice and Tom. The photograph was printed at 253 Fulton Street in Brooklyn. Tom and possibly Eunice were from the Schenck family. The Schencks were close with the Verplanck family in Fishkill. James F. Brown notes in his January 1, 1829, diary entry that he "went to a party at old Mrs. Schencks with Mrs. Verplanck and family." (Courtesy of Mount Gulian Historic Site.)

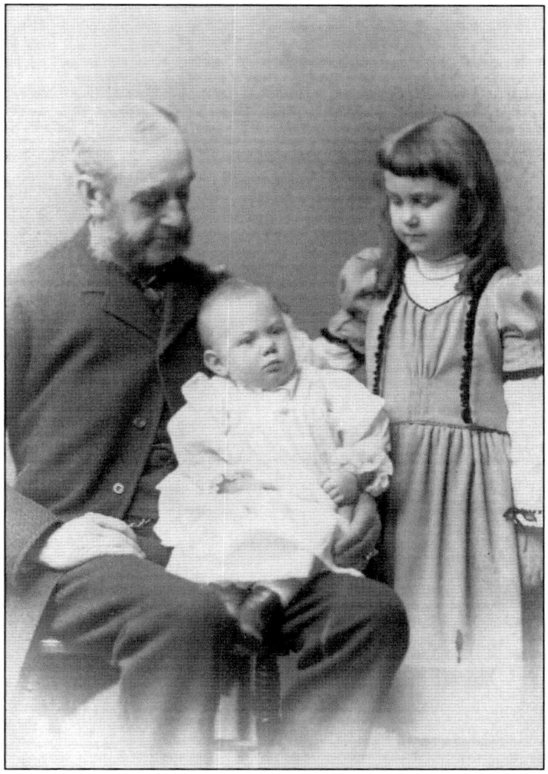

This is a class photograph taken in 1895 possibly around Fishkill. The back of the photograph lists the school as C.H.S. and the principal as C.H. Stone. A "Duke" Verplanck is listed in the second row. The first school in Fishkill was built in 1760 and was located across from the Dutch Reformed Church. The Rombout Presbyterian Church at Brinckerhoff was the location of a classical school. This school later grew into the Dutchess Academy. (Courtesy of Mount Gulian Historic Site.)

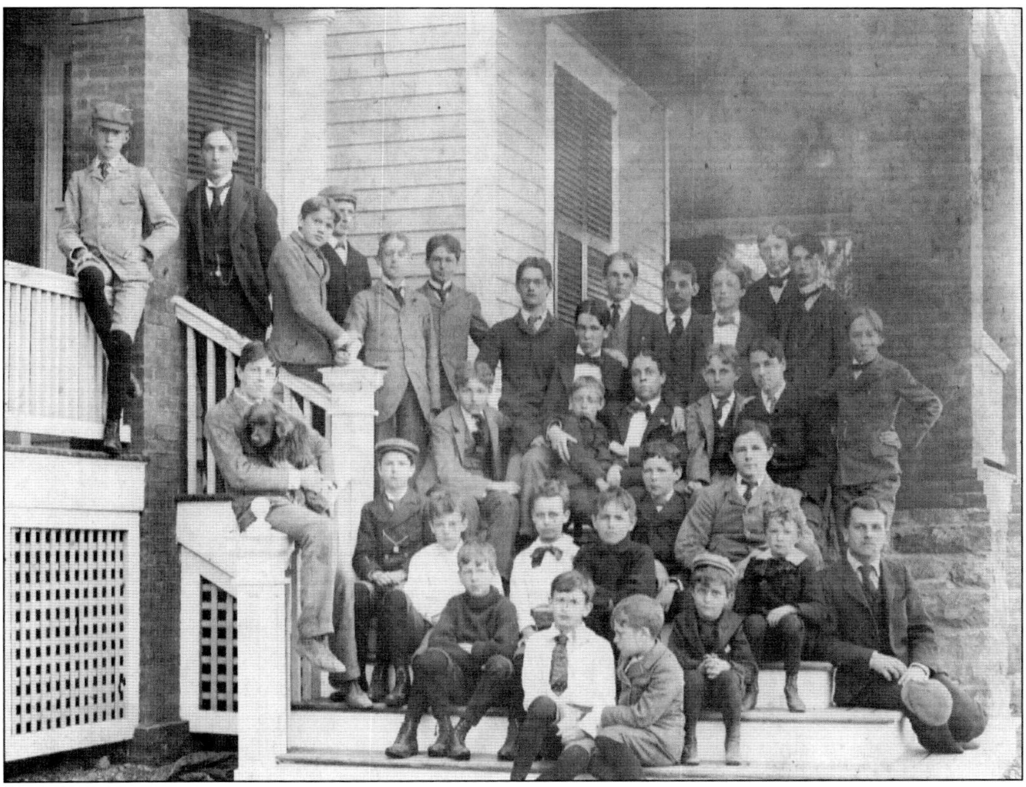

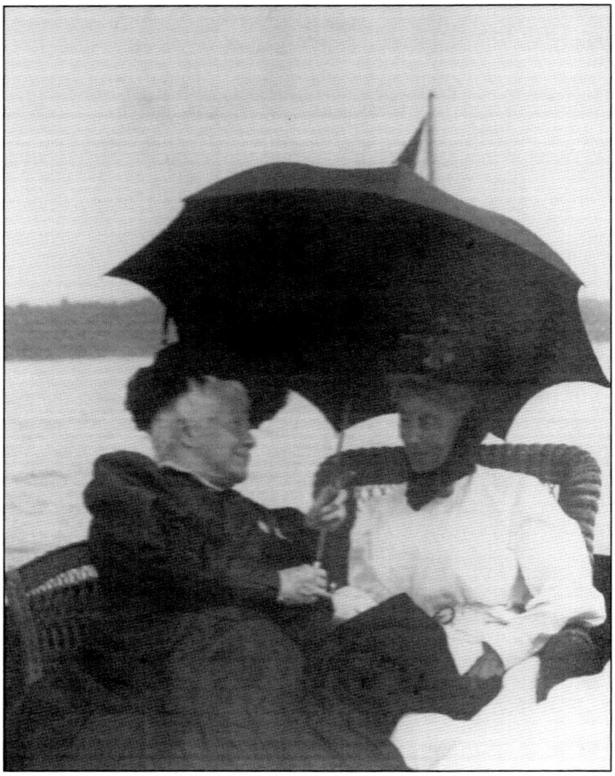

Josephine Kirby and a friend are pictured sitting on the docks. The Kirbys were close in relation to the Verplancks. The wife of Jacob Brown Kirby leased Mount Gulian Historic Site for a few summers during the late 1870s. Pamela Kirby was the aunt of Virginia Eliza Verplanck. (Courtesy of Mount Gulian Historic Site.)

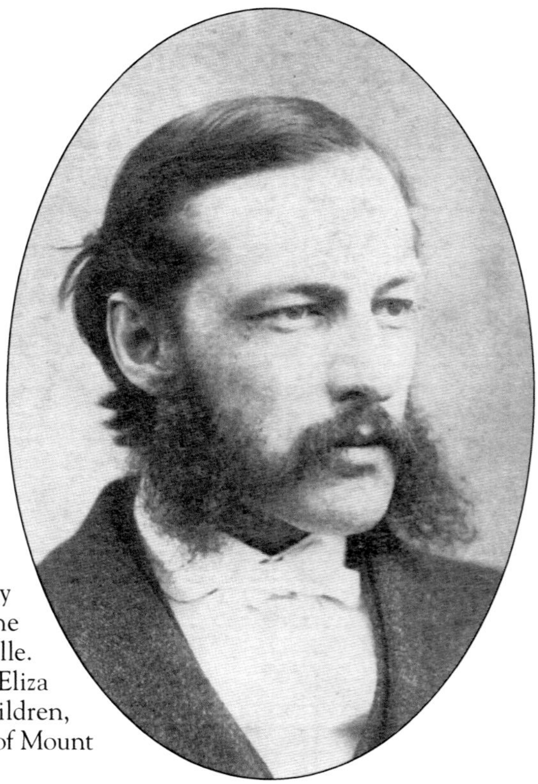

This photograph is of R.M. Kirby. Rev. Henry F. Darby's wife, Eliza Brown Kirby, was the daughter of Col. Edmund Kirby of Brownsville. Brownsville is located in Jefferson County. Eliza Brown Kirby and Henry Darby had two children, Virginia Eliza and Edmund Kirby. (Courtesy of Mount Gulian Historic Site.)

Two members or friends of the Verplanck family are depicted on their wedding day in the mid-20th century. Today, weddings are still conducted at Mount Gulian Historic Site Historic Site. As many of 150 people can be entertained in the 17th-century Dutch barn located on the property. Formal events for a smaller amount of people can also be conducted inside the Society of Cincinnati room in the house. (Courtesy of Mount Gulian Historic Site.)

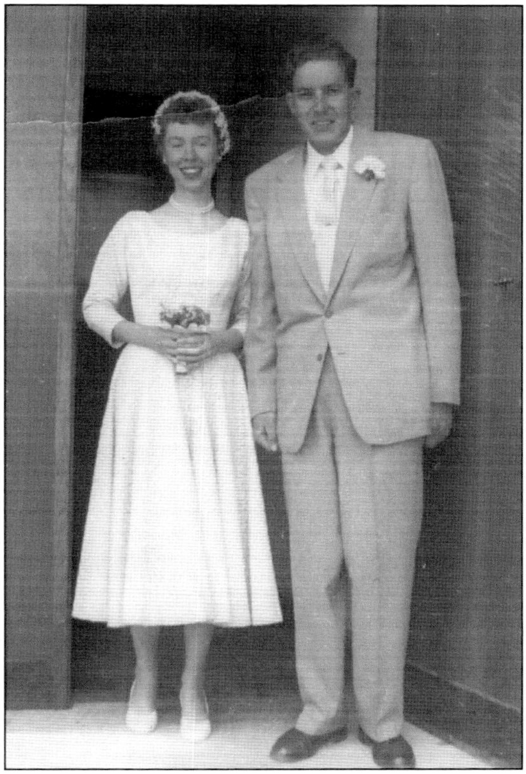

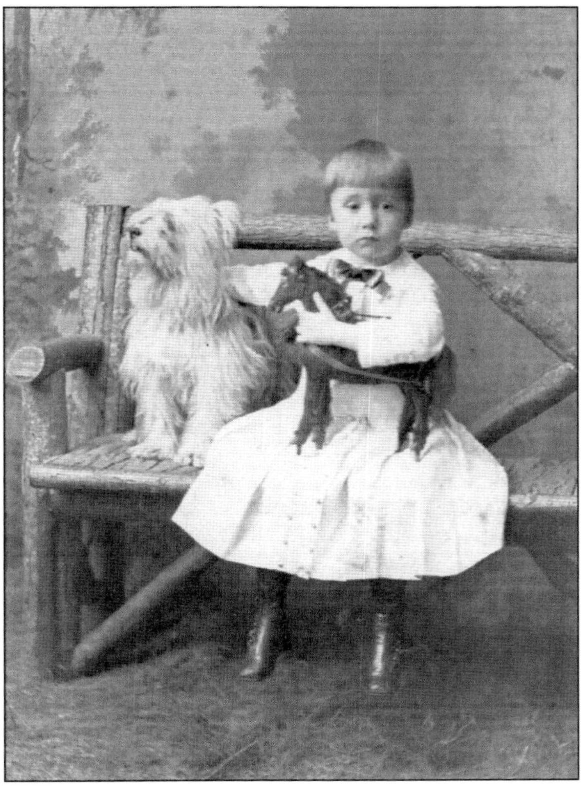

This is a photograph of John Bayard Rogers Verplanck at four years old, taken in Matteawan, New York. He was born on October 8, 1881, and died on April 6, 1955. He was a World War I pilot and eventually became a banker. (Courtesy of Mount Gulian Historic Site.)

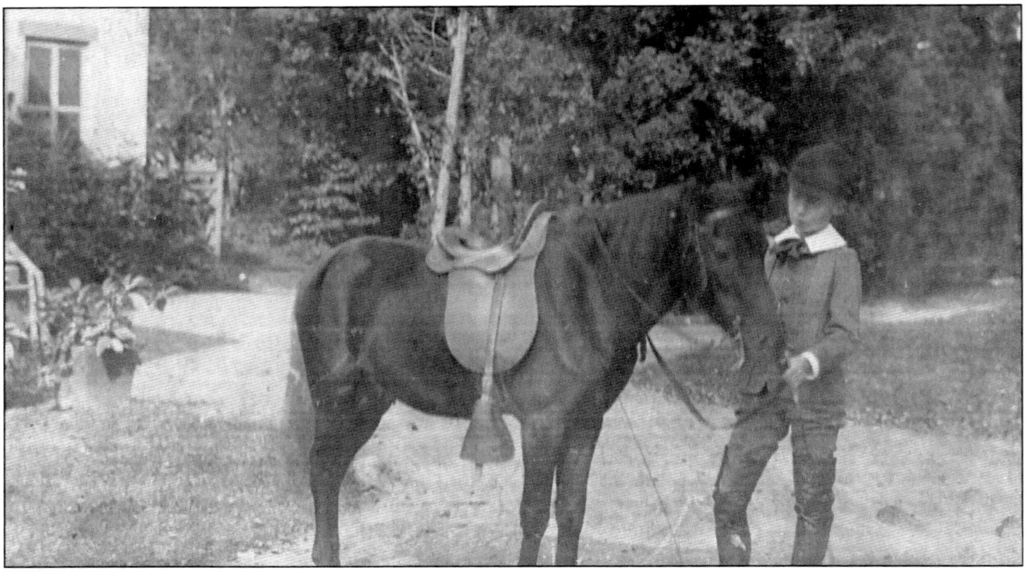

An unidentified Verplanck boy is pictured with his horse at Mount Gulian Historic Site during the early 19th century. A part of the new addition to Mount Gulian Historic Site can be seen on the far left. The Verplancks were very active people and enjoyed activities such as riding and the outdoors, as seen in this photograph. Letters written between William Samuel Verplanck and his father, Gulian C. Verplanck, often speak of their love of nature. (Courtesy of Mount Gulian Historic Site.)

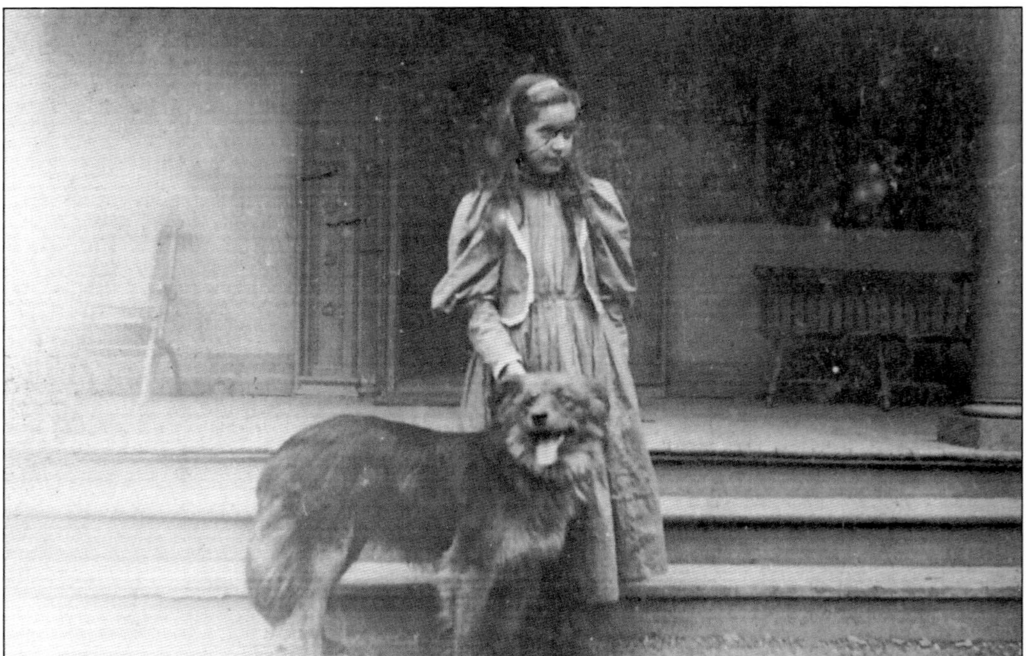

This is possibly a photograph of Virginia Darby Verplanck and her dog taken around the beginning of the 20th century. She is standing at the back of Mount Gulian Historic Site, which faces the Hudson River. Today, the Hudson River can still be seen from the back porch at Mount Gulian Historic Site. (Courtesy of Mount Gulian Historic Site.)

Four

The Land that Was Once Fishkill

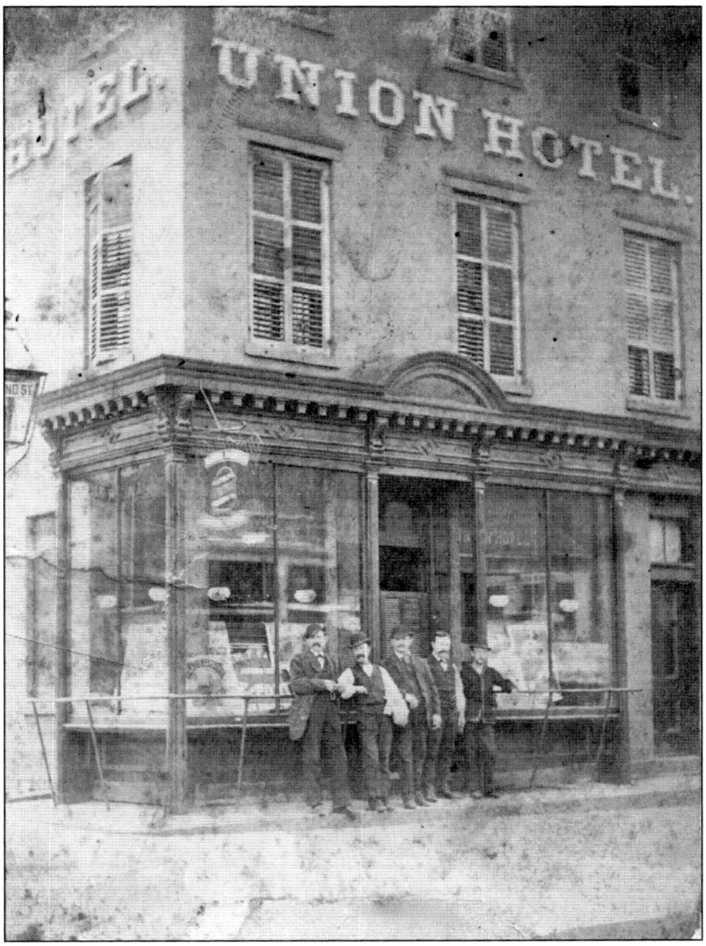

Several men are shown standing in front of a building labeled the Union Hotel. It is not clear for sure, but this building may have been the Union Hotel in Fishkill. That Union Hotel was a popular stop during the 1840s and 1850s with travelers coming through Fishkill. The Union Hotel in Fishkill burned down in 1873. (Courtesy of the Beacon Historical Society.)

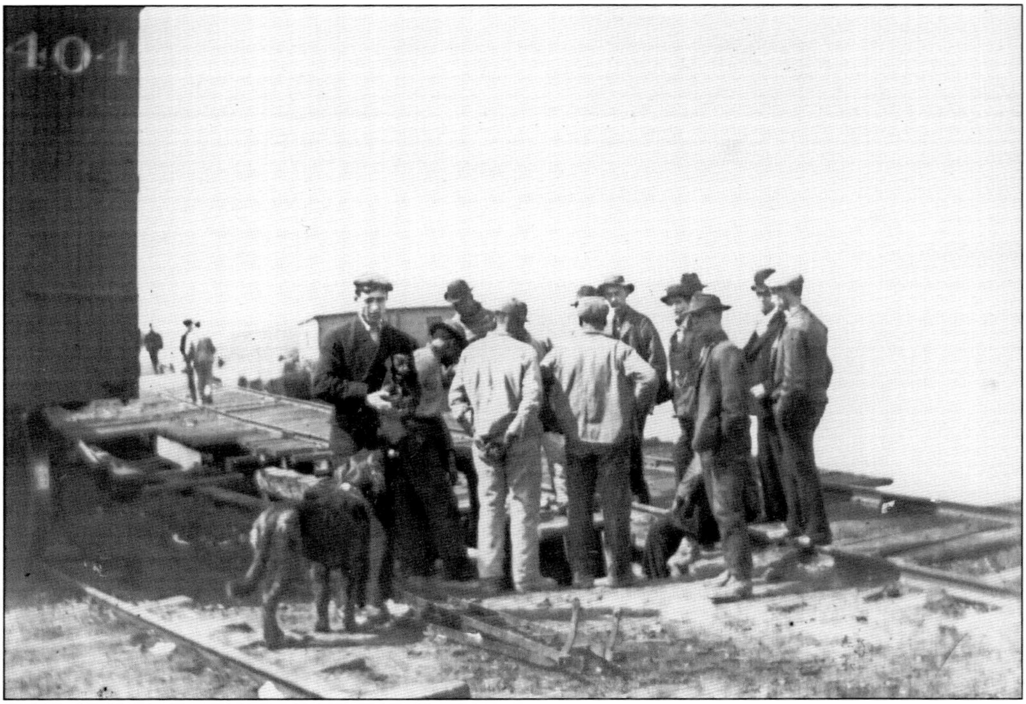

This photograph captures several men busy at work on the railroad in Dutchess Junction. Dutchess Junction is the area between present-day Beacon and Cold Spring. It starts at the Craig House and ends in the tunnel at Cold Spring. Beginning in the 1820s, brickyards like the one shown in this photograph shipped bricks to New York City and Connecticut. (Courtesy of the Beacon Historical Society.)

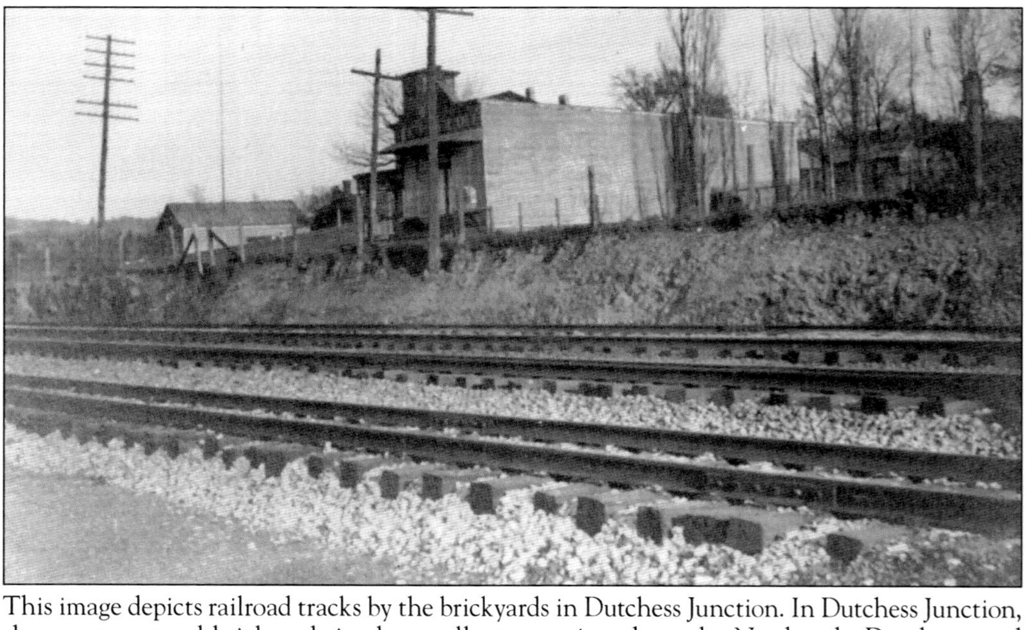

This image depicts railroad tracks by the brickyards in Dutchess Junction. In Dutchess Junction, there were several brickyards in the small community where the Newburgh, Dutchess, and Connecticut Railroad intersected with the Hudson River Railroad. Workers of the brickyard lived in tenement houses owned by the railroad. (Courtesy of the Beacon Historical Society.)

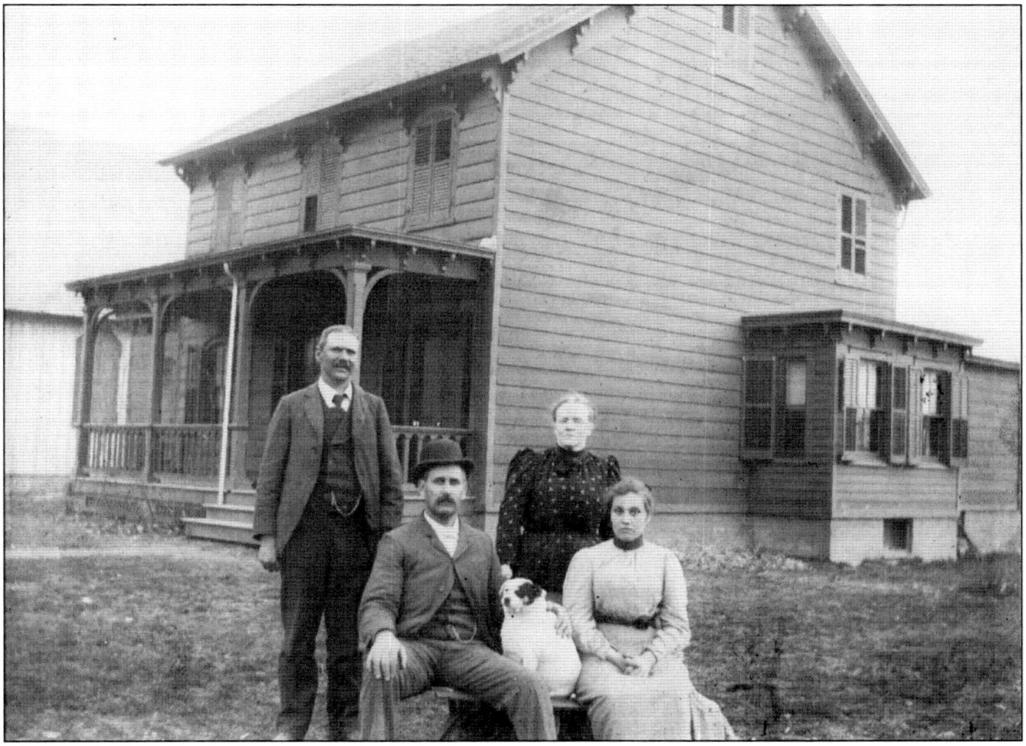

Several people are shown posing for a photograph taken in Dutchess Junction. The people in the photograph are, from left to right, Nathaniel Covert, Thomas G. Aldridge, "Punch" (presumably the dog), Mrs. Thomas G. Aldridge, and Nettie Griffin, the daughter of Janette Aldridge Griffin. (Courtesy of the Beacon Historical Society.)

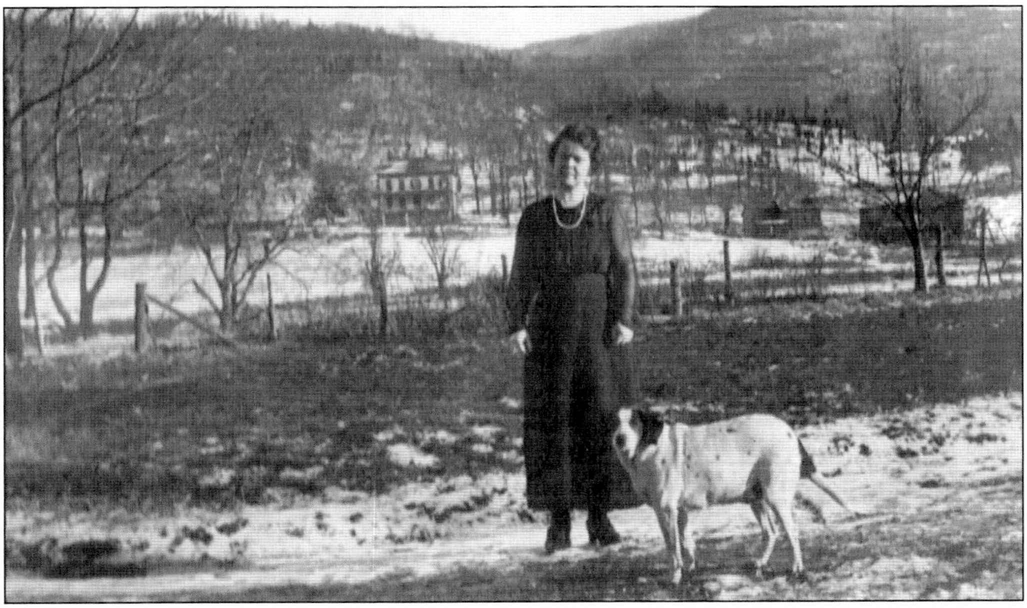

This is a photograph of Charlotte James Covert and the dog "Dotty" Aldridge taken around 1920. They are standing at the back of the house on the hill at Dutchess Junction. They are looking east towards Theodore Brinckerhoff's home. (Courtesy of the Beacon Historical Society.)

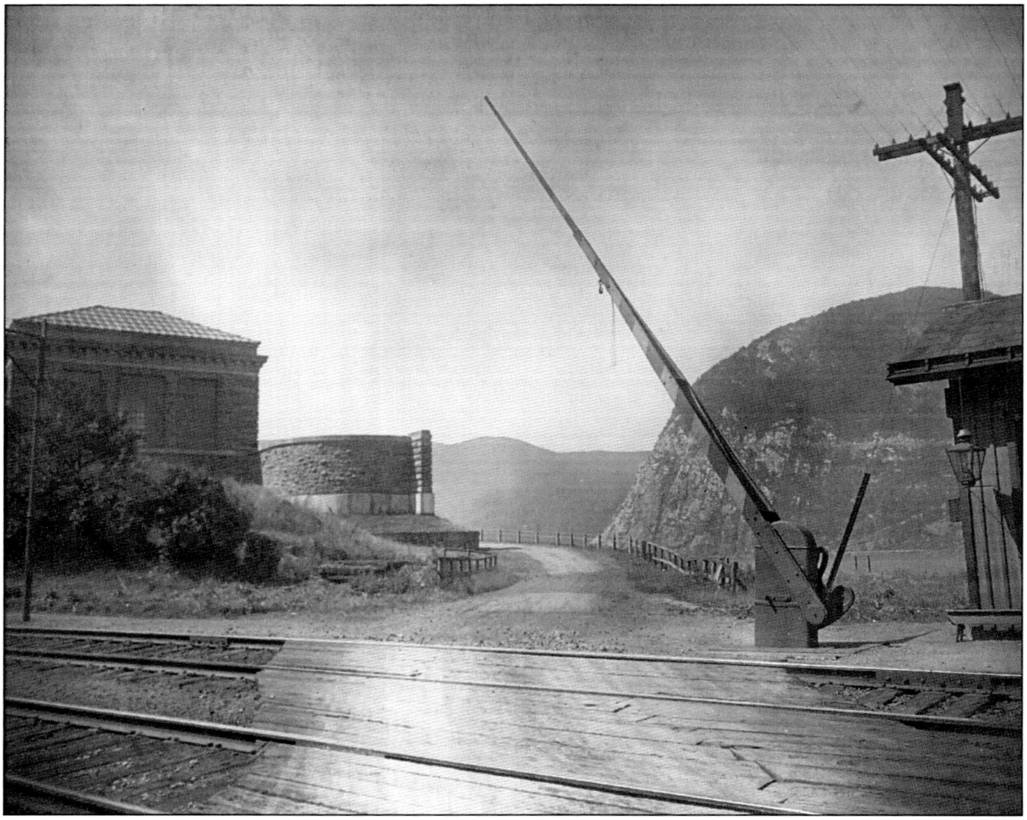

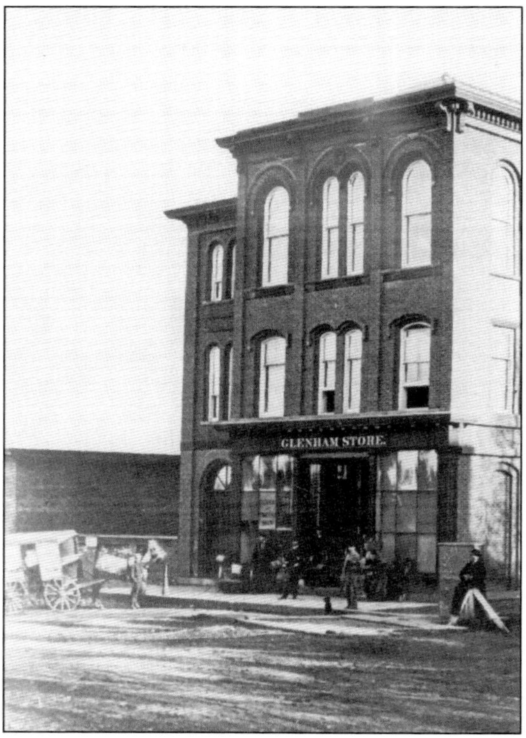

The road around the aqueduct before the tunnel at Breakneck is captured in this photograph. Breakneck Ridge is a mountain along the Hudson River between Beacon and Cold Spring, straddling the boundary between Dutchess and Putnam Counties. Part of Breakneck, which is located within Dutchess Junction, is part of the Hudson Highlands State Park. Denning's Point is also included within the Hudson Highlands State Park. (Courtesy of the Beacon Historical Society.)

The Glenham Store is captured in this photograph, taken around the early 20th century. Glenham is part of the area originally settled as the villages of Matteawan and Fishkill Landing in 1709. Beacon incorporated as a city in 1913 and amalgamated the two villages of Matteawan and Fishkill Landing as well as a small portion of the hamlet of Glenham from the town of Fishkill. (Courtesy of the Beacon Historical Society.)

Jas Miller took this photograph of Miller's store some time around 1900 in Glenham. In the 19th century, mills and factories sprang up in Glenham and Matteawan. However, the strong industry fell into decay after the Civil War. In 1931, the Texaco Research Center purchased the old mill site and established a research center there. (Courtesy of the Beacon Historical Society.)

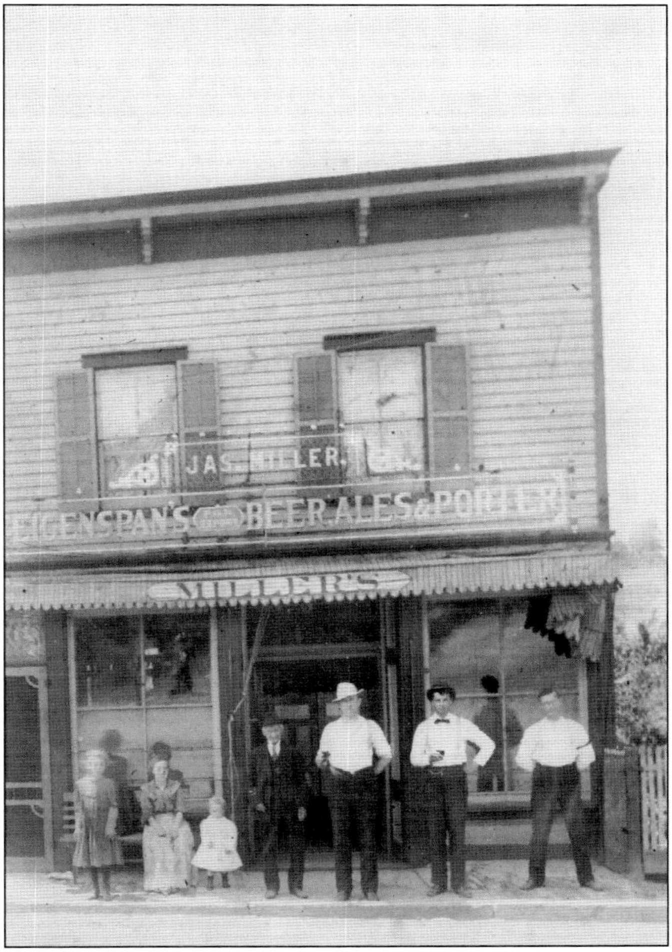

Two men pose for a photograph with a sign that reads "Happy Hill Poultry Farm" in Glenham. Today, farms are not as widespread as they were when this photograph was taken. However, several farms still exist in the area, such as Fishkill Farms. Henry Morgenthau Jr. started Fishkill Farms in 1914. He was friendly with Franklin Delano Roosevelt, who lived in nearby Hyde Park. (Courtesy of the Beacon Historical Society.)

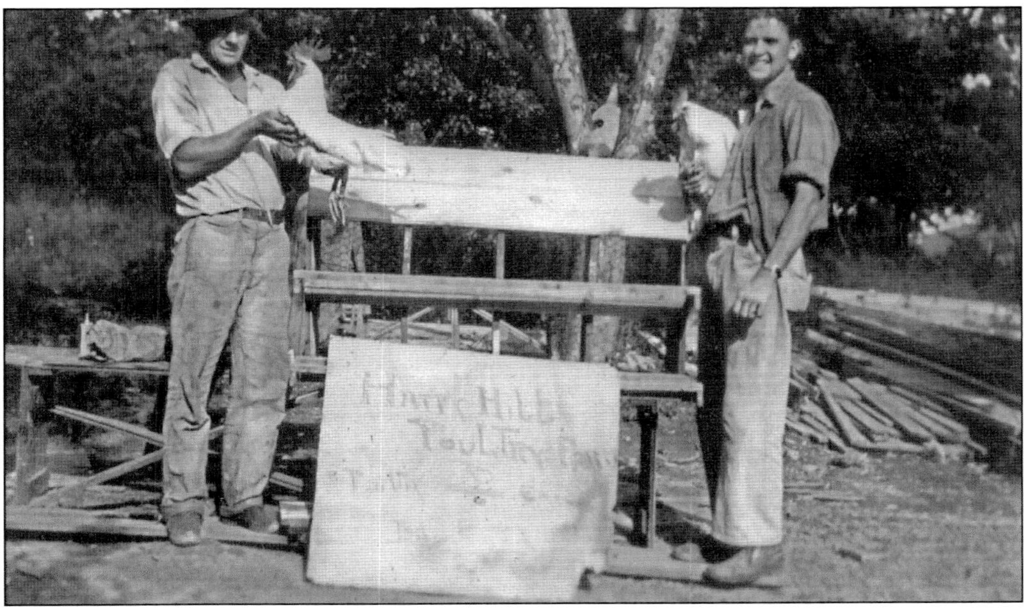

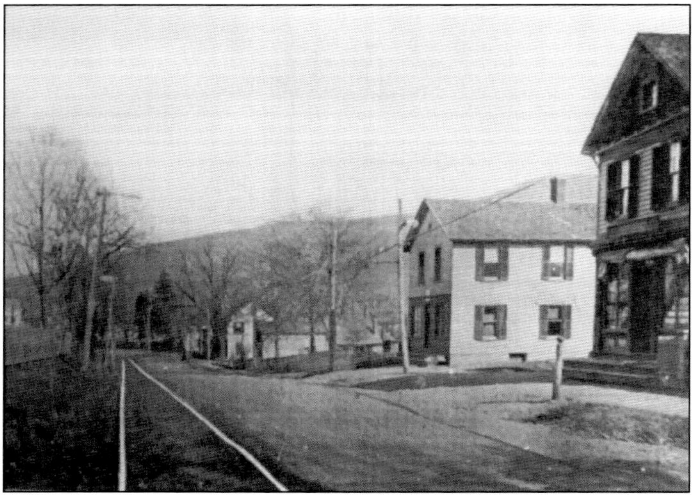

The post office and Main Street are depicted in this photograph. This is now the site of the Texaco Research Center parking lot. The store moved across the street and was converted into a home. Texaco was an independent company until it merged into Chevron Corporation in 2001. It began as the Texas Fuel Company, founded in 1901 in Beaumont, Texas. (Courtesy of the Beacon Historical Society.)

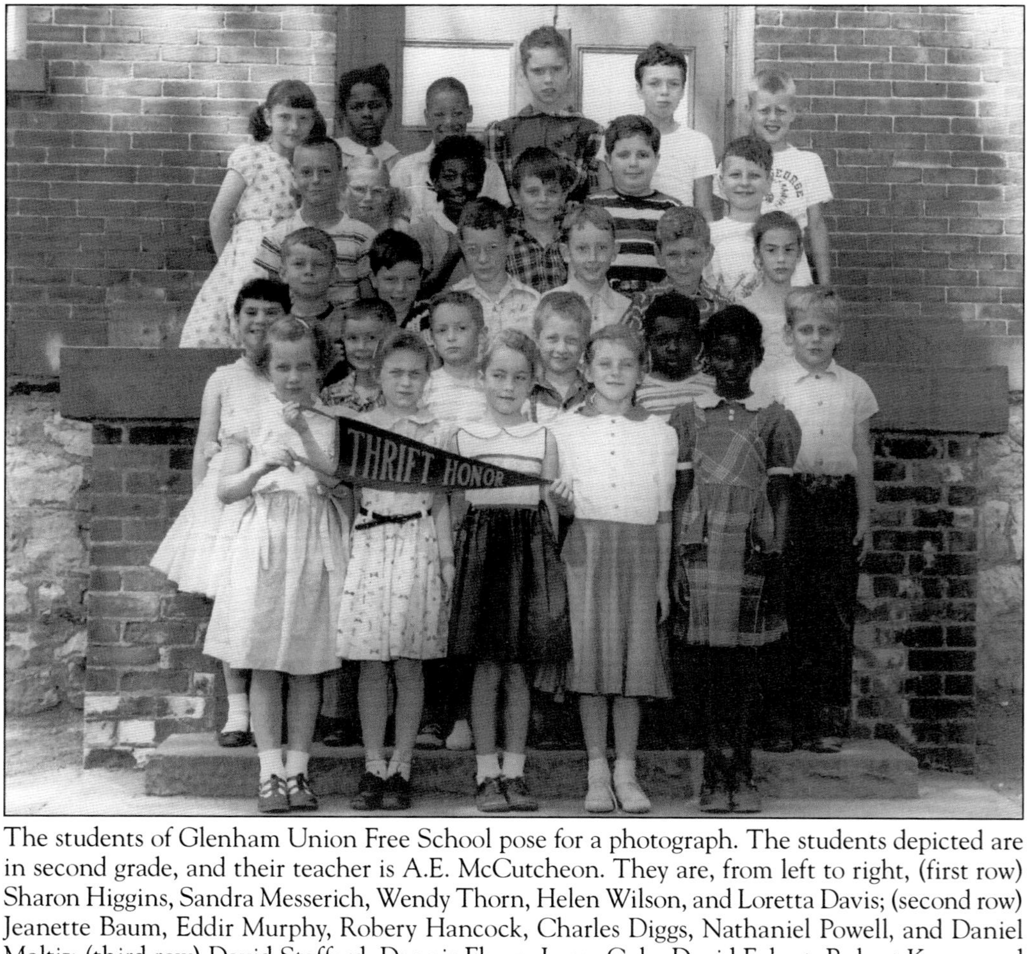

The students of Glenham Union Free School pose for a photograph. The students depicted are in second grade, and their teacher is A.E. McCutcheon. They are, from left to right, (first row) Sharon Higgins, Sandra Messerich, Wendy Thorn, Helen Wilson, and Loretta Davis; (second row) Jeanette Baum, Eddir Murphy, Robery Hancock, Charles Diggs, Nathaniel Powell, and Daniel Maltiz; (third row) David Stafford, Dennis Flynn, Larry Cole, David Eckert, Robert Kacur, and Gail Cooper; (fourth row) Dennis Cable, Marie Maher, Joyce Sharp, Eddie Wilson, Timothy Edmond, and John Higgins; (fifth row) Marsha Buck, Dolores Powell, Conway Perry, Marion Weir, Jimmie Weir, and Willard Voght. (Courtesy of the Beacon Historical Society.)

This photograph shows a different set of students at Glenham Union Free School in June 1952. The students are, from left to right, (first row) Janet Wilson, Roger Howell, and Roland Haight; (second row) Steve Katy, Paul Walsh, Elaine Mudd, Diane Micdel, Cecile Laidlow, and Elaine Robinson; (third row) James Schwartz, Ed Wesche, Albert Wilson, and John Monger. (Courtesy of the Beacon Historical Society.)

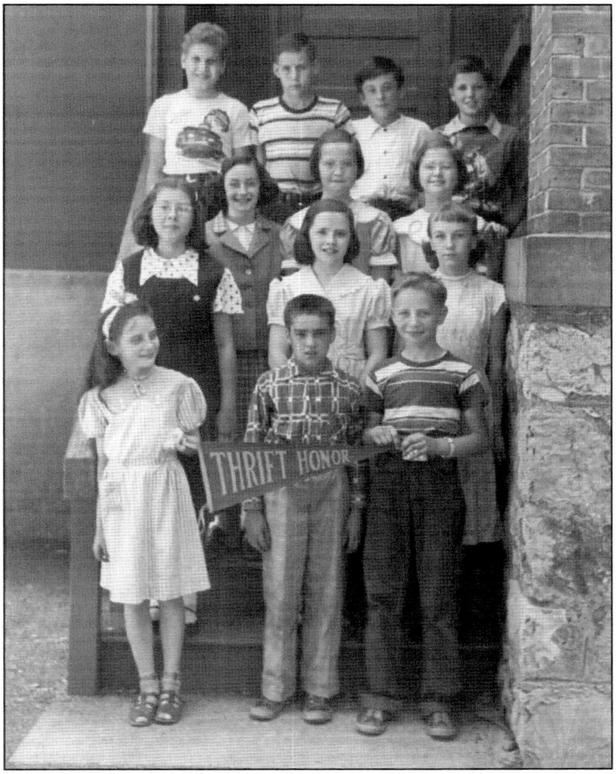

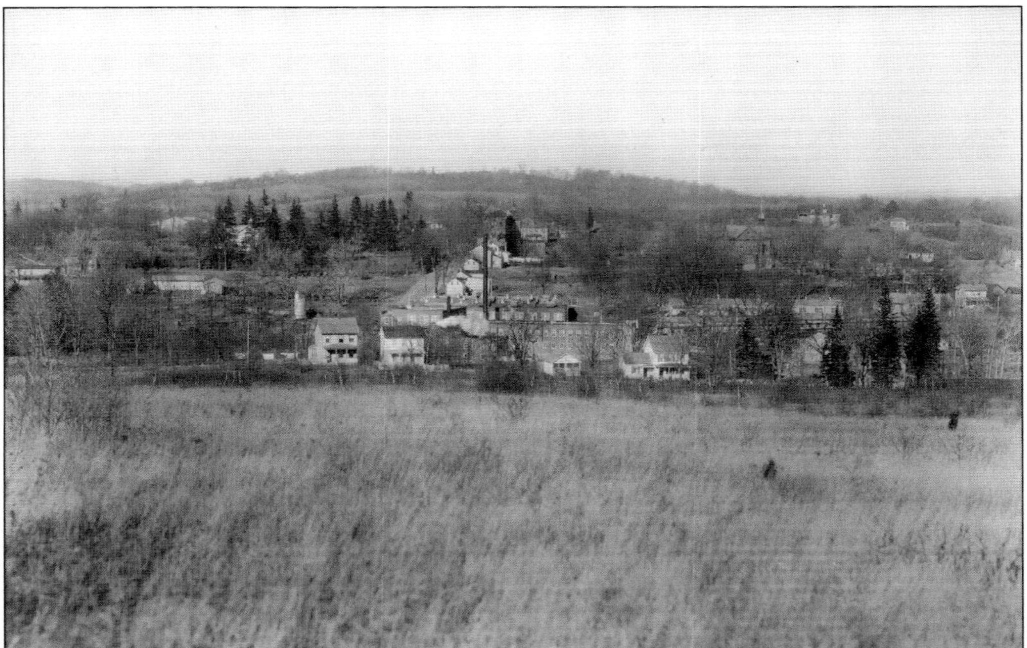

This photograph, taken during the 20th century, depicts Glenham. Glenham was viewed as an advantageous site for commercialization because of its geography. The Fishkill Creek borders the site, and Glenham has a natural waterfall. A dam was built that allowed for an ample water power supply, and the land offered space for building mills. (Courtesy of the Beacon Historical Society.)

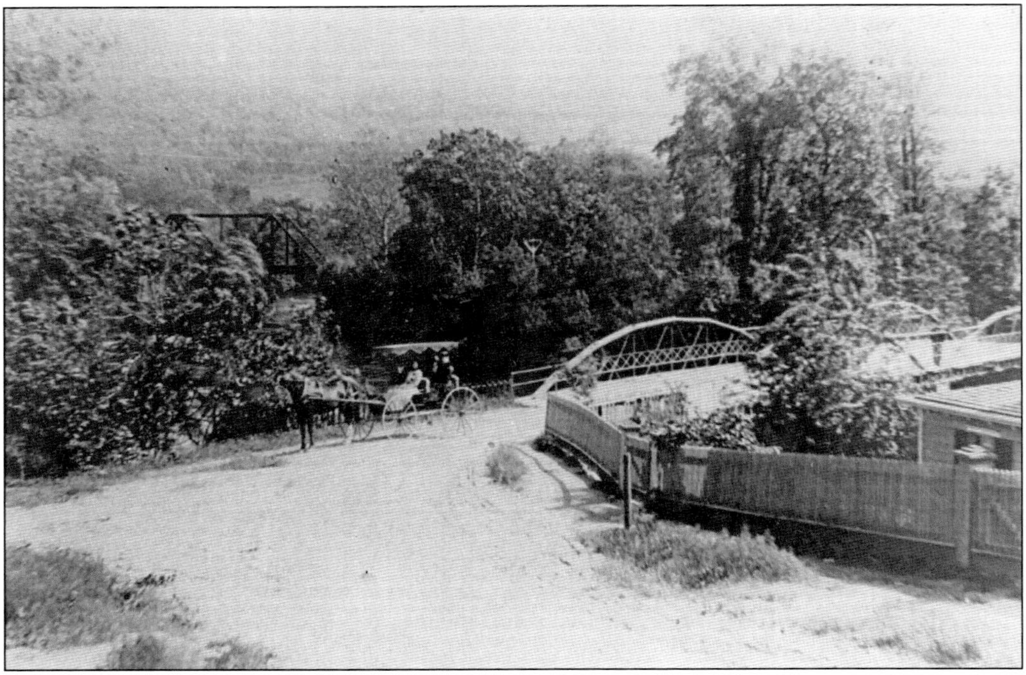

A horse and buggy are depicted crossing the Glenham Bridge in this photograph. In 1871, a railroad bridge was constructed across the Fishkill Creek. It led from the Glenham Railroad Station into the Glenham Mill Company. The bridge was used so that coal could be transported to the Glenham Mill Company. (Courtesy of the Beacon Historical Society.)

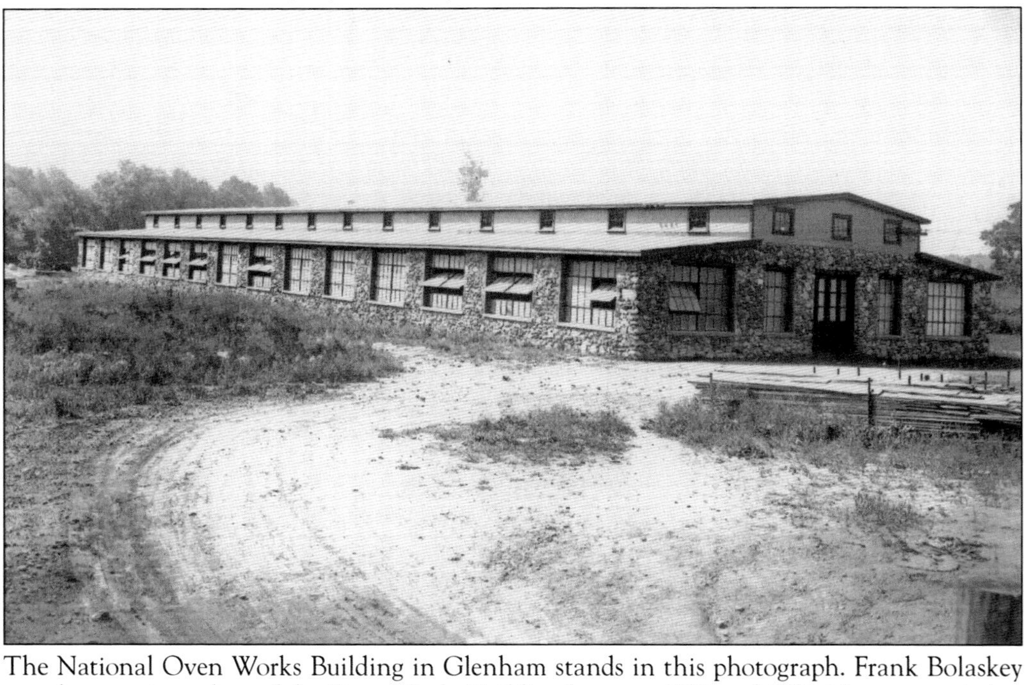

The National Oven Works Building in Glenham stands in this photograph. Frank Bolaskey was the superintendent of the Oven Works Building between 1921 and 1931. He was married to Arabella Lassman at St. Thomas Chapel in New York City on March 16, 1919. They moved to Glenham in 1921. (Courtesy of the Beacon Historical Society.)

This 1940s photograph depicts several crafts foremen at work. These men work as part of the Texaco Research Center Labs. For many years, Texaco was the only company selling gasoline under the same brand name in all 50 states as well as Canada. (Courtesy of the Beacon Historical Society.)

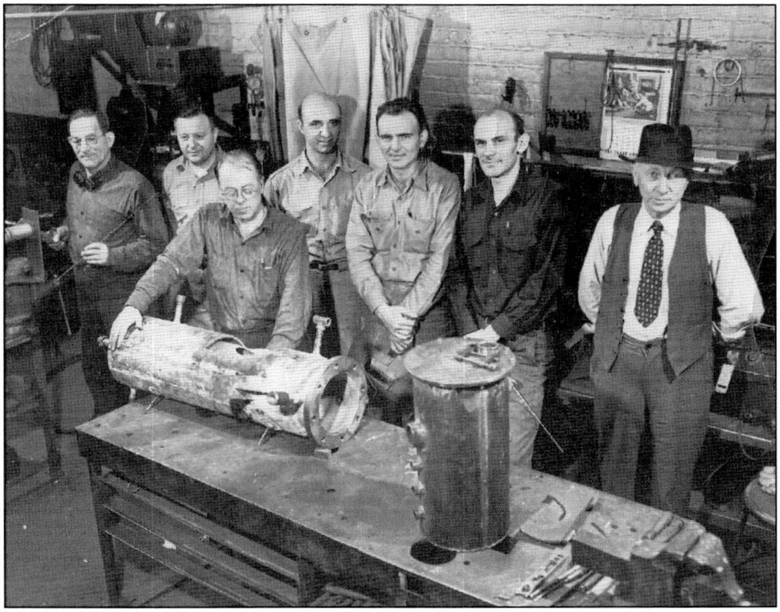

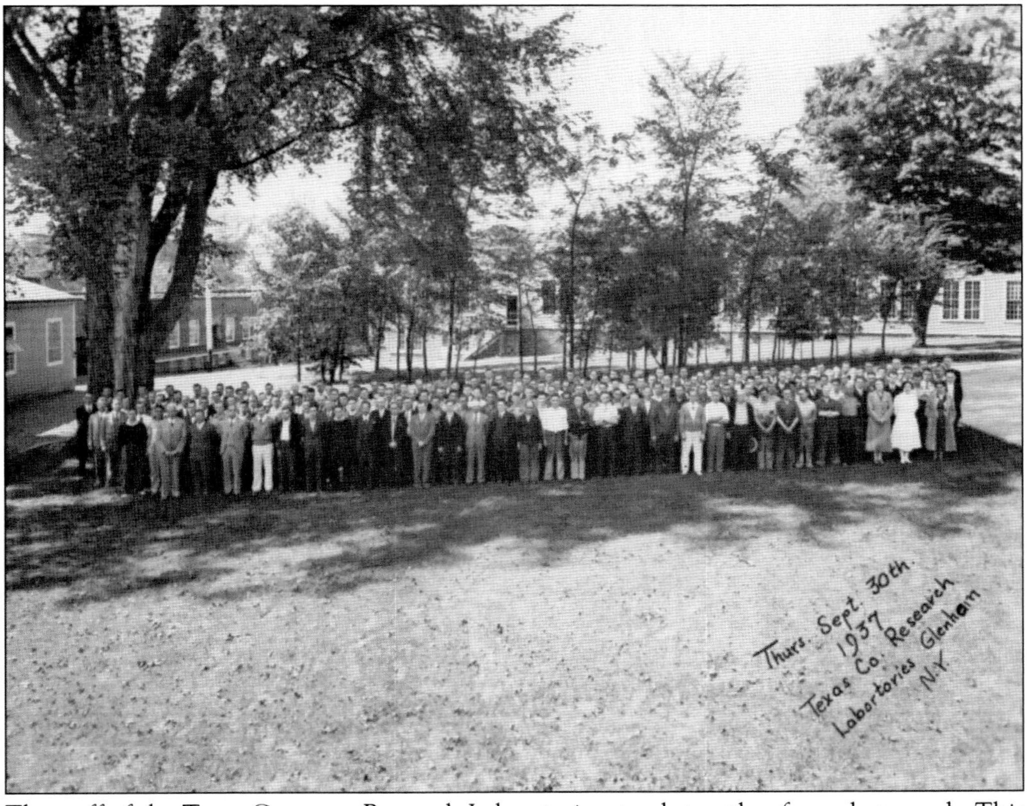

The staff of the Texas Company Research Laboratories stands together for a photograph. This photograph was taken on Thursday, September 30, 1937. The Texaco Research Center was established in 1931 as a principal research and testing center of the Texas Company. The Texaco Research Center commonly made petroleum products at the time. (Courtesy of the Beacon Historical Society.)

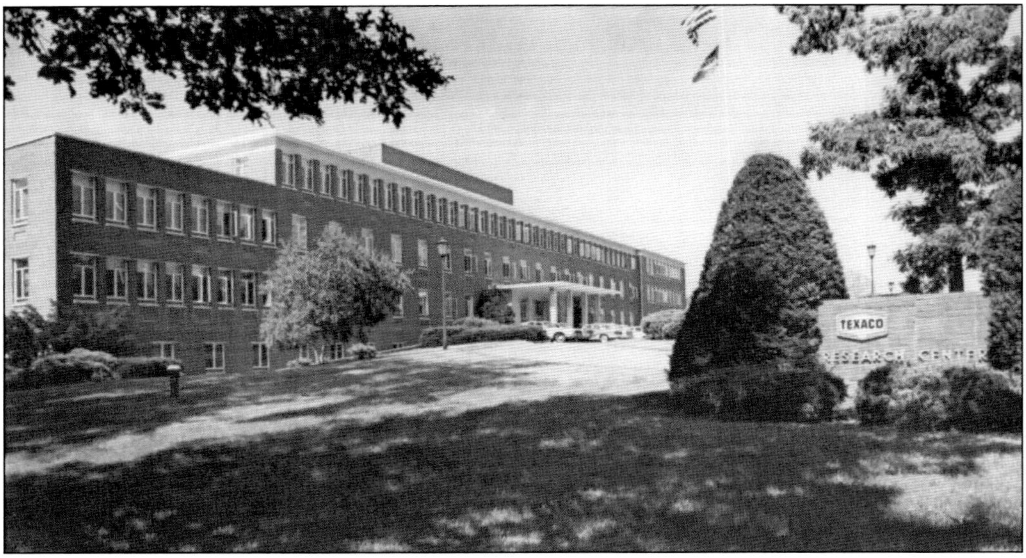

The front of the Texaco Research Center is shown in this photograph. The laboratory dealt with problems associated with the production and use of petroleum fuels and lubricants. The staff consisted of a small group of physicists and other workers. Nobel Prize–winning American physicist Clifford Glenwood Shull worked at the site in Glenham during World War II. (Courtesy of the Beacon Historical Society.)

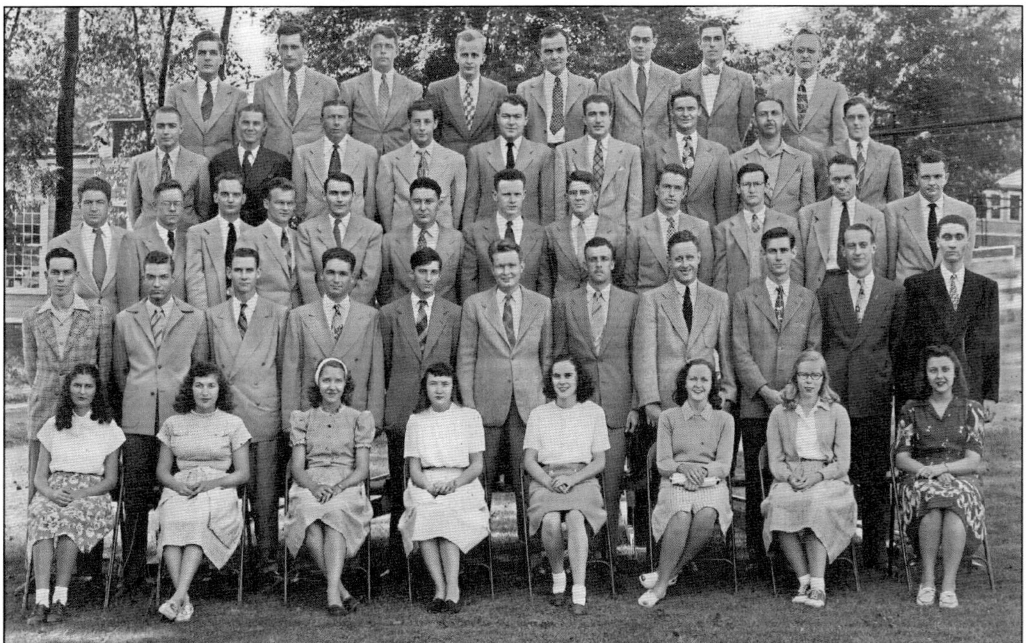

This last photograph of the Texaco Research Center depicts workers hired during the first eight months of 1947. Significantly, the first woman hired by the Texaco Research Center was in 1947. Seated in the first row are several female employees at Texaco during this year. They are, from left to right, Dixie Lee Harris, Pearl A. Leaf, Joy Rae Clark, Dona R. Harbinson, Joan A. Howley, Gloria B. Carlick, Susan A. Boulware, and Norma J. Streicher. (Courtesy of the Beacon Historical Society.)

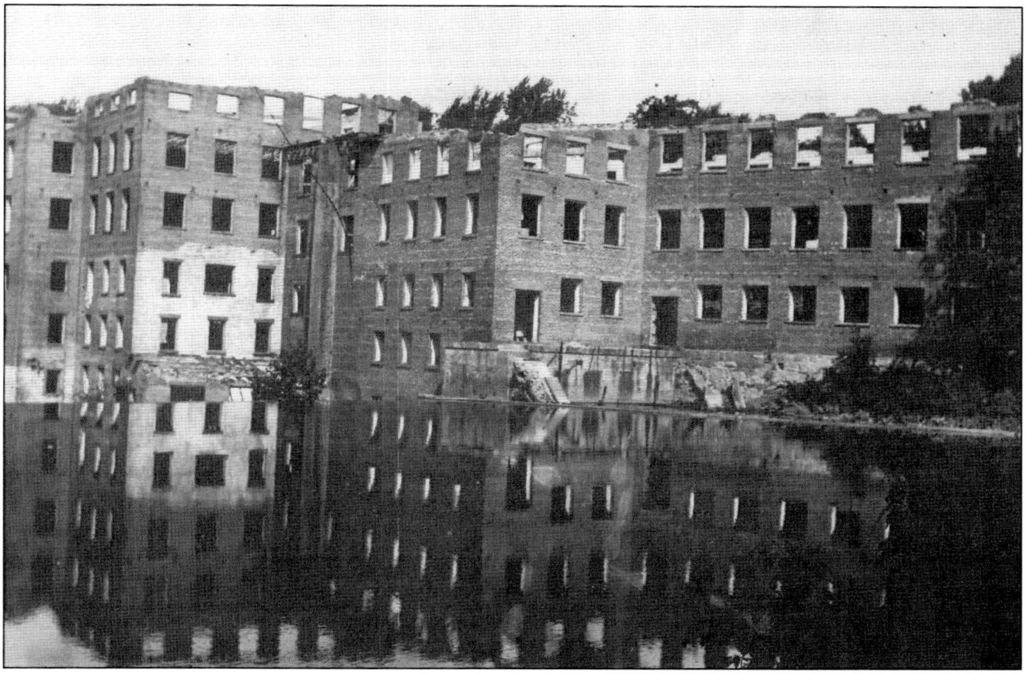

The remains of the Glenham Mill buildings are depicted in this photograph. The Glenham Woollen Mill was started in 1823. The height of the mill period in Glenham was at the start of the Industrial Revolution and lasted until the Panic of 1873. (Courtesy of the Beacon Historical Society.)

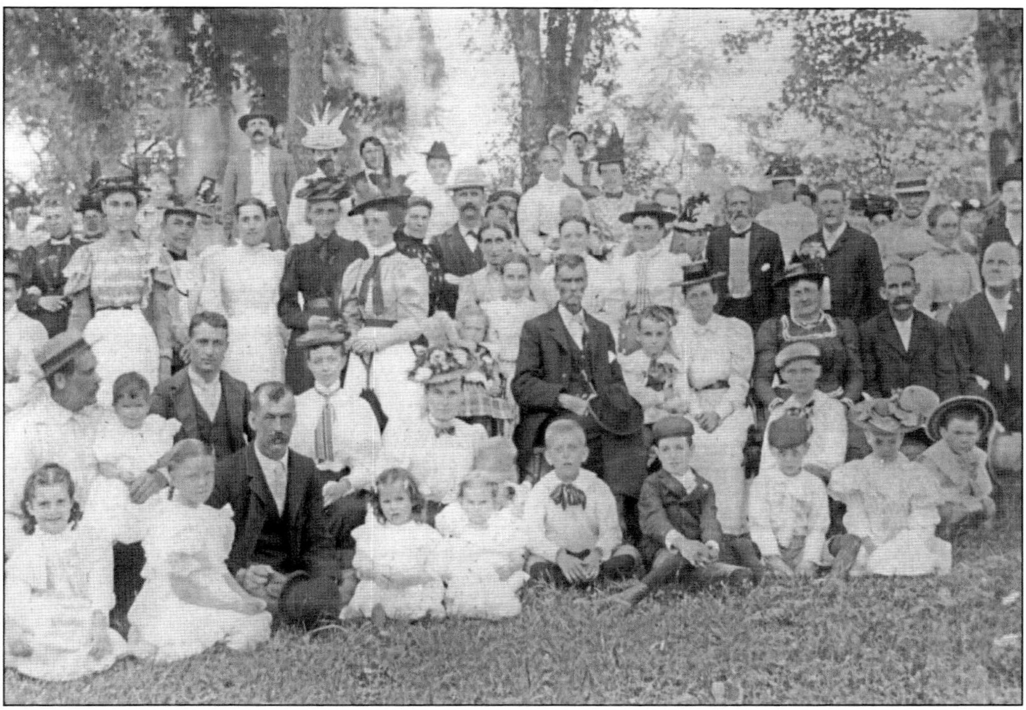

This photograph shows a large group of people dressed for an outing in Chelsea some time after 1898. Today, Chelsea is an unincorporated hamlet of the town of Wappinger. It has its own fire district and is located on the Hudson River waterfront. (Courtesy of the Beacon Historical Society.)

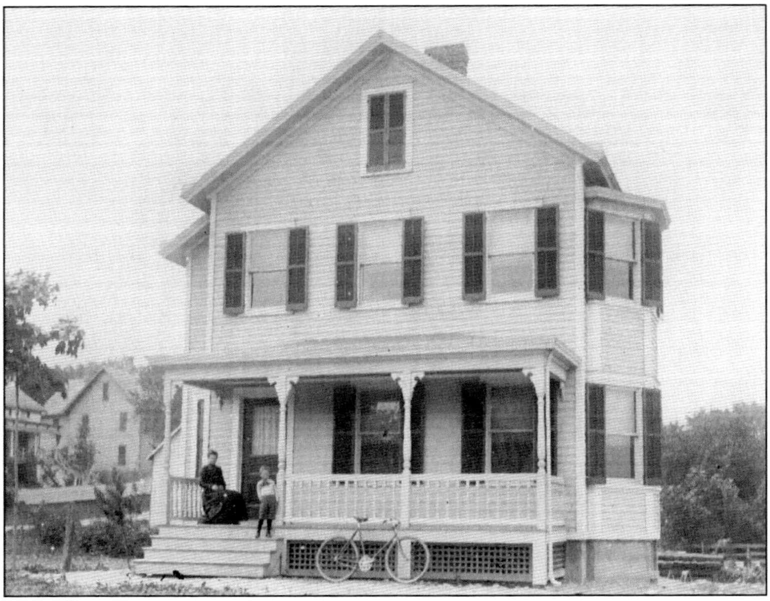

V.A. Hager and Emory J. Hager are pictured on the porch of their home in Chelsea. This home is one of the many that lie in within the small hamlet. Chelsea is mostly residential, though it does contain St. Mark's Episcopal Church, a post office, and a few stores. (Courtesy of the Beacon Historical Society.)

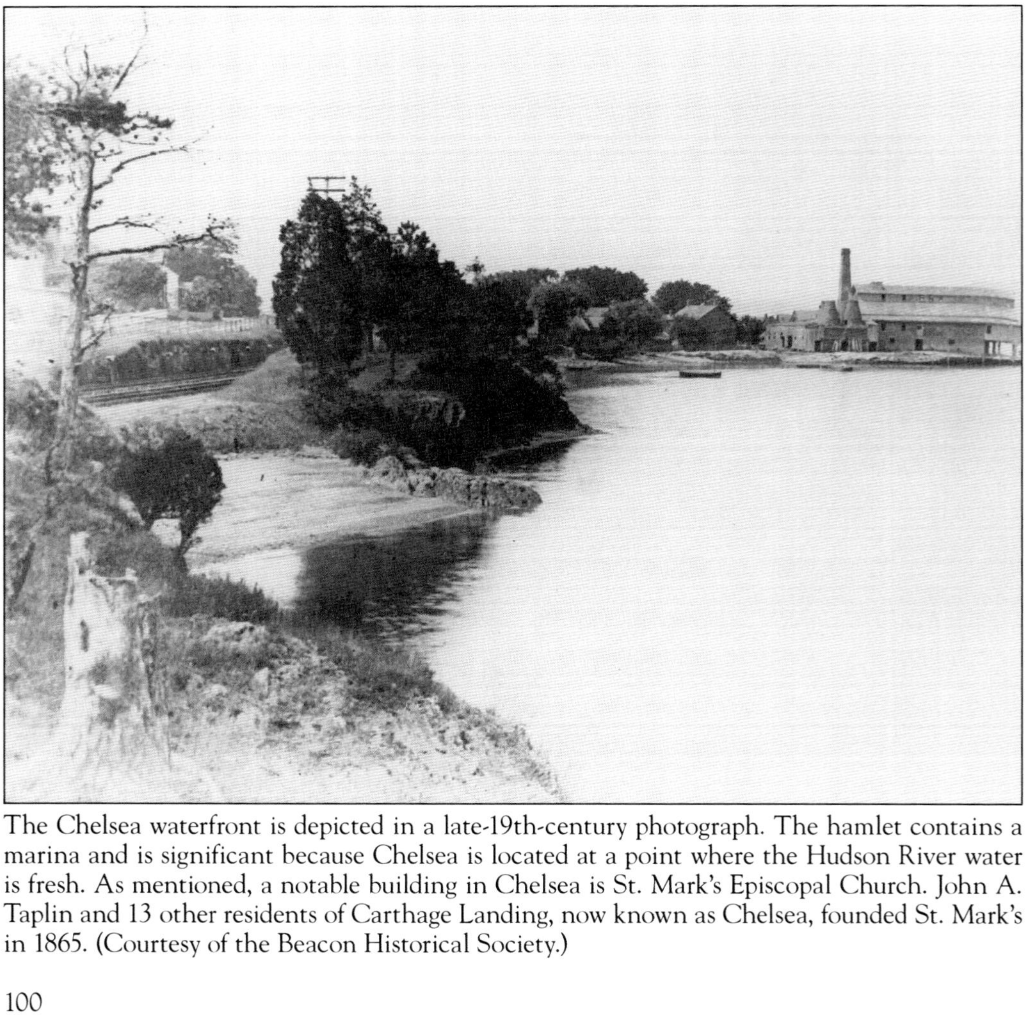

The Chelsea waterfront is depicted in a late-19th-century photograph. The hamlet contains a marina and is significant because Chelsea is located at a point where the Hudson River water is fresh. As mentioned, a notable building in Chelsea is St. Mark's Episcopal Church. John A. Taplin and 13 other residents of Carthage Landing, now known as Chelsea, founded St. Mark's in 1865. (Courtesy of the Beacon Historical Society.)

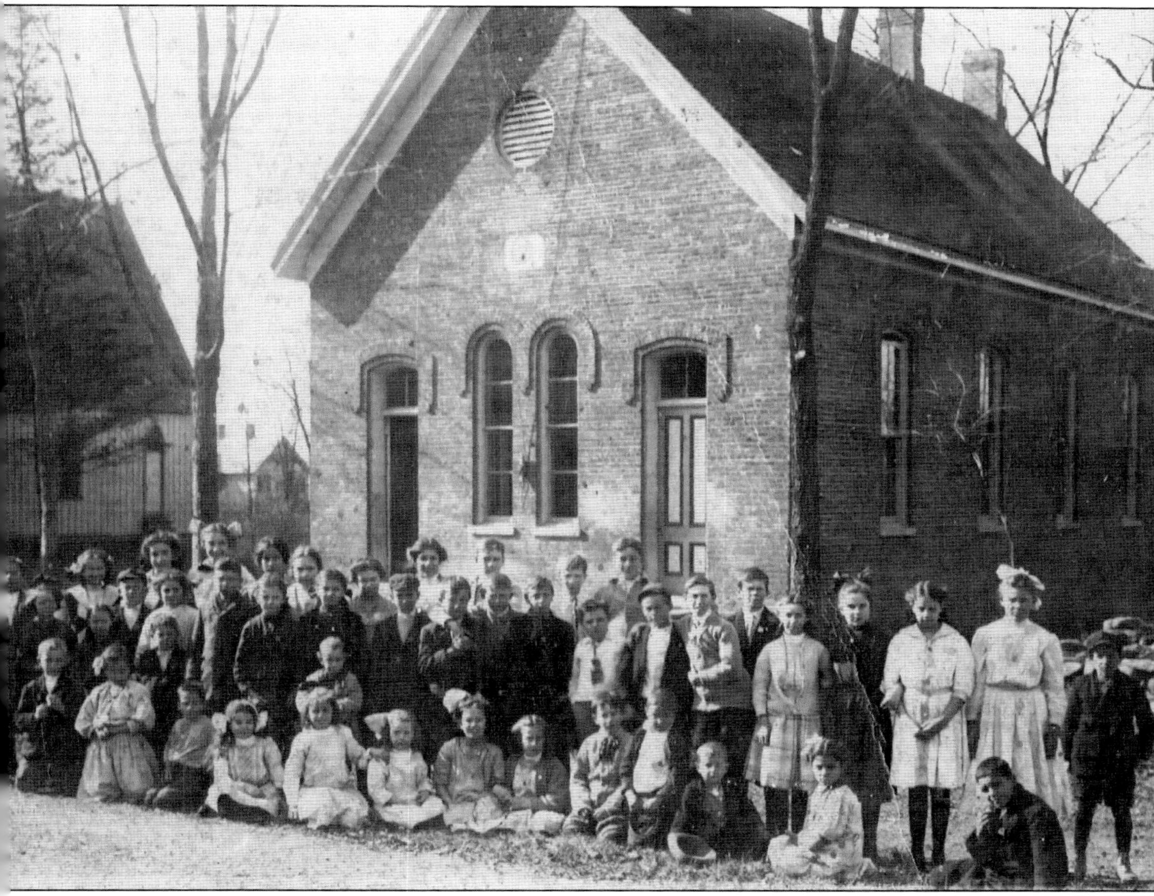

The entire 1912 Chelsea Union Free School population is depicted standing in front of its school. The school was built around 1875 on Liberty Street. It closed during the mid-20th century, but the building is still used by the Chelsea Fire Department and the post office. It is listed in the National Register of Historic Places. Today, Chelsea is part of the Wappingers Central School District. (Courtesy of the Beacon Historical Society.)

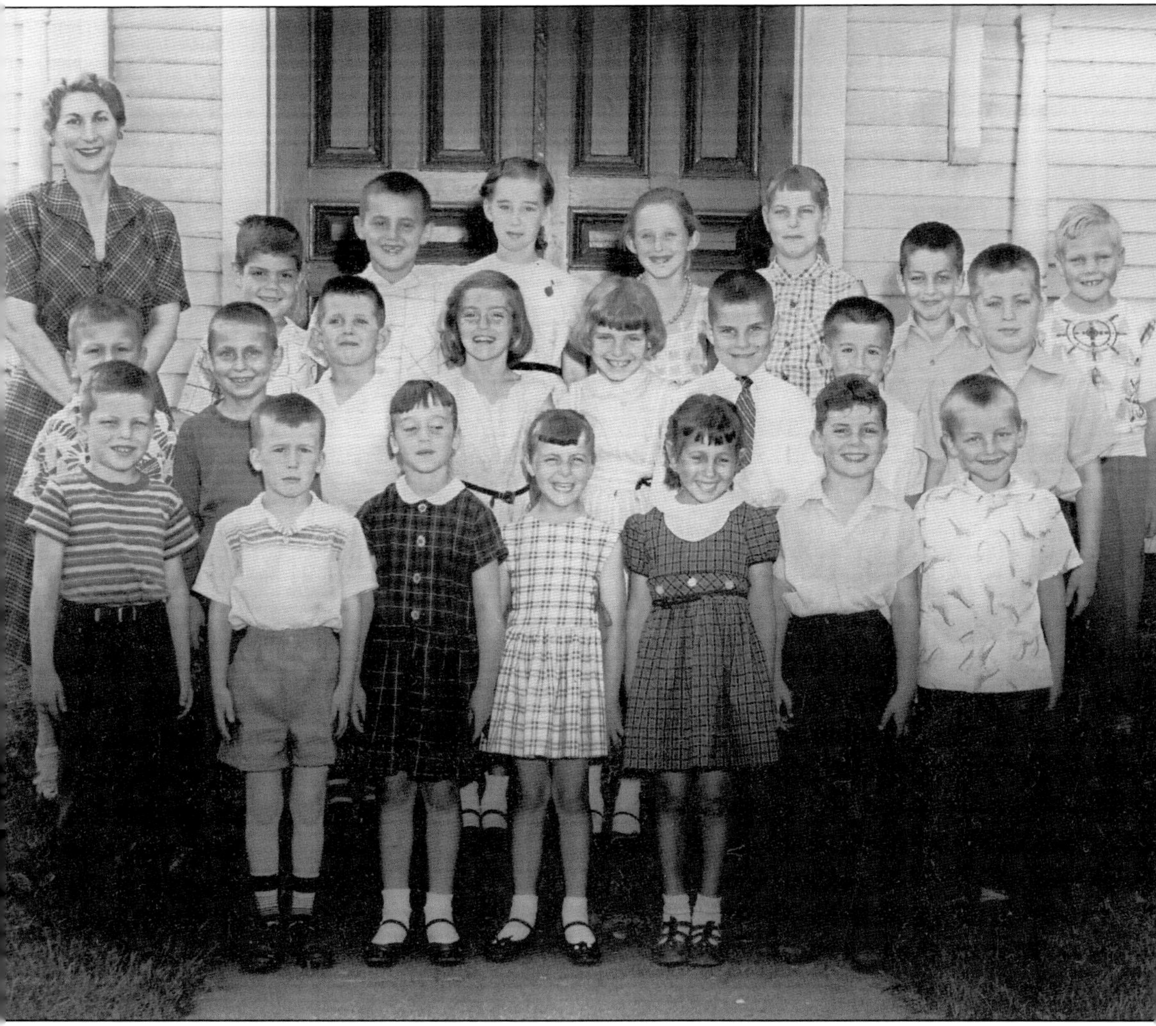

The entire school population stands for its class photograph at the Chelsea Union Free School in 1956. The teacher is Mrs. Wilson. The students are, from left to right, (first row) Joseph Fulliman, Charles Barrett, Suzanne Strickland, Susan Price, Linda Mesnick, Thomas Turco, Thomas Brickner; (second row) Thomas Sheffield, Carl Bate, Stephen Reid, Cathy Smith, Joan Greer, James Baisley, Joseph Berner, Jack Pulliman; (third row) John Todd, William Brickner, Linda Barrett, Sandra Riggs, Bette Lu Hammond, Anthony Pullian, and Douglas Robinson. (Courtesy of the Beacon Historical Society.)

Five

Fishkill, a Part of Dutchess County

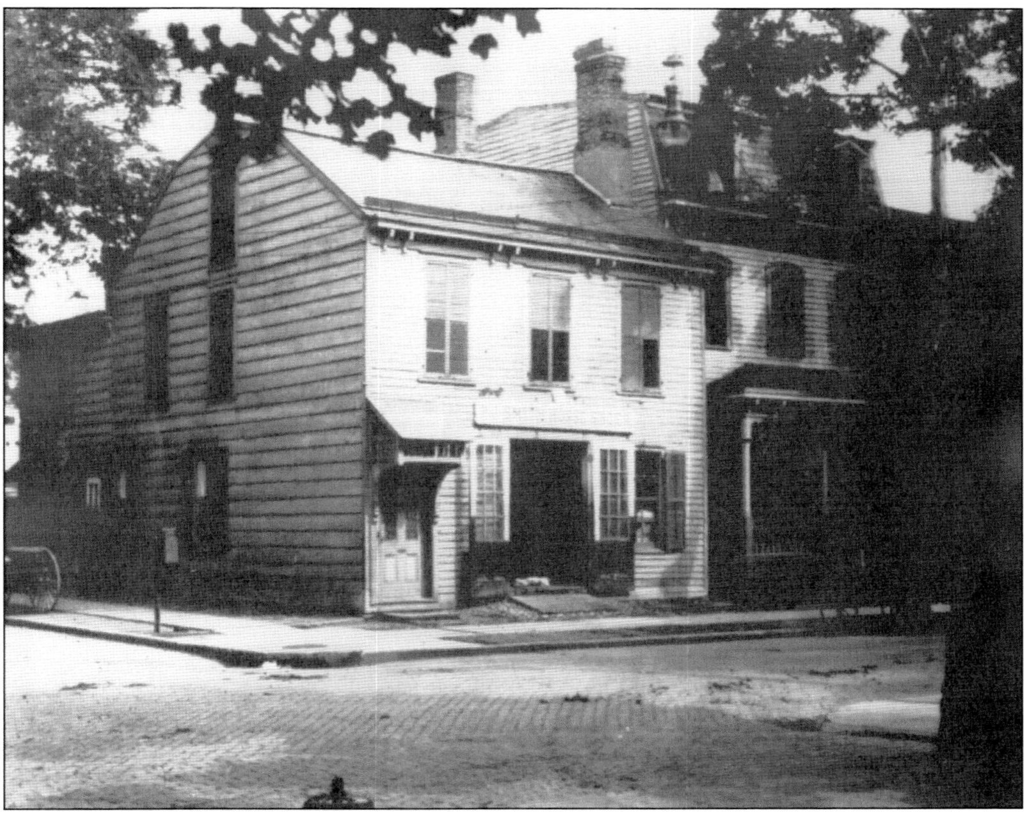

This photograph depicts a historic home in Dutchess County. Dutchess County is part of the Mid-Hudson region of the Hudson Valley. The county seat is located in Poughkeepsie. Prior to the settlement of Europeans, Dutchess County was a settlement for the Wappinger people. (Courtesy of the Dutchess County Historical Society.)

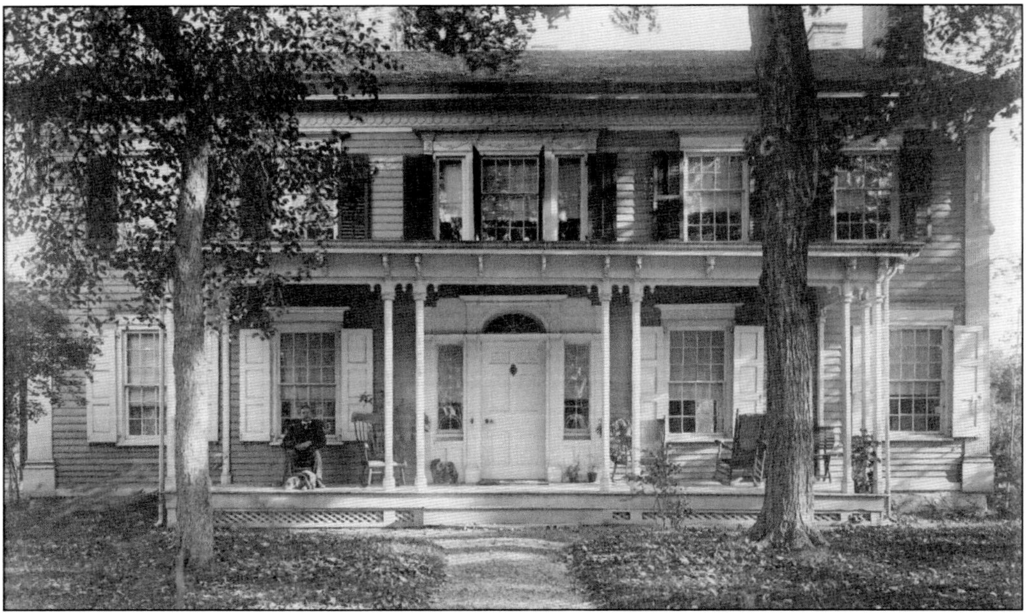

The photograph above is also of a historic home in Dutchess County. In 1683, the Province of New York established the first 12 counties, including Dutchess County. The boundaries included present-day Putnam County and parts of Columbia County. The county was named for the Dutchess of York, Mary of Modena, the wife of James II. The Rombout Patent in 1685 eventually helped with the establishment of Fishkill. Several men are pictured below shortly before 1901 at the Dutchess County Courthouse. The first courthouse was the site of New York's debate on ratifying the US Constitution, while Poughkeepsie was briefly the state capital in 1788. It burned in an 1806 fire. The second courthouse was built three years later and stood for about 100 years. The third and current courthouse was built in 1903 and was designed by William J. Beardsley in a Classical Revival style. Fishkill resident Jesse Wood, who had one of the last public executions in Dutchess County, was tried at the courthouse in 1806. (Both, courtesy of the Dutchess County Historical Society.)

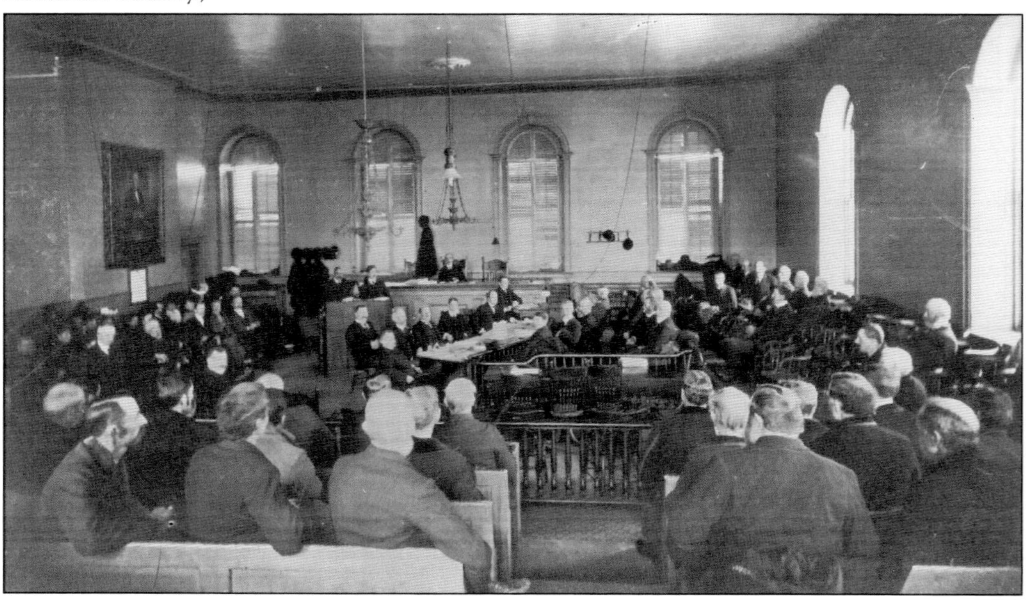

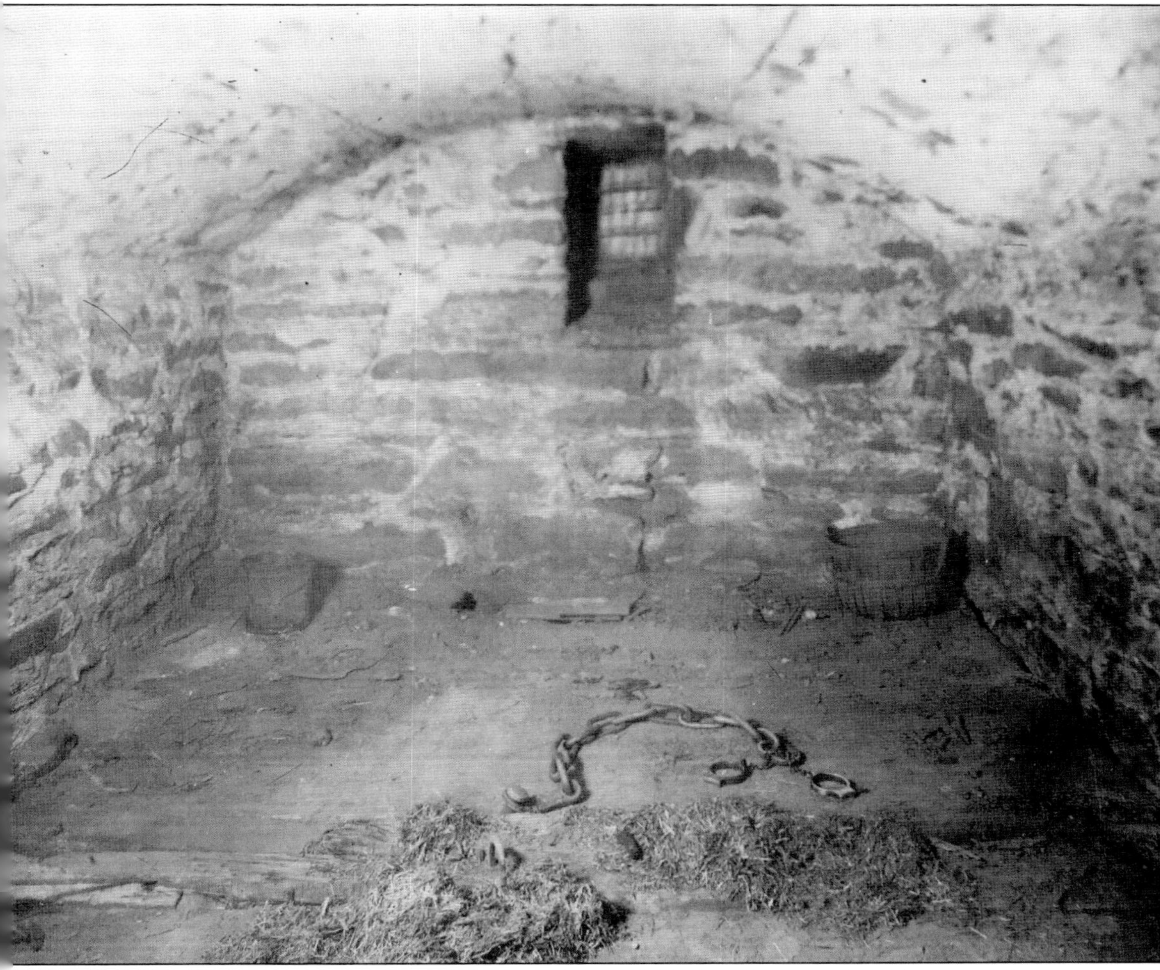

The Dutchess County Courthouse still stands today at 10 Market Street in Poughkeepsie. Three courthouses have stood on the same spot on Market Street. The first was authorized by the provincial assembly in 1717 and was built in 1720. This photograph, taken between 1901 and 1909, most likely depicts the original 1720 courthouse jail cell. The original deed requires that one of the original jail cells must remain in the basement of the courthouse. (Courtesy of the Dutchess County Historical Society.)

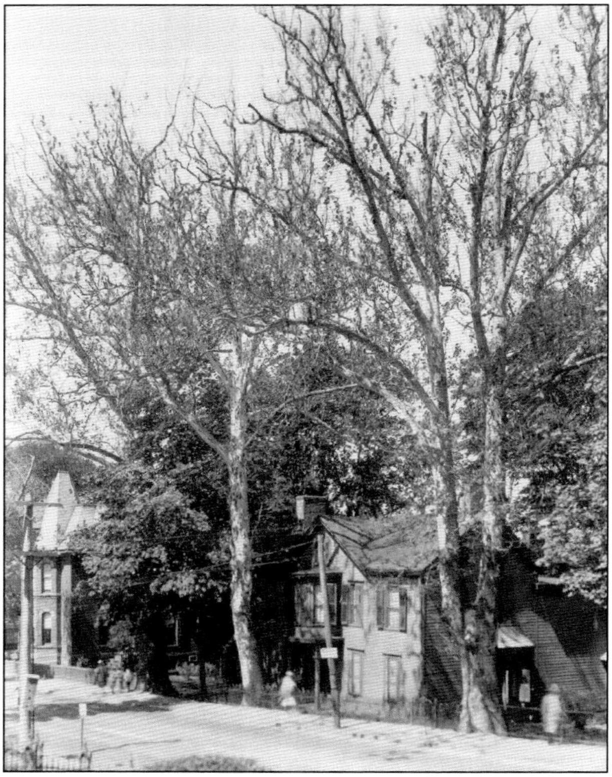

These two photographs depict historic homes in Poughkeepsie. The photograph to the left may be of the area around Raymond Avenue, and the photograph below is of 24 Cannon Street, which was removed in 1926. Poughkeepsie was originally settled in the 17th century by the Dutch and became New York's second capital shortly after the American Revolution. It was chartered as a city in 1854. The name *Poughkeepsie* was taken from the Wappinger language and roughly means "safe harbor." The Dutchess Academy, which originated in Fishkill, was moved to Poughkeepsie at Cannon and Academy Streets. (Both, courtesy of the Dutchess County Historical Society.)

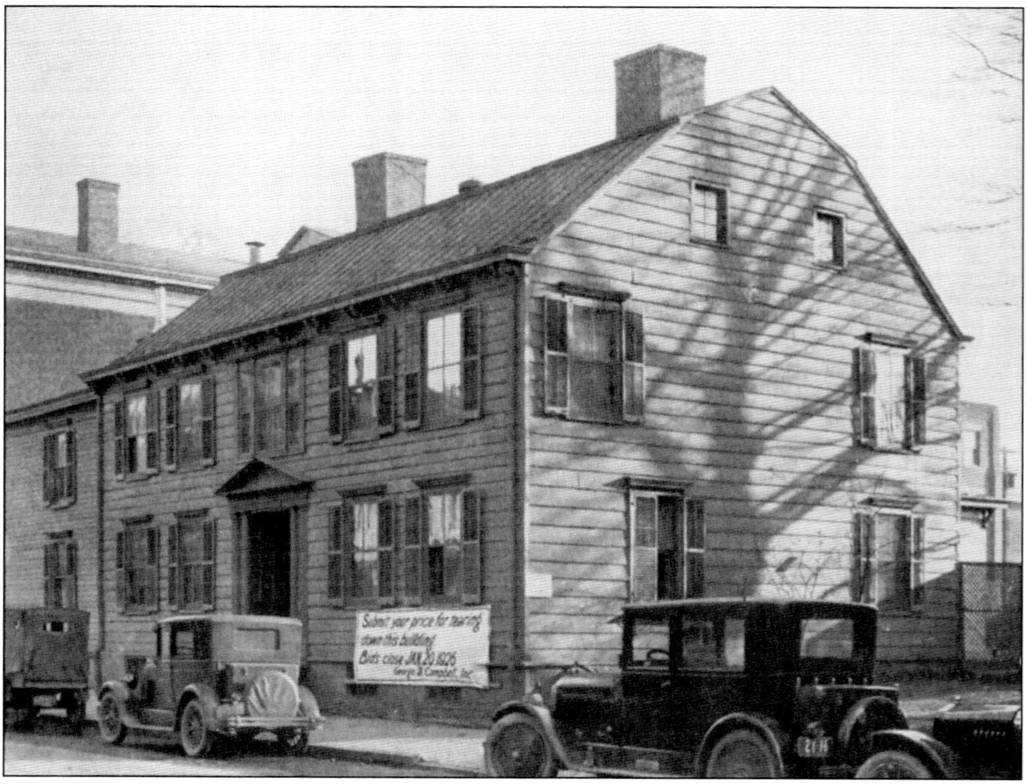

The Samuel B. Morse home or Locust Grove is located not far from Fishkill in Poughkeepsie. Samuel B. Morse acquired the home in 1847 and he used it as a summer retreat for over 25 years. He was a contributor to the invention of a single-wire telegraph system, coinventor of Morse code, and an accomplished painter. (Courtesy of the Dutchess County Historical Society.)

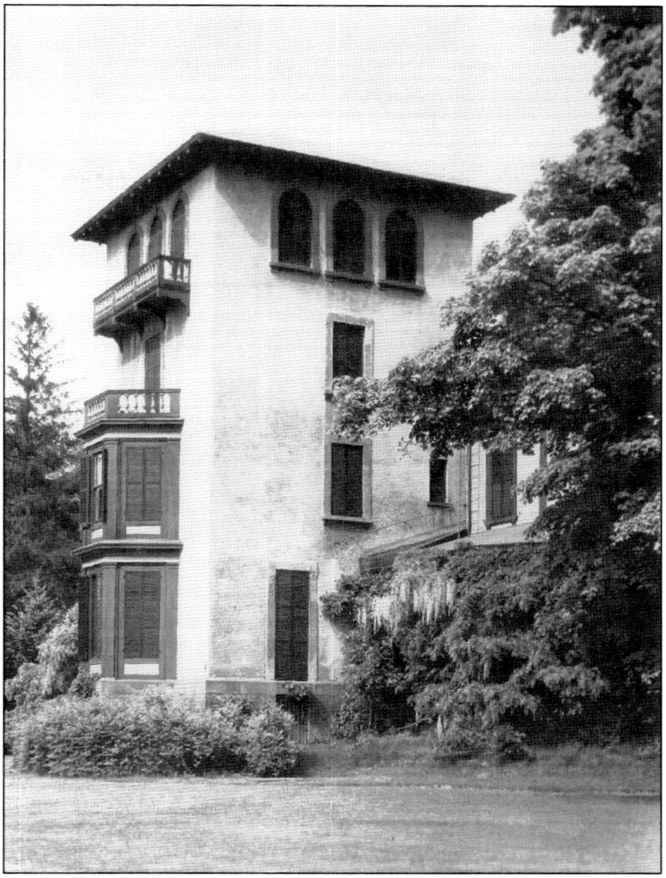

Vassar College in Poughkeepsie is represented in a 1915 photograph. Matthew Vassar, who immigrated to and settled in Poughkeepsie from England when he was very young, founded Vassar College. He was a successful brewer and merchant, and he established Vassar College as one of the first women's colleges in the United States in 1861. (Courtesy of the Dutchess County Historical Society.)

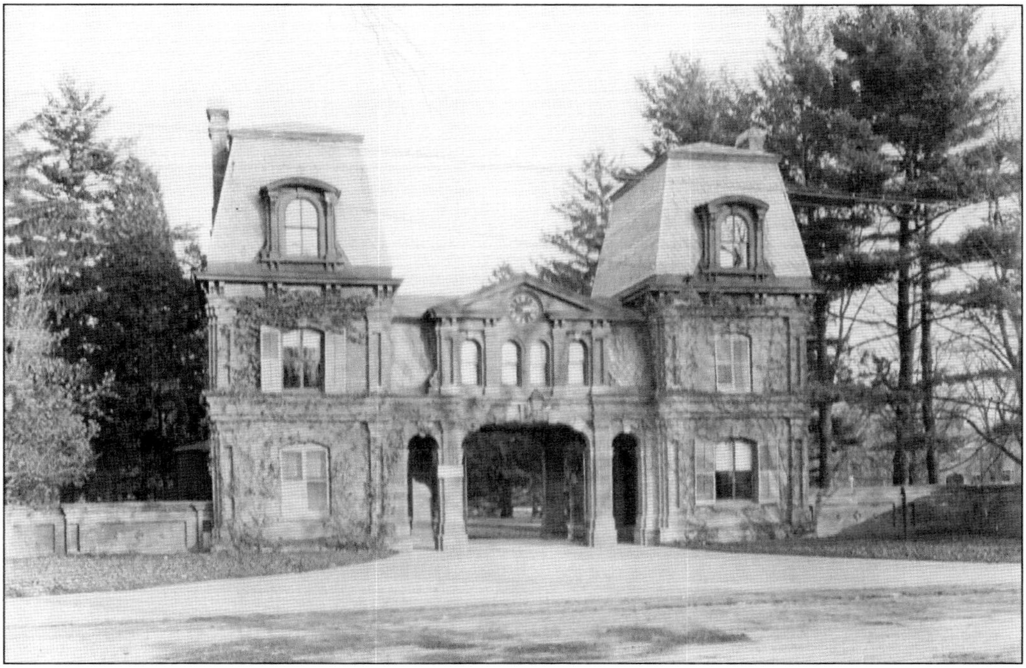

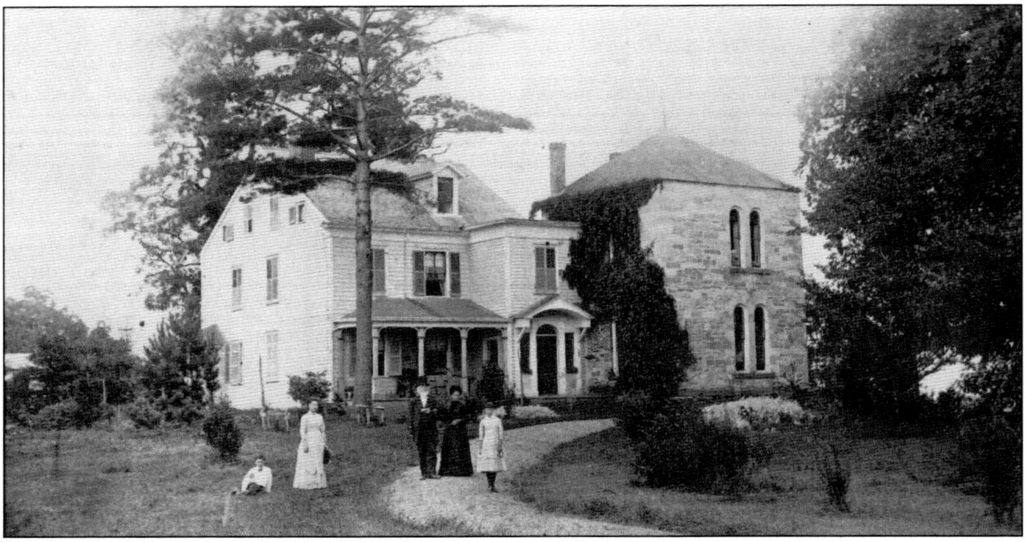

The home of Benson J. Lassing of the Ridge in Dover Plains is depicted in this photograph. He is significant to Dutchess County because he was a charter trustee of Vassar College. He was born in Beekman, and his father was one of the earliest Dutch settlers in the Hudson Valley. In 1835, Lassing became part-owner and editor of the *Poughkeepsie Telegraph*. He was also a noted American historian. (Courtesy of the Dutchess County Historical Society.)

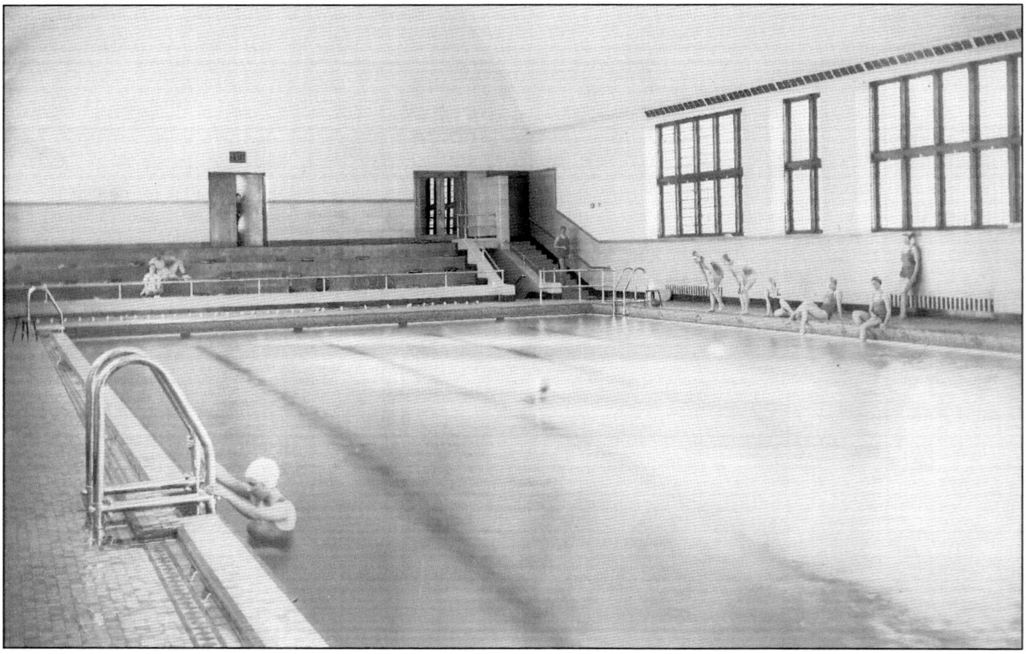

The Vassar College gymnasium is depicted in an early photograph. Edgar V. Anderson built the gymnasium. Several women can be seen enjoying the pool. Vassar College was the first of the Seven Sisters colleges that was strictly for women. The Seven Sisters are seven liberal arts colleges in the Northeast that are historically women's colleges. They are Barnard College, Bryn Mawr College, Mount Holyoke College, Radcliffe College, Smith College, Vassar College, and Wellesley College. All were founded between 1837 and 1889. (Courtesy of the Dutchess County Historical Society.)

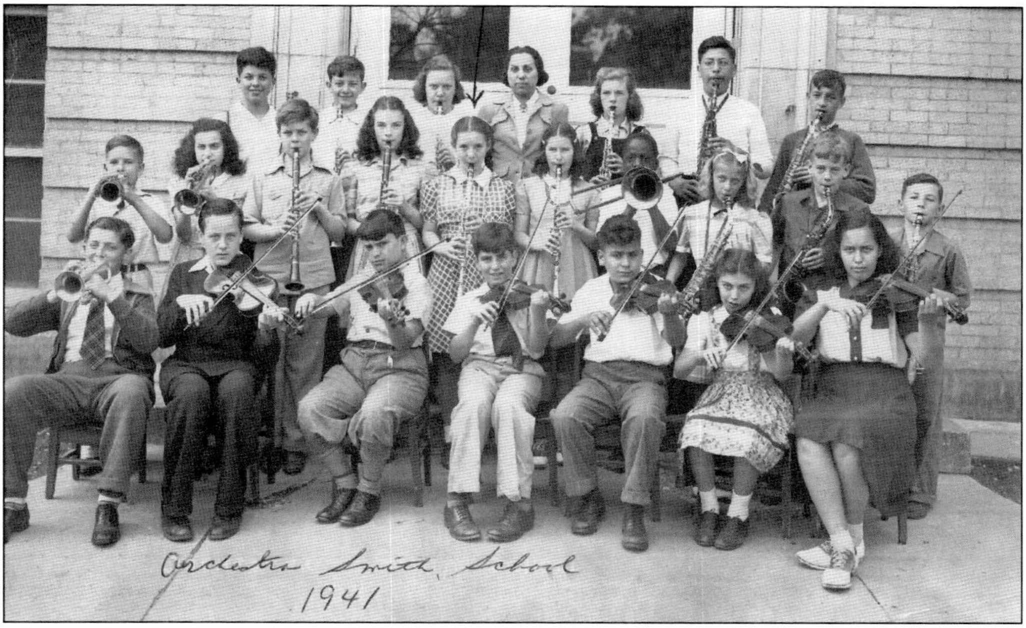

The Smith School orchestra members pose together for a photograph in 1941. The Smith School was built in 1912 and was established as a magnet school in 1987. Magnet schools are public schools with specialized courses or curricula. It was located at 400 Church Street in Poughkeepsie, and the school closed in June 2010. (Courtesy of the Dutchess County Historical Society.)

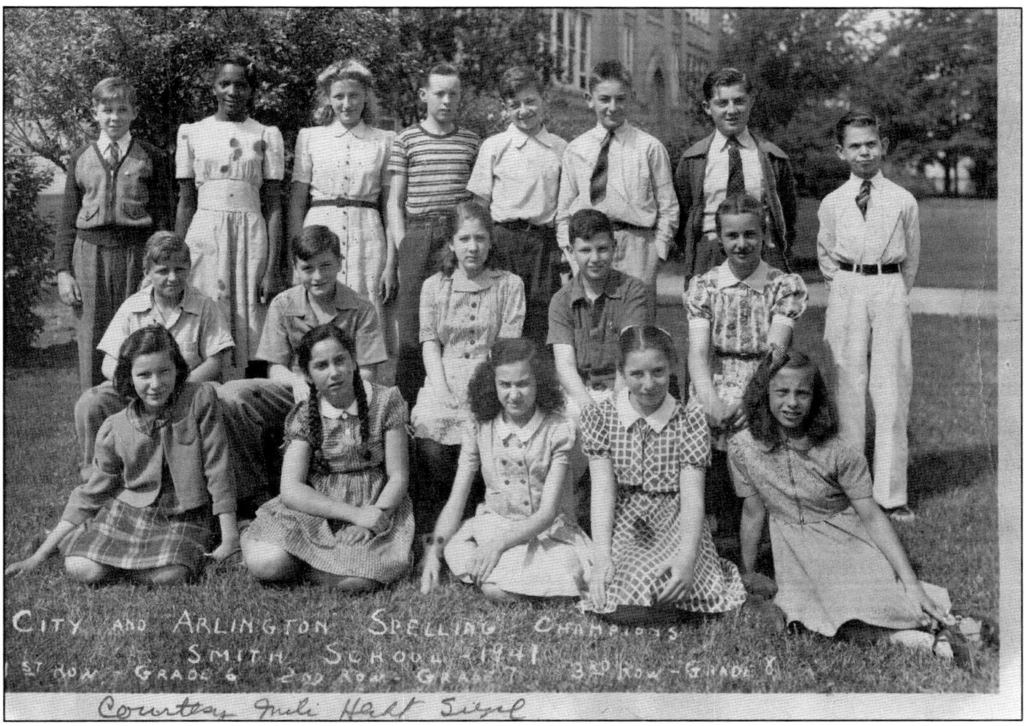

The Poughkeepsie city and Arlington spelling champs from the Smith School pose together in a 1941 photograph. The first row is sixth-grade students, and the second row is seventh-grade students. The third row is eighth-grade students. (Courtesy of the Dutchess County Historical Society.)

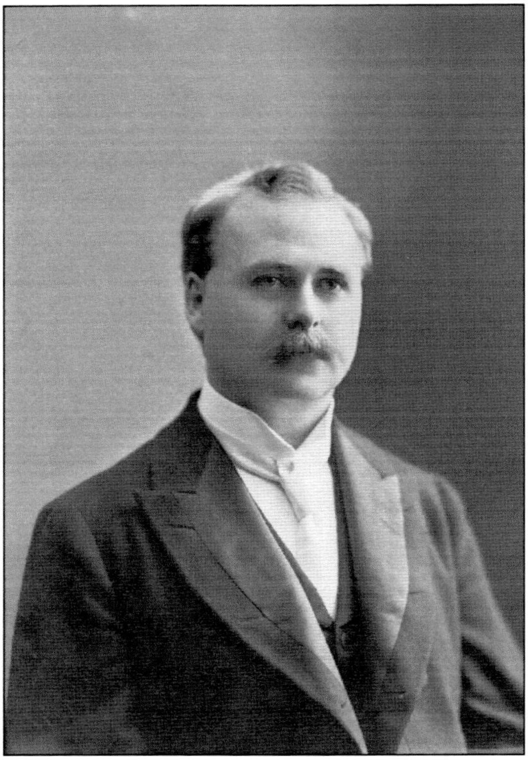

Mr. Raeusen (left) and Emily Barclett Platt Raeusen (below) are pictured separately in photographs taken on October 6, 1898. The Raeusens might have known the Livingston family, who had a home in the area. Several of the Livingstons were significant in and around the Fishkill area. Henry Livingston was a close friend of Catheryna Brett. Furthermore, his sons were taught at one of the first schools in the area, which was named Dutchess County Academy. The school was located at Brinckerhoff. Rev. John Livingston was the rector of Trinity Episcopal Church in Fishkill. (Both, courtesy of the Dutchess County Historical Society.)

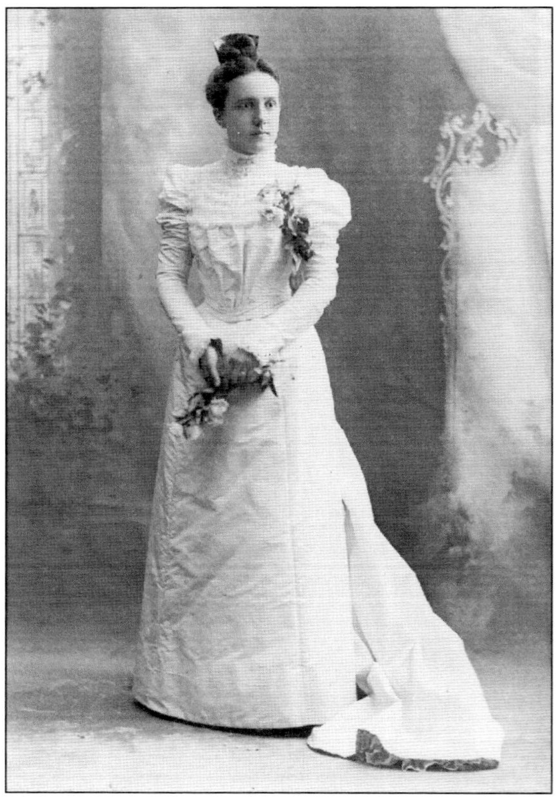

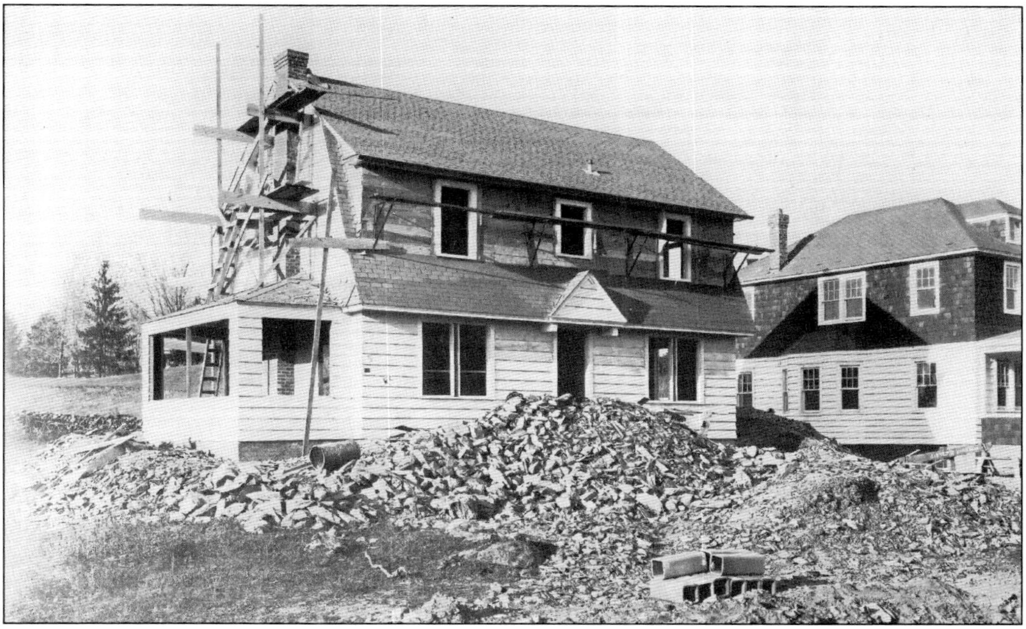

A home in Poughkeepsie is depicted in the later stages of construction during the mid-20th century. Poughkeepsie was also a major center shipping during the 19th century and hosted several breweries along the Hudson River, including some owned by Matthew Vassar, founder of Vassar College. Families such as the Astors and the Vanderbilts built Gilded Age homes nearby. (Courtesy of the Dutchess County Historical Society.)

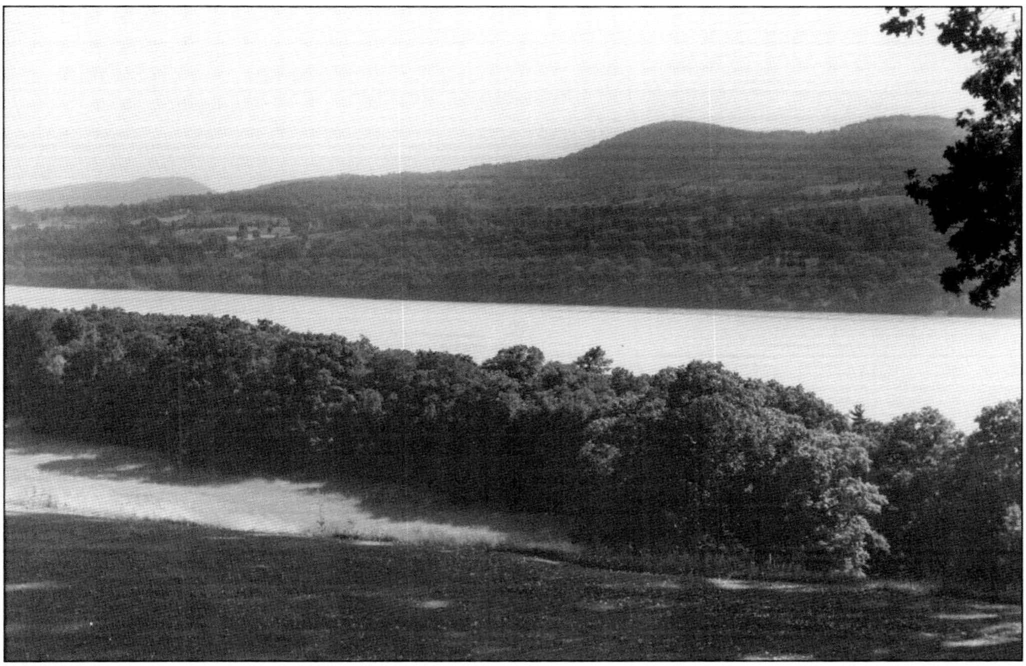

The grounds of the Vanderbilt estate are shown in this photograph with a view of the Hudson River. A landscape artist before the American Revolution laid out the grounds. The Vanderbilt Mansion National Historic Site is located in Hyde Park and is one of best examples of the country palaces during the Gilded Age. (Courtesy of the Dutchess County Historical Society.)

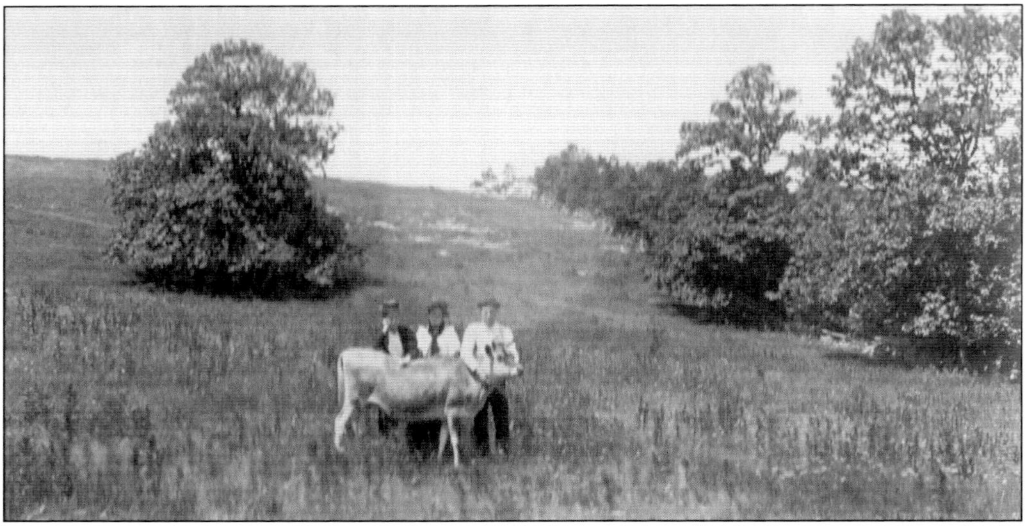

Three people are pictured with Victorie, a farm animal, on July 4, 1892. The picture was taken in Dutchess County. The creek at Fishkill and other creeks and streams in the area provide fine farming lands. The availability of farming land allowed for the development of Fishkill and Dutchess County in general. (Courtesy of the Dutchess County Historical Society.)

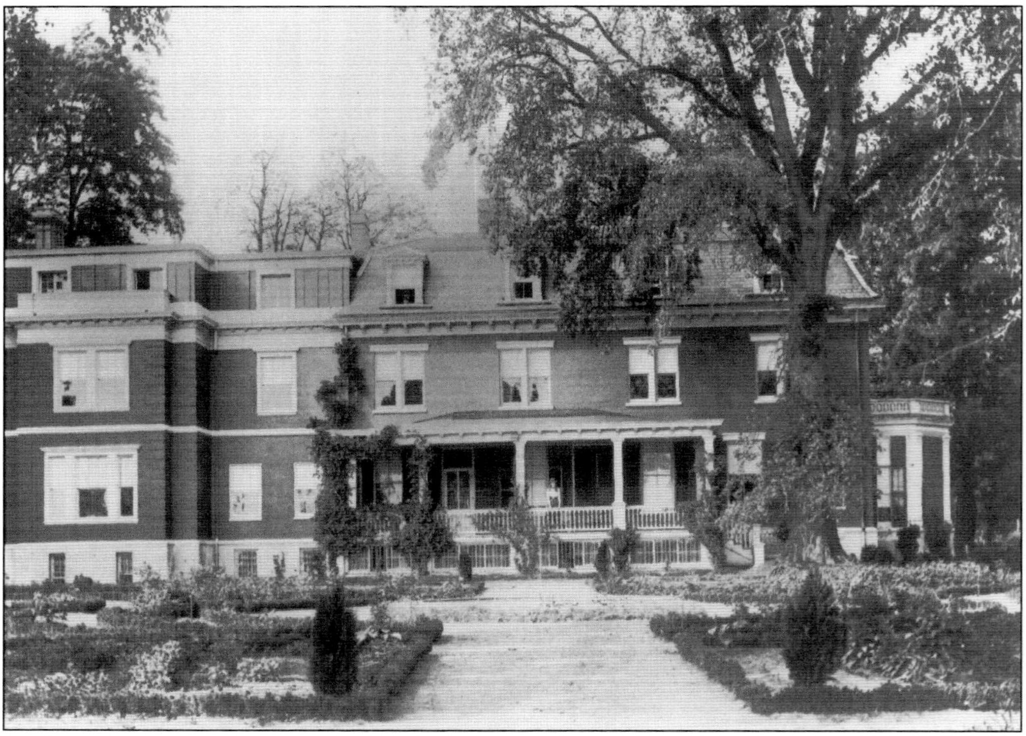

A horse and buggy stands outside the old Rhinebeck house that was remodeled by Dr. Isaac Van Vliet and was owned by H. Colton. Asa Polter constructed the building. Rhinebeck is located at the edge of Dutchess County, and early settlement was begun in 1686 by Europeans. John Jacob Astor IV, an American millionaire, businessman, real estate builder, inventor, and writer, was born in Rhinebeck. He died in the sinking of the RMS *Titanic*. (Courtesy of the Dutchess County Historical Society.)

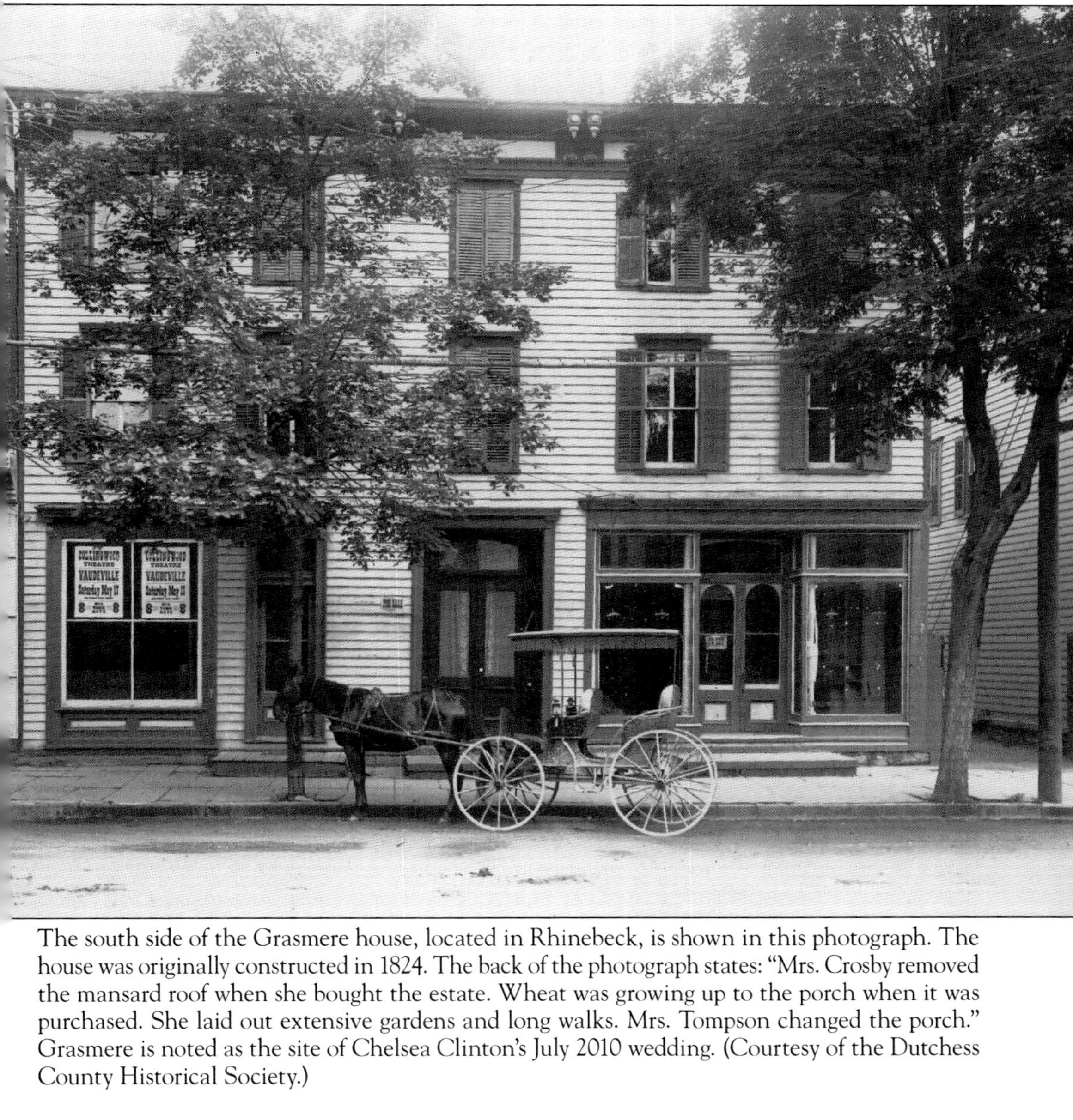

The south side of the Grasmere house, located in Rhinebeck, is shown in this photograph. The house was originally constructed in 1824. The back of the photograph states: "Mrs. Crosby removed the mansard roof when she bought the estate. Wheat was growing up to the porch when it was purchased. She laid out extensive gardens and long walks. Mrs. Tompson changed the porch." Grasmere is noted as the site of Chelsea Clinton's July 2010 wedding. (Courtesy of the Dutchess County Historical Society.)

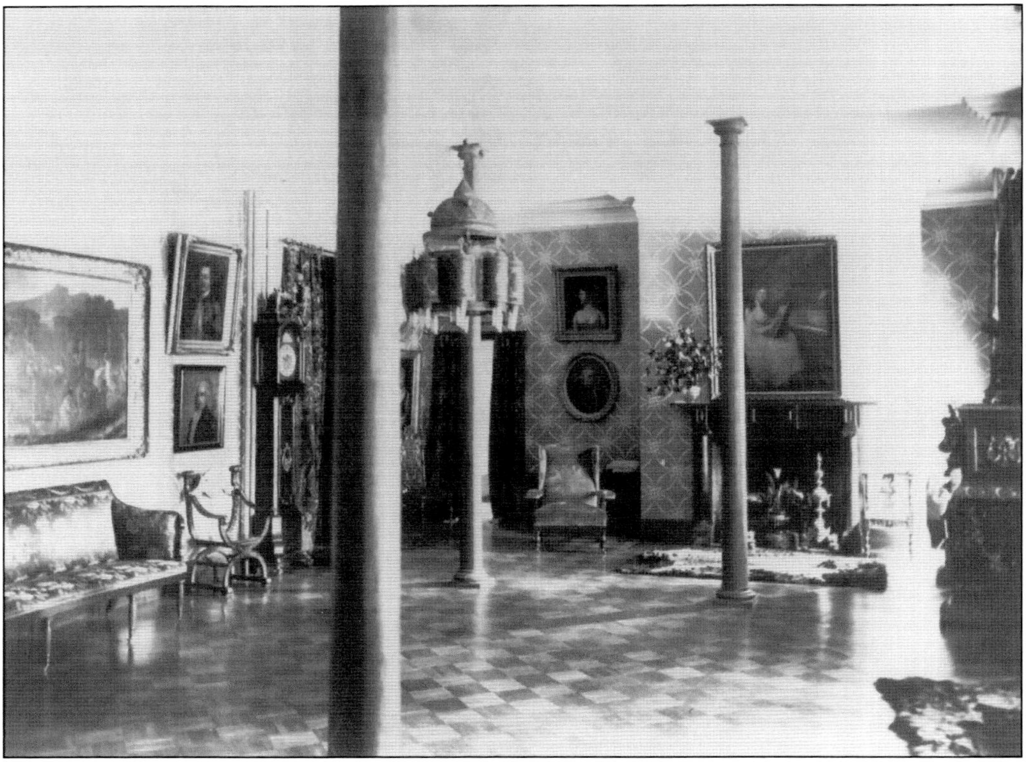

These photographs are of the front hall of Grasmere in Rhinebeck (above) and the white corner building (below). The back of the photograph for Grasmere states "Mrs. Crosby ran three rooms into one and the fireplace in the house came from a brownstone house in New York City. The 'Battle of Alexandria' hangs over the sofa. Many of the furnishings came from Judge Crosby's sojourn in Egypt as a judge at the international court. The painting over the mantel hangs now in the Winterthur Museum. The clock was Dutch." The white corner building was formerly the Rhinebeck Savings Bank. William M. Sayer was the first president. A dry goods store was located in the east part of the building. (Both, courtesy of the Dutchess County Historical Society.)

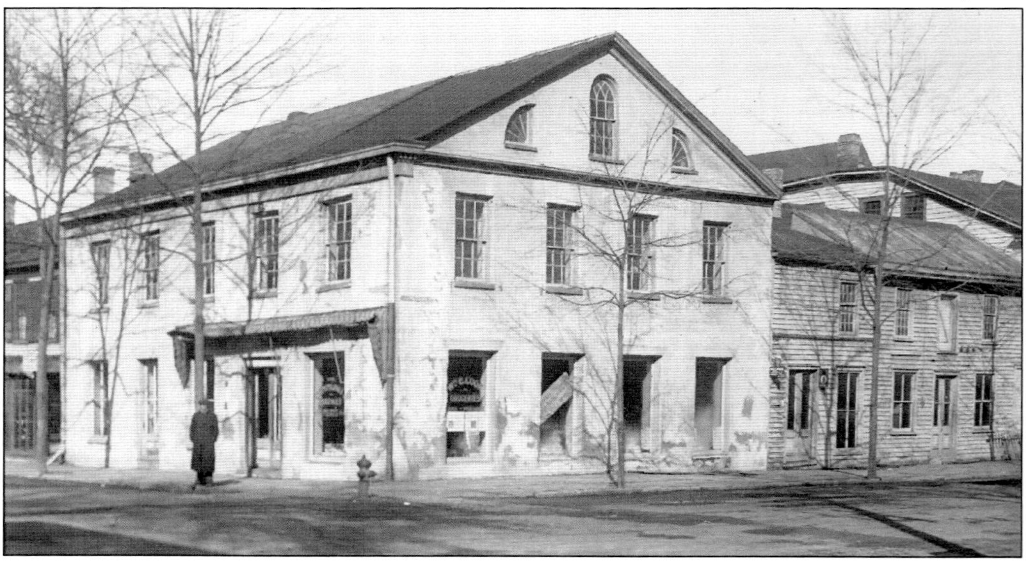

The Dutch founded the Rhinebeck Reformed Church (right) in 1731. Today, it is located on Route 9 at South Street, not far from the intersection within the village of Rhinebeck. The Stone Church (below) is depicted in 1850. The "Old Stone Church," as it is known locally, was built for the congregation starting in the 1730s. It is listed in the National Register of Historic Places. Officially, it is called the Evangelical Lutheran Church of St. Peter. Today, services are only occasionally held. The building has also been used by the Museum of Rhinebeck History. (Both, courtesy of the Dutchess County Historical Society.)

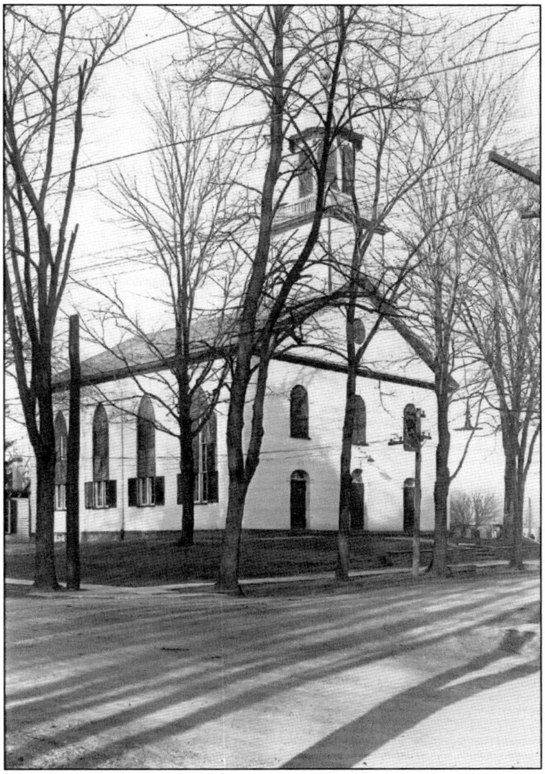

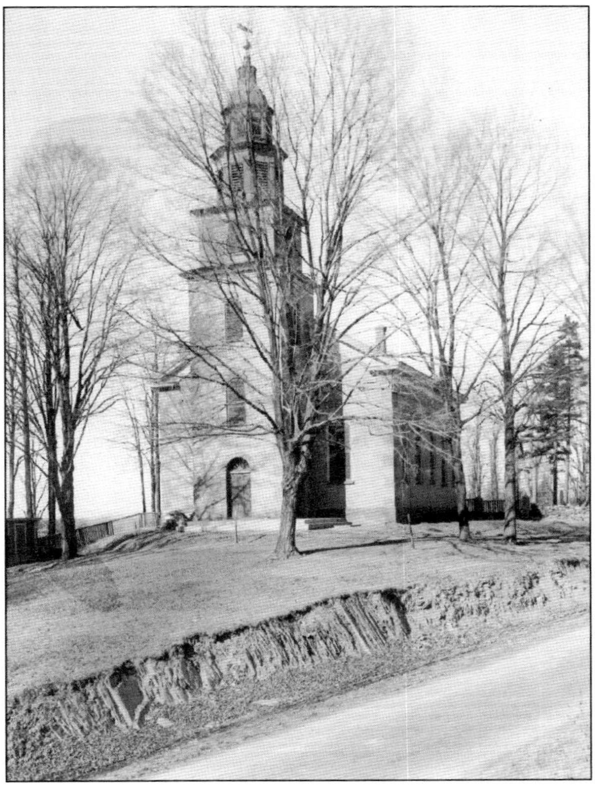

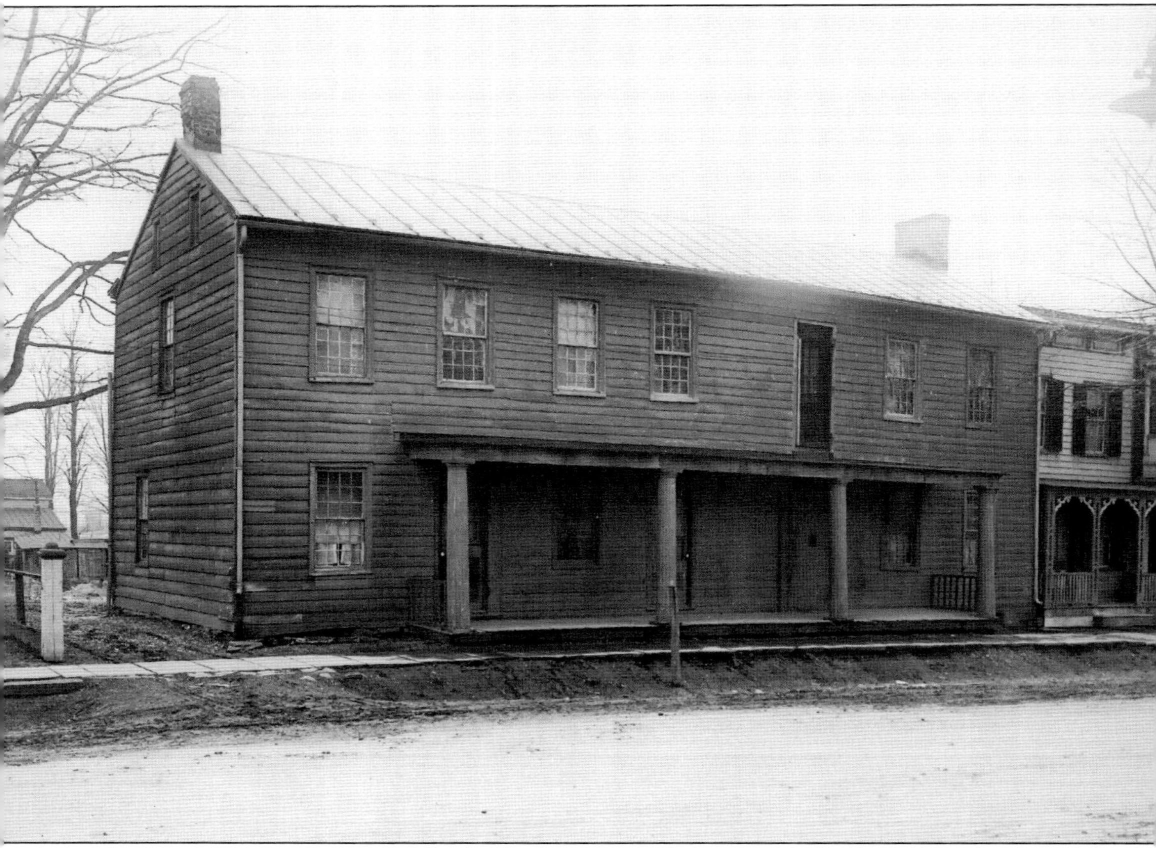

The Old Bowery House, also known as Peter Pultz's Tavern, is pictured during the late 19th century. It is located east of Mulberry Street in Rhinebeck and was known as the social center of the community. It was constructed around 1800. (Courtesy of the Dutchess County Historical Society.)

Six

Fishkill Revisited

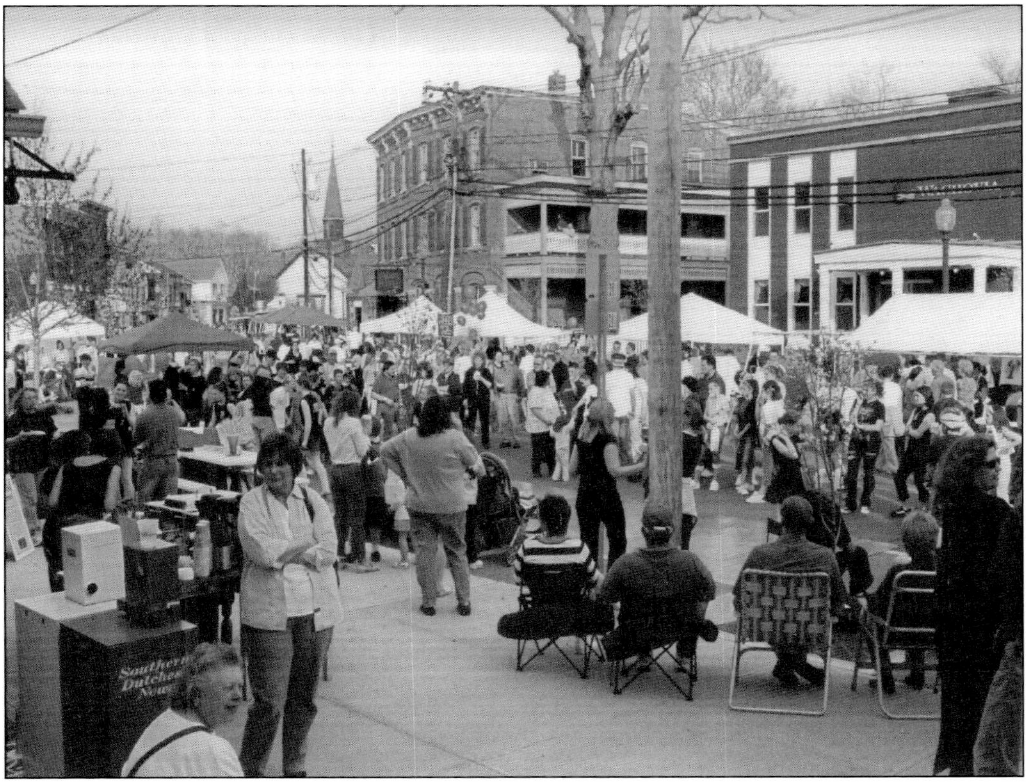

Large crowds of people are pictured celebrating the "Rock Around the Clock" block party on Main Street, which has been held in the village of Fishkill since 2005. The party lasts all day and closes Main Street. (Courtesy of Allan R. Way.)

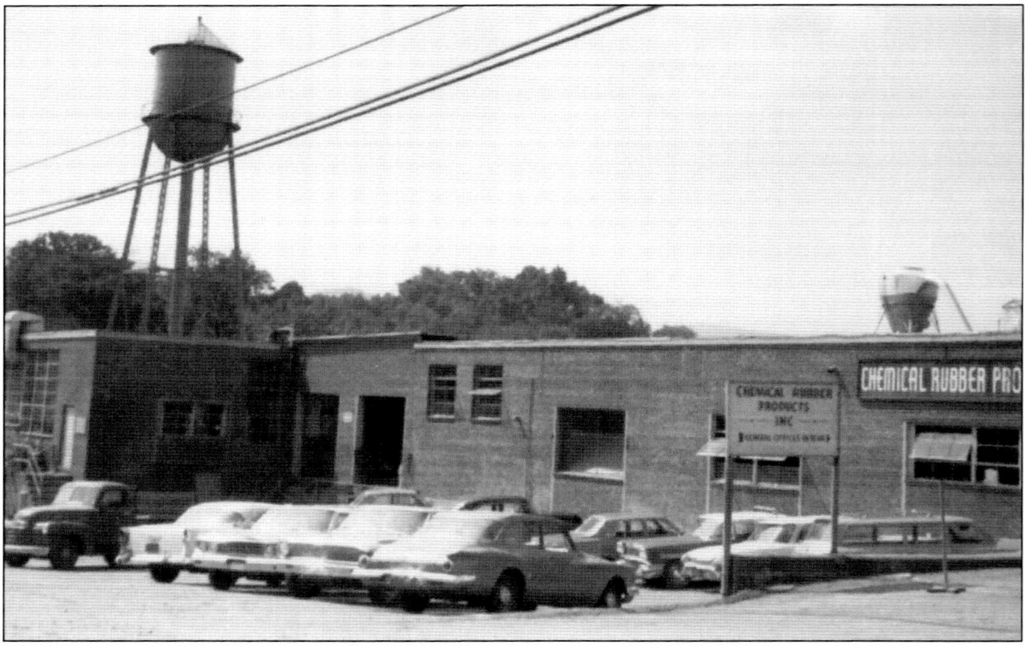

The Omega Chemical Corporation building at Fishkill Creek is depicted in a photograph taken on August 28 some time between 1965 and 1975. This photograph is a part of the Hudson River Valley Commission Collection at Marist College. As the Marist College Archives and Special Collections notes, "The Hudson River Valley Commission was formed by Governor Rockefeller and his staff to regulate the development along the Hudson River in 1966. This collection consists primarily of the findings from a series of surveys conducted by the Commission." (Courtesy of James A. Cannavino Library, Archives and Special Collections, Marist College.)

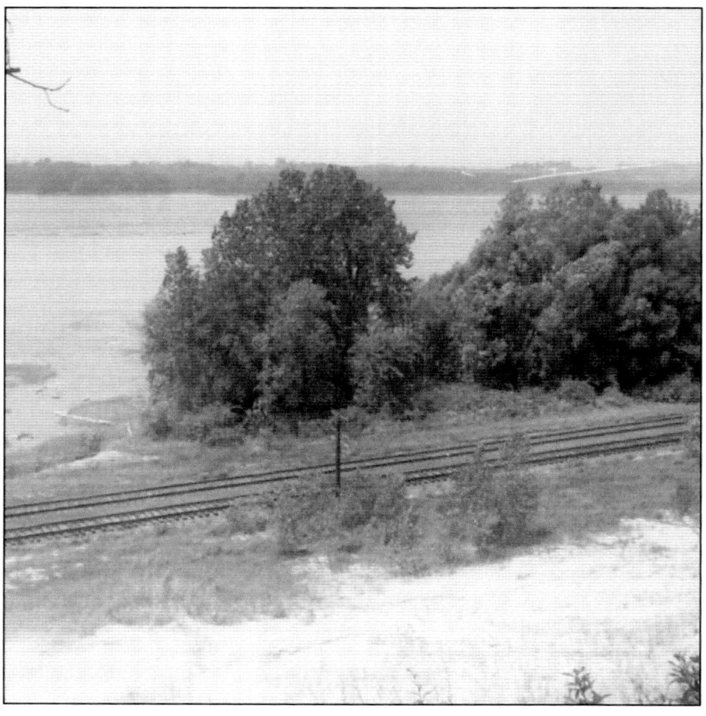

This photograph is also from the Hudson River Valley Commission Collection at Marist College. In this photograph, the Fishkill Dump is depicted. The photograph was taken on August 5 some time between 1965 and 1975 and may have been taken by or for Roger Richman. The commission was founded in order to ease concerns about the possible destruction of the scenic beauty of the Hudson River waterfront. (Courtesy of James A. Cannavino Library, Archives and Special Collections, Marist College.)

The John Jay House in East Fishkill is depicted in an aerial photograph. This is the site of the IBM expansion. John Jay, with Nathaniel Sackett, issued orders to Enoch Crosby, who may have been the influence for the main character in James Fenimore Cooper's novel *The Spy*. Crosby was confined in Fishkill at the Dutch Reformed Church and was allowed to escape after a mock trail by the Committee of Public Safety. John Jay Senior High School in Hopewell Junction is named after John Jay. (Courtesy of the Dutchess County Historical Society.)

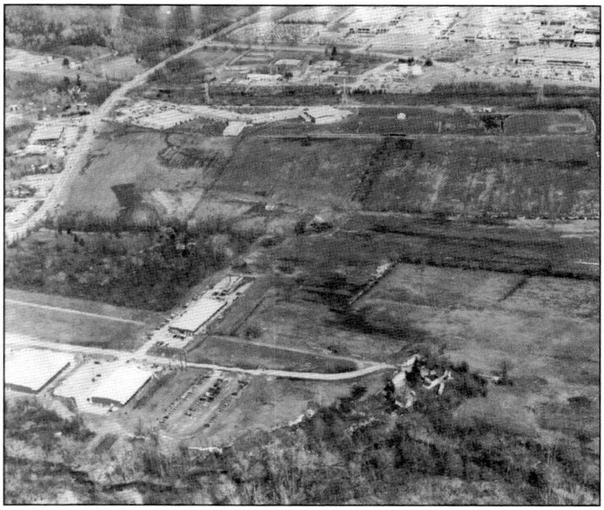

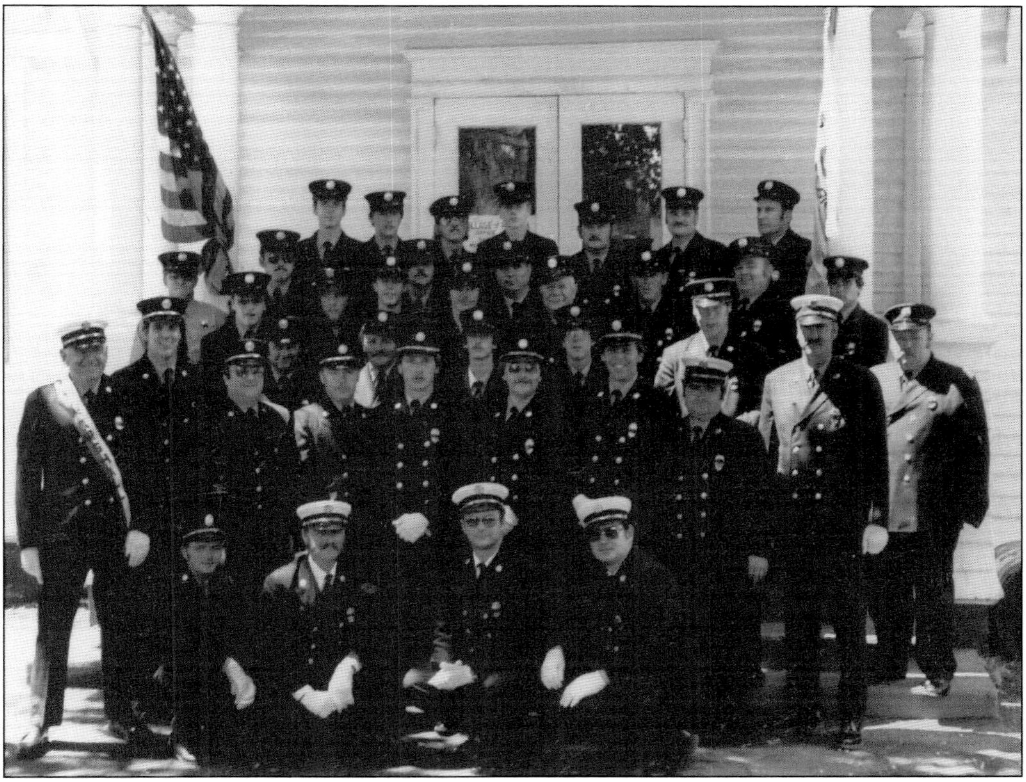

The 150th anniversary of the Fishkill Fire Department is celebrated in this 1970s photograph. Some of the people featured in the photograph are Rad Wilson, Allan Way, Joe Miculski, Jay Rollison, and Steve Rabbitt. The Fishkill Fire Department began in 1829 and continues to be a strong presence in the community. (Courtesy of Allan R. Way.)

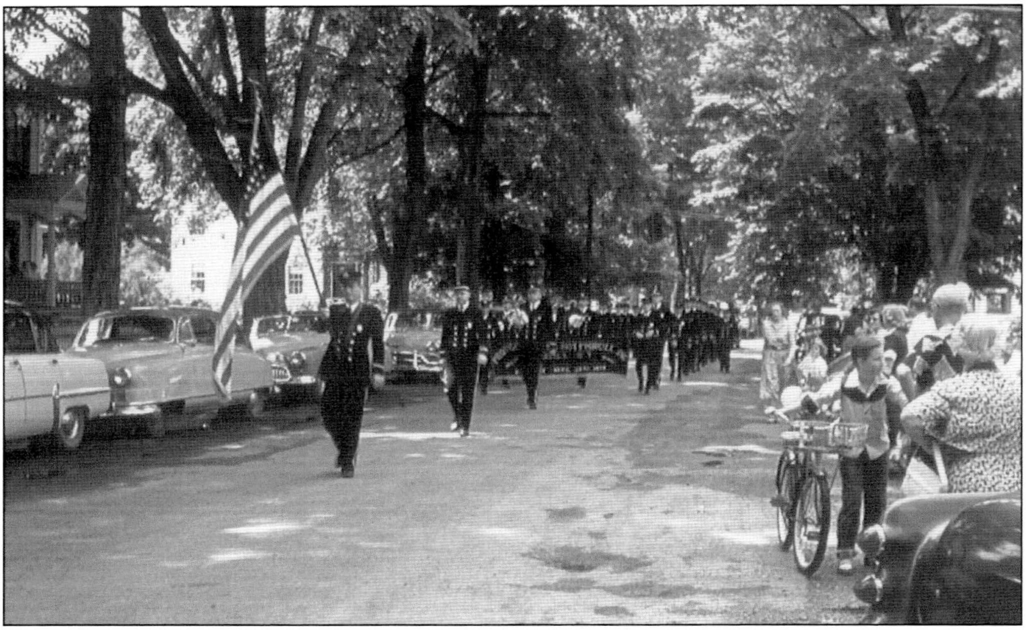

Taken on May 30, 1953, this copy of a slide depicts a Memorial Day parade on Broad Street. Today, Memorial Day services are held in front of the Dutch Reformed Church on Main Street in Fishkill. Not far from the Dutch Reformed Church, across the street between what today is know as Paula's Wine Bar and Ketchham Motors, is a statue commemorating the contributions of Fishkill men and women soldiers. (Courtesy of Frederick Villforth.)

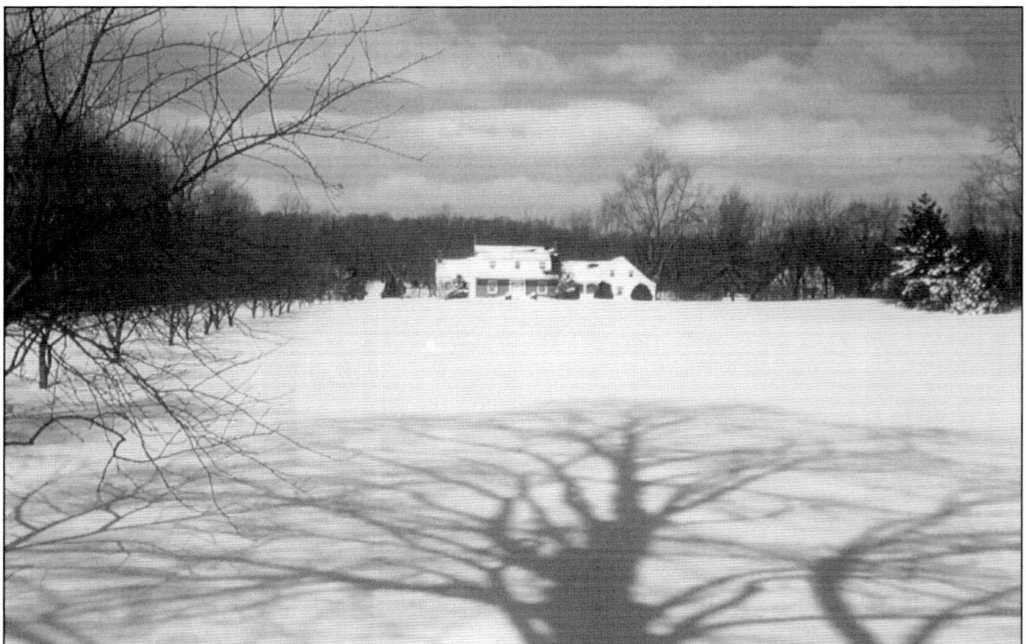

This slide is of the future site of the Fishkill Church of the Nazarene at 953 Main Street. The slide was taken between 1955 and 1956. Near this site was W. Cecil Gage's Cecilwood Theater. It was a playhouse that ran during the summer from 1948 to the 1970s. Also near this site was the Vest-Pocket Railway, which ran from 1926 until 1948. (Courtesy of Frederick Villforth.)

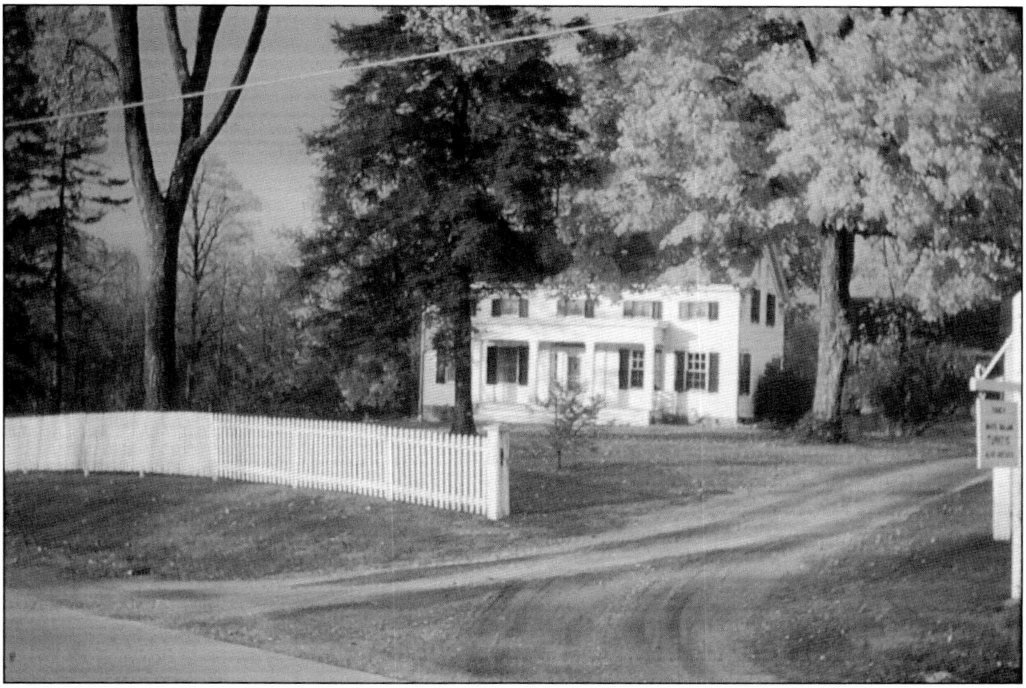

This photograph slide was taken by Frederick Villforth during the mid-20th century. After some extensive research, it was discovered by Lance A. Ashworth to be another photograph of the Cornelius C. Van Wyck House, though taken much later than the previous photograph. Unfortunately, this home was removed in 1965 to make way for the Holiday Inn on Route 9. (Courtesy of Frederick Villforth.)

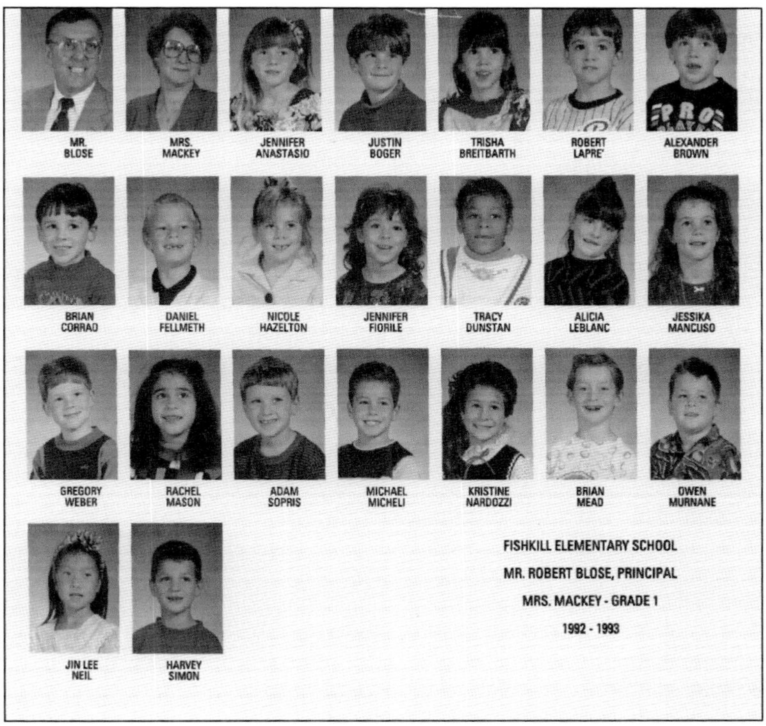

This is a photograph of a 1993 first-grade class at Fishkill Elementary. Members of this class were featured in the 1996 *Around Fishkill* book. The tower of the Fishkill Elementary School is one of the oldest public buildings that is continually in use as a school in New York State. In 2010, Fishkill Elementary School celebrated its 100th anniversary. (Courtesy of the author.)

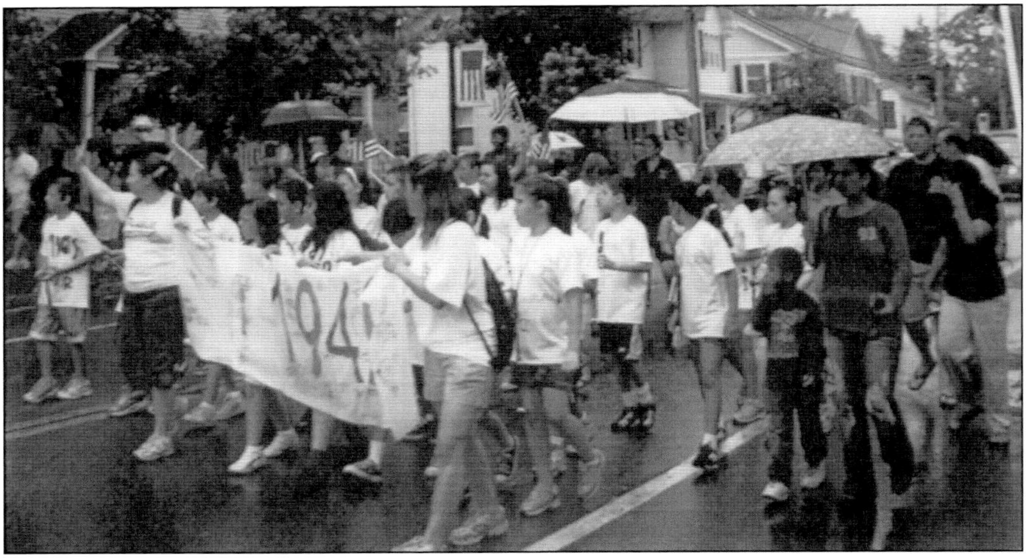

Several children and parents are depicted marching in a parade for the Fishkill Elementary School's 100th anniversary in June 2010. Each grade was given a decade to represent, and these children are holding a sign for the 1940s. This suggests that they are in the fourth grade. Fishkill Elementary School is apart of the Wappingers Central School District. This public school district is the ninth largest central school district in New York State. (Courtesy of Allan R. Way.)

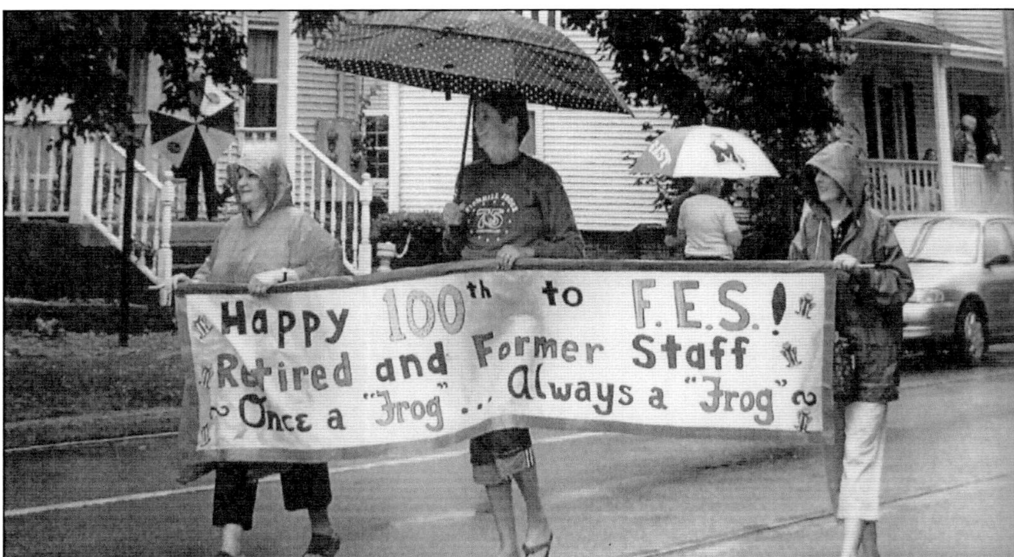

Three former teachers are shown holding a banner as they march in the Fishkill Elementary School's 100th anniversary parade. Photographed are, from left to right, R. Henneberry (retired kindergarten teacher), an unidentified woman, and Marion Peterson-Grover (retired fifth-grade teacher). (Courtesy of Allan R. Way.)

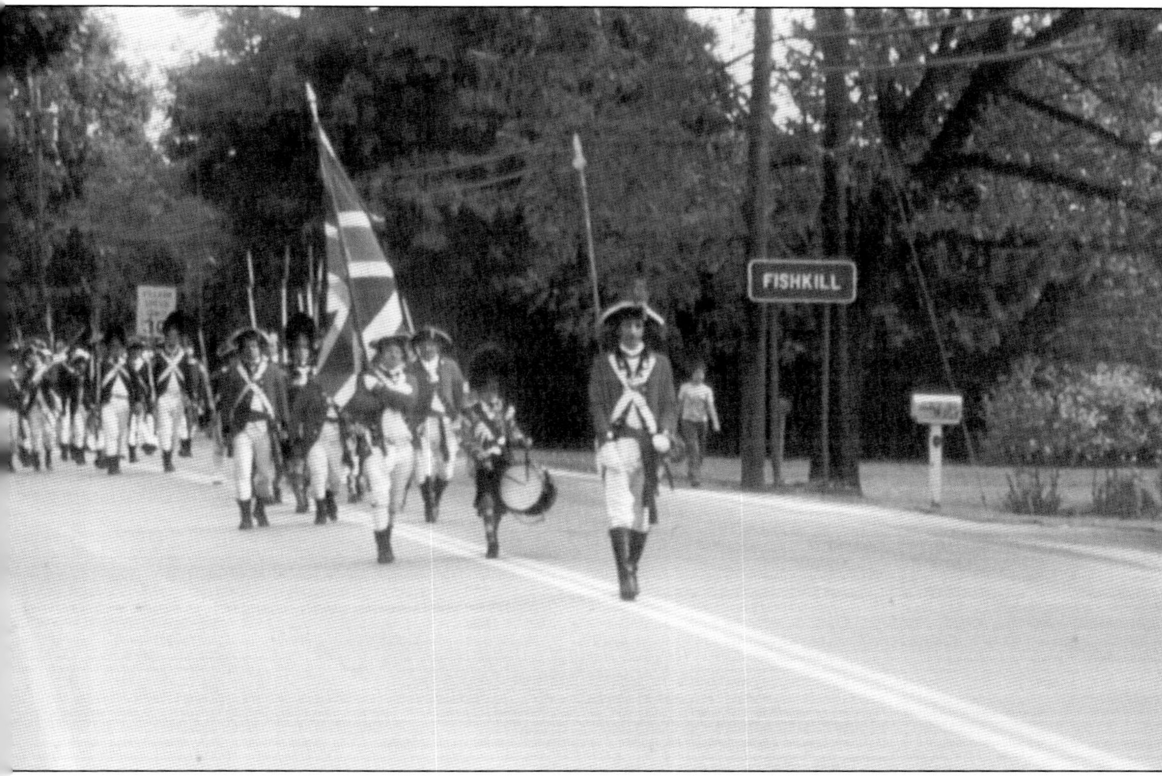

A reenactment of the Continental Army marching through Route 52 is depicted in a copy of a slide taken in September 1976. This parade was most likely part of the US Bicentennial celebrations, which paid tribute to the historical events leading up to the creation of the United States as an independent republic. The bicentennial culminated on Sunday, July 4, 1976, with the 200th anniversary of the adoption of the Declaration of Independence. When the Continental Army came through during the American Revolution, the Van Wyck Homestead became the headquarters of the Fishkill Supply Depot, which was created on the orders of George Washington in 1775. (Courtesy of Frederick Villforth.)

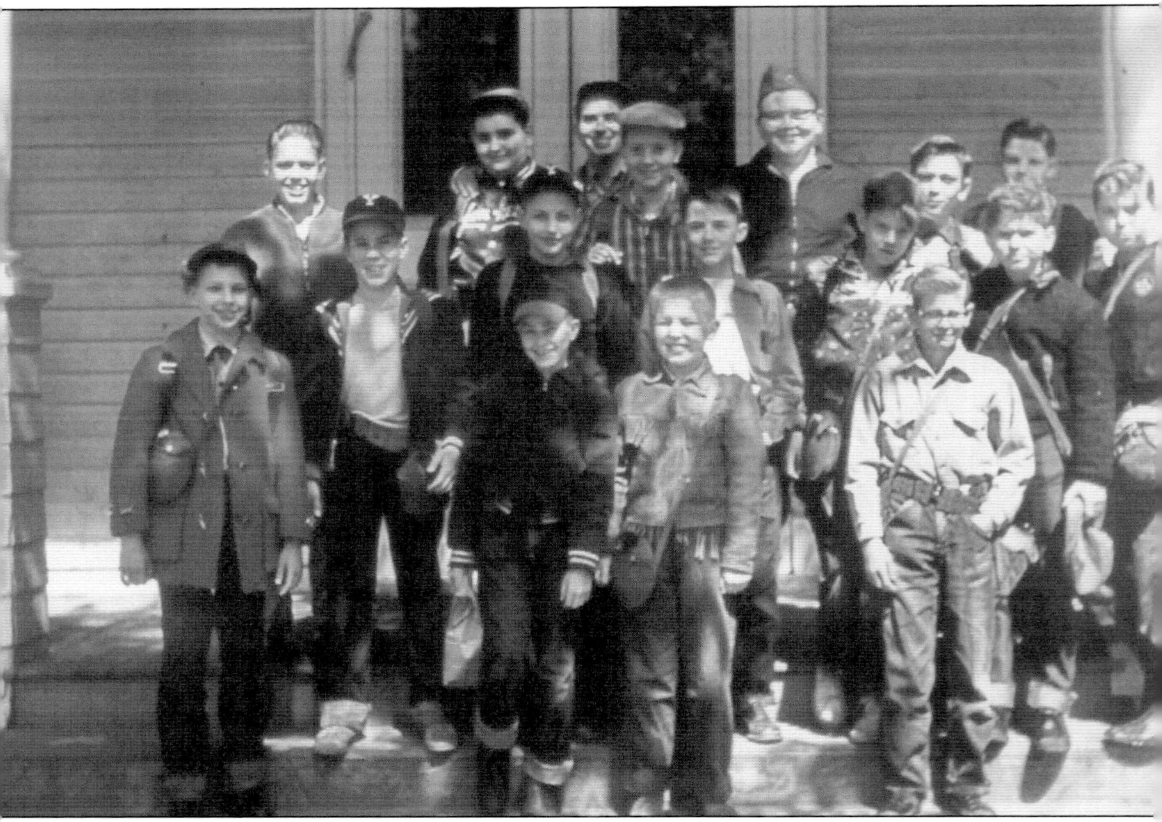

This slide of the Fishkill Boy Scout Troop was taken in 1950. The current Boy Scout troop in Fishkill is Troop 65. The troop is sponsored by the Dutch Reformed Church in Fishkill. It meets at the southern Dutchess and Putnam Sportsman's Association on Cedar Hill Road in Fishkill. The Boy Scouts are for boys 11 years old through 18 years old. (Courtesy of Frederick Villforth.)

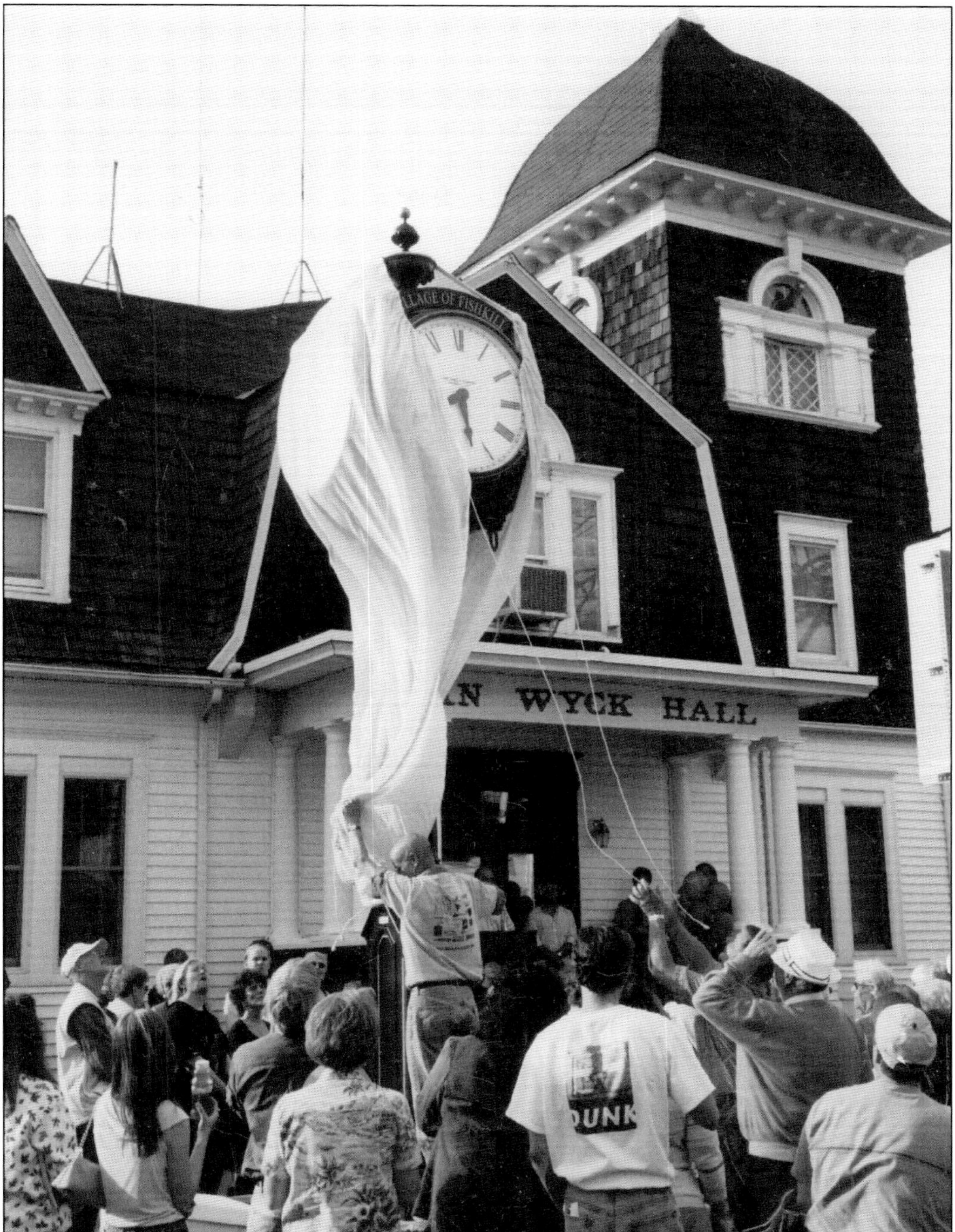

Fishkill Revisited closes on an image of the unveiling of the clock that stands in front of the Van Wyck Hall on Main Street. The unveiling of this clock around 2005 began the annual "Rock Around the Clock" block party. The block party provides Fishkill residents with various activities such as food vendors, live music, and face painting. It is a celebration of the rich history of Fishkill both past and present. (Courtesy of Allan R. Way.)

Bibliography

The Fishkill Historical Society. Images of America: *Around Fishkill.* Charleston, SC: Arcadia Publishing, 1996.

Keller, Allan. *Life Along the Hudson.* Tarrytown: Sleepy Hollow Restorations, Inc., 1976.

MacCracken, Henry Noble. *Old Dutchess Forever: The Story of an American County.* New York: Hastings House, 1956.

Skinner, Willa. *History of Fishkill, NY: 1683–1873.* Fishkill: Town of Fishkill Publishing, 1978.

———. *Remembering Fishkill.* Charleston, SC: The History Press, 2008.

Verplanck, William Edward, ed., and Charlotte VerPlanck Willman. *The History of Abraham Isaacse Ver Planck and his Male Descendants in America.* Fishkill: John W. Spaight, 1893.

INDEX